RECALLING THE BELGIAN CONGO

New Directions in Anthropology
General Editor: **Jacqueline Waldren**, *Institute of Social Anthropology, University of Oxford*

Volume 1 *Coping with Tourists: European Reactions to Mass Tourism*
Edited by Jeremy Boissevain

Volume 2 *A Sentimental Economy: Commodity and Community in Rural Ireland*
Carles Salazar

Volume 3 *Insiders and Outsiders: Paradise and Reality in Mallorca*
Jacqueline Waldren

Volume 4 *The Hegemonic Male: Masculinity in a Portuguese Town*
Miguel Vale de Almeida

Volume 5 *Communities of Faith: Sectarianism, Identity, and Social Change on a Danish Island*
Andrew S. Buckser

Volume 6 *After Socialism: Land Reform and Rural Social Change in Eastern Europe*
Edited by Ray Abrahams

Volume 7 *Immigrant and Bureaucrats: Ethiopians in an Israeli Absorption Center*
Esther Hertzog

Volume 8 *Venetian Life on a Lagoon Island*
Lidia Sciama

Volume 9 *Recalling the Belgian Congo: Conversations and Introspection*
Marie-Bénédicte Dembour

Volume 10 *Mastering Soldiers: Conflict, Emotions, and the Enemy in an Israeli Military Unit*
Eyal Ben-Ari

Volume 11 *The Great Immigration: Russian Jews in Israel*
Dina Siegel

RECALLING THE BELGIAN CONGO

Conversations and Introspection

Marie-Bénédicte Dembour

Berghahn Books
New York • Oxford

First published in 2000 by
Berghahn Books
www.berghahnbooks.com

© 2000, 2008 Marie-Bénédicte Dembour
Paperback reprinted in 2008

All rights reserved.
No part of this publication may be reproduced
in any form or by any means
without the written permission of Berghahn Books.

Library of Congress Cataloging-in-Publication Data

```
Dembour, Marie-Benedicte, 1961-
    Recalling the Belgian Congo : conversations and introspection /
Marie-Benedicte Dembour.
      p. cm. --  (New directions in anthropology , v. 9)
    Includes bibliographical references and index
    ISBN 978-1-57181-945-1 (hardback : alk. paper)
    ISBN 978-1-57181-320-6 (pb : alk. paper)
    1. Ethnology -- Congo (Democratic Republic)  2. Colonial
administrators -- Congo (Democratic Republic) -- History. 3.
Congo (Democratic Republic) -- In mass media  4. Belgium --
Colonies -- Africa -- Administration.  5. Congo (Democratic
Republic) -- History  6.Congo (Democratic Republic) -- Politics
and government.  7. Congo (Democratic Republic) -- Social life
and customs.  I. Title. II. Series.
    GN654 . D37 1999
    306'. 096751--dc21
                                                       98-50670
                                                           CIP
```

British Library Cataloguing in Publication Data

A catalogue record for this book is available from the British Library.

Printed on acid-free paper

ISBN 978-1-57181-945-1 (hardback), 978-1-57181-320-6 (paperback)

Contents

Preface	ix
Note on use of language and pseudonyms	xi
List of translated technical words	xiii
Maps and Illustrations	xvii
1. Introduction	1
Writing about colonialism	1
Discordant colonial memories	3
The ever-transforming process of memory	5
A reflexive and diaological ethnography	7
Why 'Recalling the Belgian Congo'?	11
2. A glossary in disguise	17
The territorial service: creation, ranks and numbers	17
The territorial functions	22
The council of chiefdom	22
The judicial organisation	24
Native accounts	29
The distribution of tasks in practice	29
Internal organisation: Transfers, itinerance and control	30
The territorials as a group of Belgian men in a wider society	37

3. My project — 45
Original prejudice against colonialism — 45
Seeking to appear unthreatening — 49
In search of the real Congo — 54
A matter of interpretation — 60

4. Their expectations — 68
Muted voices — 68
The chance to be recognised by the outside world — 77
The objective witness — 81
   Deceit as a non-issue — 82
   Different kinds of facts — 85
True history will not take over — 92

5. Our dialogues — 99
Significant modalities — 99
   The guarantee of anonymity — 100
   The time and place of the interviews — 105
   The record of the interview — 107
The terms of the dialogue — 109
The value of memory — 112
   Getting started — 113
   The transformative work of memory — 113
   Memory and history — 120
   Remembering well — 123
Unavoidable misunderstandings — 124

6. My story — 133
Being immersed: The pretence of closeness — 134
   A sense of immersion — 134
   Speaking of occupation — 138
   The figure of the ménagère — 139
Preferring the authentic African: An expression of imperialistic nostalgia — 143
   Downplaying change — 143

Regretting change	146
Enhancing one's authority	149
Acting through persuasion: Prestige as violence	153
The idiom of prestige	154
No prestige without the whip	160
A concern for distinction	162

7. Their response — 169

Resorting to inadequate concepts: A rather common peculiarity	170
Leaving out the texture of life: A rigid picture	176
Inventing screens: A prejudiced approach	179
Lacking experience: An action reduced to a discourse	186

8. Conclusion: The anthropological position — 194

The argument so far	194
The need to go beyond the native voice	196
In limbo between distance and empathy	198
The seeming arrogance of anthropology	201
My findings	202
The value of anthropology	205

Appendices — 209

Bibliography — 214

Index — 231

PREFACE

*A*ll Belgian schoolchildren used to be taught that Belgium had a colony which was eighty times its size. Even though the Congo had been independent for a year by the time I was born in 1961, I also learnt at primary school about this vast territory which one of our previous kings had 'given' to his people. I remember wondering what life was like for the Belgian adults I knew were living in Zaire, as the country was renamed from 1972 to 1997. I also have a rather vivid memory of a photograph of Zairean children crossing a river by holding onto a rope and splashing about in shallow waters. This sounded like good fun to me, even though I was told they were poor and unfortunate. The missionary and economic links Belgium maintained with its former colony ensured that the existence of Zaire remained dormant in the back of my consciousness.

It was brought to the fore when Jacques Vanderlinden asked me, as a masters student, to write a paper on colonial punishment in Belgian Africa. Soon after this, I received funding to do a doctorate, and became interested in the question of how one administers a colony as large as the Congo. How many men do you need? What can you control? What do you fail to control? And most important of all, how does it feel to be a colonial administrator? In my mind (at least then), the colonial administrator, by being on the side of the coloniser, was the oppressor. How could he justify this? I started to interview former colonial officers in Belgium. Between Christmas 1987 and the summer of 1990, I met some forty of them. These meetings provide the material for this book. Its overall aim changed as the research proceeded – I would now phrase

Introduction

it as follows: to explore the way the Congo is remembered in Belgium, the way we evaluate past and present events, and the way we hold on to supposed knowledge.

When I embarked on my research project, I thought I knew what colonialism was about – economic exploitation and cultural oppression. I was also quick to pass judgment on the people who had participated in what appeared to me as a politically and morally dubious enterprise. The conversations I held with former colonial officers made me question my initial assumptions. What was it that I knew so well? And who was I to pass judgments on others whose experience I found touching? By analysing our conversations, this book traces my own efforts towards introspection. In doing so, it invites the reader to re-call the Congo, i.e. to apprehend it in other terms than the bad name by which it is generally known.

I would not have been in a position to re-call the Congo were it not for the men and more rarely women who accepted to recall, this time literally, recollections of the years they spent in the Congo. I shall not acknowledge them individually, so as to preserve their anonymity. Among them, however, 'Milnaert' stands out. I shall also wish to thank Jean Eloy, José Clément and the late Alfred Ameel, for whom anonymity is or was not a concern. This study owes much to Jacques Vanderlinden who first taught me as a law undergraduate at Brussels, and has since encouraged me in all my intellectual pursuits. Michael Gilsenan who supervised my doctorate at Oxford has been a major intellectual influence as well as a source of support. I have found the work of Johannes Fabian and Kirsten Hastrup particularly inspiring and was therefore thrilled to receive their encouragements, which the former accompanied with detailed comments on the thesis. Many other people helped along the way. I wish to single out Elisabeth Chilver, Helen Callaway, Rosemary McKechnie, Jane Cowan, Nikki Cooper, Karel Arnaut and Bob Morton. Anna Zaniewicka improved my sense of English and Rémy Bethmont provided translations from the French – and insights. The Belgian Fonds National de la Recherche Scientifique financed the doctoral research through a research post.

Beyond academic pressure to publish, I have written this book in the hope that it can foster better listening, and hence more understanding, between human beings. In this regard, two people have taught me a lot in the last three years. They are my partner, Bob Morton, and my niece, who was called Isaline. This book is dedicated to his love and to her memory.

Easter 1998

NOTE ON USE OF LANGUAGE AND PSEUDONYMS

*F*rench was the language used by the colonial administration in the Belgian Congo. As a result, it was possible to conduct all the interviews on which this study is based in French, even when the interviewee was Flemish. Translations from interviews and from texts and publications in French are mine.

While translating administrative and legal terms is fraught with difficulties, I nonetheless decided it was a better option than keeping foreign words in the text. I have adopted translations which are close to the French original and sound satisfactory in English, except when this would induce misleading results. For example I translate '*territorial*' as 'territorial' and '*administrateur de territoire*' as 'territorial administrator'; but '*magistrat*' as 'judge' and '*juge de police*' as 'magistrate of police'. Because the *commissaires de district* of the Belgian Congo were responsible for an administrative unit much larger that the district commissioners of the British colonies, I translate '*commissaire de district*' as 'district commissary' rather than 'district commissioner'. A complete list of the translations I have used is provided below.

Many geographical names were changed under the regime of General Mobutu. I use the names which were in application during the colonial period, except when I refer to events which took place after they were transformed. I also use some terms, for example 'native' and 'Black', which can appear derogatory today, but were part of the colonial vocabulary. When using them, I have not put them in inverted commas so as to avoid overloading the text. No offence is meant through this usage.

Personal names which appear in inverted commas are pseudonyms of interviewees. I explain why I decided to impose anonymity on my informants in chapter 5.

A good annual personal report (1955)

List of translated technical words

a) From French into English

Administrateur de territoire	Territorial administrator
Administrateur territorial assistant	Assistant territorial administrator
Administrateur territorial assistant principal	Principal assistant territorial administrator
Administration d'Afrique	African administration
Agent	Officer
Agent territorial	Territorial officer
Agent territorial principal	Principal territorial officer
Appel	Appeal
Assesseur indigène	Native assessor
Auxiliaire	Auxiliary
Bleu	Fresher
Caisse auxiliaire indigène	Native auxiliary account
Centre extra-coutumier	Extra-customary centre
Chefferie	Chiefdom
Chicote	Whip
Circonscription indigène	Native circumscription
Commissaire de district	District commissary
Commissaire de district assistant	Assistant district commissary
Comptable-gardien de prison	Accountant-jail warden
Contestation entre indigènes	Dispute between natives
Cour d'appel	Court of appeal
Dame auxiliaire volontaire	Volunteer auxiliary lady

Diplôme d'humanités	Humanities degree
District	District
Fonctionnaire supérieur	Senior functionary
Gîte d'étape	Rest-house
Gouverneur de province	Governor of province
Gouverneur général	Governor-General
Haut fonctionnaire	High functionary
Homme adulte et valide	Adult and able-bodied man
Inspection du travail	Labour control
Journal de route	Road diary
Juge [au tribunal] de police	Magistrate [to the tribunal] of police
Justice indigène	Native justice
Magistrat	[Professional] judge
Notables	Dignitaries
Officier de police judiciaire	Judicial police officer
Pièces annuelles	Annual reports
Politique indigène	Native policy
Poste detaché	Detached post
Province	Province
Révision	Revision
Secrétaire provincial	Provincial secretary
Secteur	Sector
Service	Service
Territoire	Territory
Jour d'itinérance	Touring day
Tribunal de centre	Tribunal of centre
Tribunal de parquet	Standing tribunal
Tribunal de police	Tribunal of police
Tribunal de première instance	Tribunal of first instance
Tribunal de secteur	Tribunal of sector
Tribunal de territoire	Tribunal of territory
Tribunal européen	European tribunal
Tribunal indigène	Native tribunal
Tribunal of district	Tribunal of district
Université Coloniale	Colonial University

List of Translated Technical Words

b) **From English into French**

Accountant-jail warden	*Comptable-gardien de prison*
Adult and able-bodied man	*Homme adulte et valide*
African administration	*Administration d'Afrique*
Annual reports	*Pièces annuelles*
Appeal	*Appel*
Assistant district commissary	*Commissaire de district assistant*
Auxiliary	*Auxiliaire*
Chiefdom	*Chefferie*
Colonial University	*Université Coloniale*
Court of appeal	*Cour d'appel*
Detached post	*Poste detaché*
Dignitaries	*Notables*
Dispute between natives	*Contestation entre indigènes*
District	*District*
District commissary	*Commissaire de district*
European tribunal	*Tribunal européen*
Extra-customary centre	*Centre extra-coutumier*
Fresher	*Bleu*
Governor-General	*Gouverneur général*
Governor of province	*Gouverneur de province*
High functionary	*Haut fonctionnaire*
Humanities degree	*Diplôme d'humanités*
Touring day	*Jour d'itinérance*
Judicial police officer	*Officier de police judiciaire*
Labour control	*Inspection du travail*
Magistrate [to the tribunal] of police	*Juge [au tribunal] de police*
Native assessor	*Assesseur indigène*
Native auxiliary account	*Caisse auxiliaire indigène*
Native circonscription	*Circonscription indigène*
Native justice	*Justice indigène*
Native policy	*Politique indigène*
Native tribunal	*Tribunal indigène*
Officer	*Agent*
Principal assistant territorial administrator	*Administrateur territorial assistant principal*
Principal territorial officer	*Agent territorial principal*
[Professional] judge	*Magistrat*

List of Translated Technical Words

Province	*Province*
Provincial secretary	*Secrétaire provincial*
Rest-house	*Gîte d'étape*
Revision	*Révision*
Road diary	*Journal de route*
Sector	*Secteur*
Senior functionary	*Fonctionnaire supérieur*
Service	*Service*
Standing tribunal	*Tribunal de parquet*
Territorial administrator	*Administrateur de territoire*
Territorial assistant administrator	*Administrateur territorial assistant*
Territorial officer	*Agent territorial*
Territory	*Territoire*
Tribunal of centre	*Tribunal de centre*
Tribunal of district	*Tribunal of district*
Tribunal of first instance	*Tribunal de première instance*
Tribunal of police	*Tribunal de police*
Tribunal of sector	*Tribunal de secteur*
Tribunal of territory	*Tribunal de territoire*
Volunteer auxiliary lady	*Dame auxiliaire volontaire*
Whip	*Chicote*

Map 1: *Relative Surface Areas of Europe, Belgium, and the Belgian Congo.*

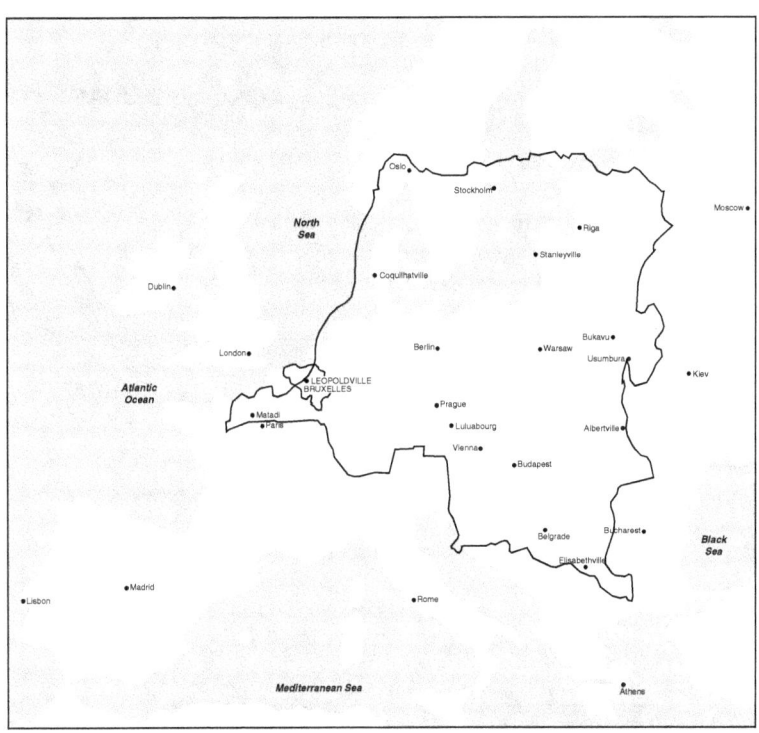

Europe: 10,000,000 km²; 560,000,000 inhabitants; 56 inhabitants per km².

Belgium: 30,500 km²; 8,700,000 inhabitants; 290 inhabitants per km².

Belgian Congo: 2,343,930 km²; 12,000,000 inhabitants; 5 inhabitants per km².

Adapted from Réalités Africaines: Le Congo belge et le Ruanda-Urundi, 1957 (Casablanca: Les éditions Fontana, p. 21). See also, for a similar map, Michiels and Leude 1938: 5.

Map 2: *The Belgian Congo in the 1950s.*

Source: CRISP

Furniture inside this official's home is the 'Louis-Box' style

Reaching small villages during a tour

The paperwork never leaves the territorial alone

The comfort of the Guest-House is rudimentary

1: Introduction

Writing about colonialism

This book is based on interviews I conducted in the late 1980s with senior men in Belgium. Middle-class and generally retired, they lived in comfortable homes, spoke of trips abroad they had taken or were about to take, had pictures of their grandchildren displayed in their living-rooms, could have been experiencing family, health or financial worries which they did not share with me. They were both tall and short, large and slim, intelligent and dull, prompt to smile and severe, listening to themselves or attentive to comments expressed by others. Nothing in their dress, speech or demeanour distinguished them as a group from their peers of the same nationality, class and generation. They share[1] one thing, however, and this is that they began their adulthood as colonial officers in the Belgian Congo.

A few decades ago when they were in their early twenties, they had joined the main branch of the Belgian colonial administration, i.e. the territorial service, more commonly known as the Territoriale.[2] The oldest among my interviewees had become territorials in the late 1920s, but the great majority had done so soon after the Second World War had ended. The latter left the service ten to fifteen years later, at a time when they had not completed a full territorial career. The riots which broke out in January 1959 in the capital, Leopoldville, triggered the unforeseen process towards independence, which was declared on 30 June 1960. Most territorials then returned to Belgium, often in a precipitous way and sometimes narrowly escaping the violence which erupted a few days after the declaration of independence.³ They were not prepared for this sudden and stressful return. By all accounts, the first months in Belgium were difficult. But, in time, they found good jobs, moved into proper accommodation, developed a social circle of friends and acquaintances. They blended back into Belgian society. When I met them, most were in their late sixties, some older and a few slightly younger.

I was asking them to talk about a subject which they normally avoid today. (When I say 'today', I refer loosely to the period during which this research was conducted). The Congo is no longer an active part of their present. It has become less and less relevant to their day-to-day concerns, less and less worth talking about. As one interviewee said without any apparent nostalgia, 'it has ceased to interest anyone.' One could simply say that time has passed on. But this fading-away process, arguably common to all past events, is combined with a definite reluctance on their part to talk about a period which many qualify as the most beautiful time of their life. Such reserve can be attributed to a double bitterness. On one hand, these men watch the continual disintegration of the country in which they worked, and this fills them with sadness and regret.⁴ On the other, they prefer to 'shut up' rather than expressing reminiscences aloud and thus risking being labelled colonialists.

'Colonialist', the big word has been uttered. It obviously derives from 'colonialism'. The latter term is one which I had carefully avoided in the first draft of this work, for I had sensed my informants would instantly and persistently object to it. Instead, I had used the term 'colonisation', presuming that it constituted an appropriate translation of the French '*colonisation*'. I was wrong. The two words differ more than by their respective pronunciation. The French term can refer to the 'colonial regime', i.e. the set of institutions put in place in order to ensure the effective governing of a colony. By contrast, the English term can only refer to the action of 'colonising'. In other words it connotes the idea of moving in and establishing oneself where one has yet to set foot, without being able to encompass the idea of a colonial regime already in place. To express this idea in English, one needs to turn to the term 'colonialism'. Thus the Oxford English Dictionary defines 'colonialism' in the following way: '1.a. The practice or manner of things colonial ... 2. The colonial system or principle' (1989). The Concise Oxford Dictionary similarly offers a 'down-to-earth' definition of 'colonialism': 'a policy of acquiring or maintaining colonies' (1989). Both dictionaries go on to note that 'colonialism' has acquired a derogatory sense and is now frequently used to refer to an 'alleged policy of exploitation of backward or weak peoples by a large power'. However, they do not present this definition as the first meaning of the term. By contrast, the Lexis-Larousse (1989) provides the following definition of '*colonialisme*': doctrine which only considers the interest of the coloniser in colonial practice.[5] Considering the way in which the term '*colonialisme*' is predominantly used in French today,[6] the reader will not be surprised to hear that the interviewees who read my work were not happy with my repetitive use of the term 'colonialism'.

My explanation that 'colonisation' did not offer an appropriate English translation to its apparent French equivalent failed to satisfy them. For them, my insistence on using the word which ended in 'ism' proved that I held the colonial experience in a negative light. The semantic discussion above could suggest otherwise. At the same time, I have to accept that the pejorative connotations of the term 'colonialism' cannot be brushed aside. Furthermore, I cannot but see that we, the former territorials on one hand and me on the other, hold different and perhaps irreconcilable memories of colonialism.

Discordant colonial memories

The juxtaposition of two texts can usefully introduce our respective memories of colonialism. The first text comes from the degree thesis of a Belgian historian graduate who had worked on the Territoriale. As she explains in a subsequent piece of writing, she considers herself to be the 'faithful interpreter' of the former territorials she interviewed (Tancré-Van Leeuw 1992: 410). The second text is extracted from a book written by two leading political scientists on Zaire. They would probably wish to dissociate themselves from the group of the colonisers. To quote them in turn:

> [The territorial administrators] were up early and late to bed. Their nights were sometimes interrupted to perform duties as judicial police officers. Holidays could not always be respected, annual vacations not always taken. Touring took about half their time, and they were sometimes the only Europeans amongst the Africans. Confidences shared at night around the fire, storytelling … Moments of grace which made it possible for them to know, understand and value the African auxiliaries and the administered populations. … The territorial administrators were always a principal driving force behind the colonising enterprise (Tancré-Van Leeuw 1992: 401–02).

> Basically, Africa was called upon to organise and finance its own subjugation and exploitation. The only reproductive resource for accomplishing this pur-

pose was African labor. Very quickly, colonial states directed their attention to self-financing means for its expropriation.

The primary instrument for accomplishing this end was direct taxation. Although its revenue yield was not great, in the early stages it made a significant contribution to colonial budgets. More importantly, the fiscal obligations coerced rural populations into cash crop production, the exported portion of which could be taxed again. In addition, young men were driven into the labor market (Young and Turner 1985: 23).

The first quotation conveys a sense of territorial devotion, genuine interest in the Africans, and indispensible presence in the colonial machinery; the second places oppression at the centre of the colonial project. One could say that each emerges from a different memory of colonialism: the first from a memory of '*colonisation*' (as in colonial days), the second of '*colonialisme*' (as in colonialist pursuit) – to return to the distinction made by the French language. One can further suggest that these two memories correspond, broadly speaking, to the different memories with which the interviewees and I entered the research project. The text of Tancré-Van Leeuw would represent the memory of the interviewees, that of Young and Turner mine.

It may seem strange to refer to my holding a memory of colonialism. Considering I was born one year after the Congolese independence, I obviously do not have any personal reminiscences of the colonial days. Nevertheless I have heard about the Congo since I was a child, and this has shaped my memory of colonialism. By the time of my young adulthood, I possessed the 'knowledge' that colonialism was synonymous with domination and oppression – two concepts I did not bother to distinguish. This I had learnt by accepting, and associating myself with, a discourse prevalent in various circles of society, but most visibly among leftist activists, journalists and scholars. I would readily have denounced colonialism for its presumably absolute and unredeemable imperialistic, exploitative and racist evils. In other words, my memory is an emanation of a collective memory, a personal variation on a theme widely shared in society.

By contrast, my informants obviously have reminiscences of the years they spent in the Congo. In this sense, they hold plural memories of the colonial experience. I nonetheless feel entitled to suggest that they share a distinctive, and almost single, memory. This is so not only because they worked in broadly similar conditions in the Congo, but also because they have been confronted since their return to Belgium with the same judgment on colonialism, against which they have had to react. In other words, their memories are organised along sufficiently similar lines to be contrasted, as a whole, to my own memory of colonialism.

Introduction

The ever-transforming process of memory

When the interviews took place in the late 1980s, a minimum of three decades had elapsed since the events they evoked had occurred. After such a time, the interviewees' accounts could only take the form of general statements and allegoric stories about 'what the Congo was like'. Of course, each territorial experience had been unique. A territorial career had led a man through a series of posts which all had a specificity of their own. Each post had been inscribed in a particular geographical milieu. It regrouped smaller or greater numbers of Whites, was inhabited by long-rooted or migrant populations, which all held diverse traditions. Africans were engaged in different economic activities, ranging from 'traditional' agriculture, to work on plantations and in the mining industry, to trade and services. There must have been a real diversity of places,[7] but also of times. The 1930s, for example, had little to do with what happened in the Second World War, or these years with the 1950s (to mention but three periods). However, the interviews hardly unravel this diversity. What emerges from them is a fairly uniform sketch. Listening to the interviewees, the singularity of each individual history can easily be missed. The minute details of what had happened here and there, at such and such a time, are most often lost. This lack of contextual and historial contours need not be seen as a defect, even though it must be reckoned with. In particular, I think one would be ill-advised to attempt to reconstruct the histories of the social configurations which constituted the '*terrain*' of the colony solely from interviews of the kind I conducted. This is why I like to stress that this book is about memory, the act of *recalling* the past, rather than being about the past as such.[8] Let me therefore say a few words about the way memory works. More will be said about it in chapter 5.

The first crucial fact about memory is to recognise that its primary function is not to store and keep the past intact, but to help the individual adjust to the requirements of the present (Hunter 1957). To live in the present, we need to be aware of our past (as well as our future). Memory organises our past for us. It does so through processes such as structuration and synthetisation, which can only distort the past reality. The interviewees obviously presented me with a transformed vision of their past experiences. I did not conceive this as a major problem though, for I am not attempting to provide the reader with a historical account of the Congo. Instead I wish to discuss the ways in which we remember the Congo today and what these ways tell us about ourselves – our visions of life, ethics, self and other.

The second crucial fact about memory is that it is not a process that takes place internally in the mind of an individual, as if in isolation. The social environment in which it takes place directly influences its direction and outcome. In his seminal work on collective memory, Maurice Halbwachs (1925) had already noted that it is most often an external request which prompts us to remember. His observation applies to the interview situation where the interviewer asks the interviewee to recall events, atmospheres, situations. Were it not for me, the former territorials I interviewed would not have searched their memory for reminiscences the way they did. There is more, however, to the social dimension of memory than the mere prompting of answers through questions. The overall social context influences how things get remembered. Thus, both the memory of colonialism of the former territorials and my own developed in response to the way in which the colonial past is talked about, reflected upon, and remembered in Belgium today.

That memory is a social process comes through in chapters 3 and 4. In chapter 3, I describe the way the memory of colonialism I built in my childhood and young adulthood influenced the way I formulated my research project. I also discuss the unexpected influence which meeting and listening to former territorials had on the original project. In the following chapter, I concentrate on the interviewees' memory. I show that what they told me was as much shaped by the present memory of colonialism in Belgium, coming through the media, as by their original experience – which itself combined individual and social elements at the moment it was originally lived. In other words, their memories were not made up of reminiscences *directly* dating back to the 1930s, 40s or 50s. It was also a response to the way in which the Congo has been talked about in the 1960s, 70s, and 80s.

This has to be so, for memory is never static. It is constantly transformed through the present lens, which soon becomes a past layer to be reckoned with in the next act of remembering. Adopting such an approach is not to deny that 'facts' occurred in the past – as they do in the present and will in the future. The development of revisionist theories regarding the Second World War poignantly demonstrates the need to recognise the existence of facts which cannot be interpreted, reinterpreted, or simply erased.[9] To try to get out of this conundrum, I could say that I am leaving to historians the task of questioning informants' statements before considering them as evidence. But this would amount to an unacceptable cop-out. I somehow have to assess the plausibility of the statements I have heard. What I can say is that I have attempted to write this book with historical awareness. At the same time, my main interest nonetheless lies with what both myself and the former territorials have to say, or feel like saying, about colonialism, how this is in tune with our respective memories of colonialism, and what this in turn can tell us about the anthropological project.

A reflexive and diaological ethnography

The debates about colonialism which recurrently take place in Belgium made me acutely aware that I was 'in the way' of the material I was setting out to collect (Agar 1980). On that count only, I felt my influence on the interviews was worth examining. This exercise could be assimilated to a critical assessment of the sources of my work. While necessary, I would argue that this kind of reflexivity would not be going far enough. My 'voice' also deserves scrutiny because it is as socially determined as the voice of the interviewees (Kapferer 1988: 95). In my view, this made it compelling to consider myself as a personage whose immediate role in the interviews and position in the prevailing discourse on colonialism must be an object of analysis (cf Spencer 1989: 157). This task, which I tackle throughout the book but especially in chapter 3, can be seen as the hallmark of a reflexive approach. To me, however, my reflexive intention is most crucially expressed in my attempt to elucidate the way my involvement with the former territorials made my thoughts evolve.[10]

In the last paragraph, the reference to 'my voice' or 'personage' is misleading in that it conceals the fact that there were various 'I's in the course of the research – and in the text. At least three can be distinguished: the naively anti-colonial at the outset of the research, the almost converted to the view of the informants during the early and most intense interviewing period, the analytically critical at the time of writing. But even this typification is a simplification, for these three different persons were not as chronologically situated as the description above seems to indicate. In effect, they did not so much succeed each other as co-exist in various degrees at all times, with all the contradictions this implies. How and why they had, and have, to overlap, is a central concern of this work. To demonstrate the impossibility of a definite synthesis between the various 'I's of the research – and thus between the conflicting memories of colonialism, I adopt a reflexive approach, which pays explicit attention to my succeeding states of mind(s).[11]

Reflexivity is sometimes heralded as a guarantee of transparency. There is no reason why this should be the case. Jules Romains recognised exactly that, some sixty years ago, when he remarked in one of his novels that the author of a scientific essay never allows his reader to share the whole process which led him to his results. To quote him, speaking through the main character of the novel: 'In fact, [the scientist] has done the real work for himself, previously, and we shall only ever know of it what he is willing to let us know' (1972: 11). This sensible remark is true of any work, however reflexive it claims or attempts to be. Transparency seems to imply that everything relevant would be revealed. This is not possible both because memory constantly operates a selection and because the construction of an intellectual argument dictates what will be said – and not said. How to judge the relevance which guides this process is bound to be judged differently by various people, over time and contemporaneously. What is more, the author who engages in a 'reflexive' exercise presents a self-image which she constructs both consciously and unconsciously, both to shield and to disclose personal elements (in the same way as the informant is recognised to do in front of the anthropologist). As Romains says, the reader will only ever know what the author is willing to tell her readers.

Moreover the inclusion of the self in the ethnography can never, in itself, guarantee a better grasp of the reality discussed. For this to be the case, the implication of the presence of the self must be worked out, rather than left to speak for itself. As with any other data, insertion of particular elements calls for clarification and interpretation if these are to become meaningful. In my own effort to achieve meaningfulness, the question which has guided me is: how is it that the interviews turned out to become what they did? To answer this question, I had to pay attention not only to my informants but also to myself, for only our relationship (taking place not only between us as individuals but also between the 'worlds' we stand for) could provide the key to this process. This leads me to the dialogical aspect of my work.

As chapter 5 illuminates, it is clear to me that the data and knowledge I acquired in the course of the interviews were not out there, ready to be discovered, but produced through my soliciting, reacting and generally relating with the former territorials. Johannes Fabian refers to this process as 'the intersubjective nature of ethnographic investigations', the emphasis of which 'signals an intent to go beyond positivism and scientism' (1990c: 765). However, as Fabian notes, including lengthy quotations by informants will not 'automatically preserve the dialogical nature of the knowledge process' (ibid: 764). He continues: 'To preserve the dialogue with our interlocutors, to assure the Other's presence against the distancing devices of anthropological discourse,[12] is to continue conversing with the Other on all levels of writing, not just to reproduce dialogues' (ibid: 766). This is what I attempt to do in chapters 6 and 7 where I put in parallel my own reading of the interviews with the analysis of my work by my best informant, without giving one of us the final word. In doing so, I have not merely reproduced the exchange I have had with my informants through conversations and correspondence during a clearly defined period of fieldwork. I did not wish to do that. Not only is the 'trick of representing dialogue at one and the same time as data and its autopoetic transformation into data' an impossible one (Tyler 1987: 339), but also such finite reproduction would not do justice to the ongoing nature of our exchanges. Even as I revise this introduction four years after my thesis was examined, I expect our dialogues, and certainly the thought they provoke, to go on. It is the sense of a never-ending process which I wish to convey in this book.

Dennis Tedlock (1987) observes that collections of 'native texts' are generally written in the absence, as it were, of the anthropologist, while anthropological ethnographies are written in the absence, as it were, of the informants whose words are included only to support the points made by the anthropologist. He describes the situation in the following powerful words: 'There's a kind of apartheid here; it's as if anthropologists would not allow the natives to be articulate between the same two covers where they themselves were trying to be articulate' (ibid: 326). He makes a similar, but arguably stronger, point elsewhere, where he adds to this image of the absence of co-articulateness the following remark: 'There are, of course, those ubiquitous "native terms", but they do not constitute articulate speech, to say nothing of eloquence' (Tedlock 1983: 324). In other words, the articulateness of the informants is suppressed (see also Cohen 1992: 225). I tend to think that Tedlock identifies a serious defect in much anthropological writing. But this is an easy position for me to take, considering that I happen to have met an informant who is very articulate, highly eloquent, and who was ready to be dragged into my research project, despite the pain this must have caused him.[13] Not only did I meet him for long hours during the interviewing period, but he read my written work and commented on it at greater length than anyone else. This allowed me to write chapter 7 as his response to my own analysis of the colonial experience. His power of thought, however, emerges throughout the book, for I constantly refer to him.

This is not to suggest that I have given voice to him. On one hand, I do not wish this to be the case for I agree with Adam Kuper that trying or pretending to give voice to the other is paternalistic (1992: 69). This is especially so in the case of this study which deals with a relatively privileged group of people who enjoy fairly good access to the public sphere. On the other hand, and more importantly, the ultimate voice in this book is none other but mine. Whether Tedlock likes it or not, the quotations of the interviewees I include illustrate *my* points. This is not to deny the (various degrees of) articulateness of my informants; this is just to recognise that the book is *my* project, and cannot be subsumed within the projects which my informants pursue, or contemplate pursuing. Stephen Tyler blatantly asserts: '[The dialogic impulse] is a trick, a deception intended to make the observed believe they are equal participants' (1987: 340). From my experience, Tyler's critique is overstated: my 'best informant' was certainly not deceived – nor did I intend him to be. In actual fact, as chapter 7 makes clear, he has kept on telling me that I have failed to grasp what he has been trying to tell me over the years.

His observations demonstrate that we, as individuals and holders of explicit or implicit projects, are far apart. At a superficial level, such incommensurability could be seen as a failure. Although I have taken back, to borrow Tedlock's word (1987: 328), the metanarrative of the book to the field and have put it to the test of a further dialogue, our continued disagreement could mistakenly be seen to point to the limits of my approach. Such an analysis, however, would rest on a naive view of what a dialogical anthropology entails. It would turn into non-sense the anthropological project, which is to go beyond the native voice and to try to understand 'how people construct, change and deconstruct their ... social spaces' (Hastrup 1995: 157; see also conclusion). Anthropology can only be dialogical in the sense that it explicitly recognises the dialogical production of ethnographic knowledge, the subjectivity of anthropologist and informants, and the articulateness of both participants. But it cannot refer to a common project (ibid: 148–50).

In her rehabilitation of, and indeed call for, ethnographic writing in the present, Kirsten Hastrup notes exactly that (1992, see esp.: 122). Her analysis of the 'state of the art' is of compelling clarity. It deserves to be read carefully, and here I shall quote at some length a passage where she explains the dialogical nature of anthropological research, the transcendence of anthropological knowledge, and the imperative to use the present tense. To quote her:

> The monograph presents the confrontational knowledge of a particular ethnographer. At the confrontational level acting and speaking are made by

subjects, ethnographers and informants [...]. The anthropological text itself, however, is a discourse about something. [...] What we write is the meaning of action and speech, not the actions and speeches themselves as events. And meaning is positioned, just as discourse is addressed (ibid.).

It is because 'ethnographic knowledge transcends the empirical' (ibid.: 128) that the disourse can or rather should be conducted in the present tense:

> Although fieldwork took place some time in an autobiographic past, the confrontation continues. The past is not past in anthropology; it is ethnographic present' (ibid.: 125). [...] By a narrow historicising approach *we* claim to have exhausted a moment. We have not; meaning is infinite, and the 'other' may have her own project which we should not violate. The discourse must be conducted in the present tense, and by an identified author (ibid.: 128).

Hastrup clarifies why it is that the ultimate voice in an anthropological text must be the anthropologist's. She also infuses goal and optimism in anthropology and demonstrates that taking on board the valuable points raised by postmodern theorists does not need to lead to the conclusion that doing research and writing is an 'impossible' enterprise (see also Hastrup 1995). It is precisely the spirit in which I have tried to write this book.

Why 'Recalling the Belgian Congo'?

The direct and short answer to the question I have just put is that recalling the Belgian Congo is an interesting thing to do. I first started to delve into materials related to the Belgian colony after I was asked to write a paper on colonial punishment in Belgian Africa in 1986. What I discovered astounded me. I had not expected to find *such* blatant racist statements filling page after page of the relevant legal colonial literature, but this is what I felt I was reading. The research opened a new world to me, which rather disgusted me, but which I felt was all the more worth studying.[14] It puzzled me that colonialism belonged to our recent past. Its legacy was bound to mark our present. I was eager to join in the current research on colonialism which was developing in anthropology.[15] Having completed the study, I remain convinced the Congo was worthy of scholarly attention, although perhaps for different reasons. What strikes me now is that my research illuminates general human processes. I would say that its major significance lies less with either an understanding of the thoughts of Belgian former colonial officers (however these may be needed)[16] or an implicit critique of the literature on the 'colonial discourse'[17] than with an acute perception of the difficulty of attaining knowledge in anthropology. In turn this should make us, as human beings, morally humble and wary of any claim whose legitimacy derives from an easy brand of political correctness. Such a conclusion is not specific to colonialism; it applies to all walks of life.

But let us leave my conclusions for chapter 8 and return to the particular focus of this book. I have entitled it 'Recalling' the Belgian Congo for two reasons. The first is that my informants obviously recalled for me their reminiscences of the years they spent in the Congo.[18] This is an active process, which warrants to use the verb in the present continuous tense. The second reason is that my encounter with former territorials convinced me that the Belgian Congo had too much of a bad name: in Belgium among people like me who know very little about it, but also in Britain where I was based as a student. I encountered the same kind of comments whenever I was asked about my research in this country: 'Oh yes, the Belgians have done terrible things in the Congo, so horrible that they certainly deserve to be recorded.' These comments were expressed not only by the average person (whomever he or she is), but also by educated people, for example a journalist working in the African section of the BBC World Service and a University Professor whose doctorate had been on colonialism, although admittedly in a different part of the world. These comments are mistaken, but suggest that the 'red-rubber' atrocities constitute the only episode which has penetrated British consciousness.[19] In this sense one can say that the Belgian Congo has been given an excessively bad name in the UK (and probably elsewhere too). While atrocities indeed took place in the Congo Free State under Leopold II's personal rule, these unacceptable events precede, and therefore cannot be attributed to, the era when the Congo became a colony of the Belgian state. The year 1908 saw the so-called *reprise* (literally 'taking back') by Belgium of the Congo, precisely because of the international protest which developed against Leopoldian abuses. As far as I can see, the Congo after that was no worse a place for the Africans to live in than other African colonies. It is therefore crucial to give the Belgian Congo another name than the one through which it is generally known in the UK. Accepting to re-call the Belgian Congo is important. The book invites the reader to do that.

The book is organised as follows. Chapter 2 (A Glossary in Disguise) provides historical and technical clues which allow the reader to follow the subsequent text and analysis. Chapter 3 (My Project) describes my perspectives on the research project, the state of mind with which I started it and the way my views changed as I proceeded. Chapter 4 (Their Expectations) operates the same kind of decoding as far as the interviewees are concerned, i.e. it discusses how their position in Belgium could affect the way they responded to my project. Chapter 5 (Our Dialogues) attempts to problematise our conversations by looking at a number of issues, including the guarantee of anonymity, the working of memory and the way misunderstandings between researcher and informants easily creep in. Chapter 6 (My Story) presents my own reading of the colonial experience and points at paradoxes in the discourse of the former territorials: maintaining distance with the Africans while claiming to have been close to them, regretting change while working towards development, resorting to violence while seeing persuasion as the main tool of administration. Chapter 7 (Their Response) presents the main objections which my best informant levies against my analysis and my work, namely, that I cannot get rid of my prejudices towards colonialism and that I do not grasp the implications of active engagement with the world. Chapter 8 (Conclusion) raises questions on the production of knowledge and the meaning of understanding in anthropology.

Notes

1. Writing in the past or in the present tense has been a vexing dilemma. I think that Kirsten Hastrup provides the key to this dilemma when she writes: 'Truly, fieldwork takes place in an autobiographic past – but we are *not* writing autobiography. We are writing ethnography, and the discourse presents an implicational order which must have a general validity beyond the moment of the recorded events' (1992: 127). For reasons to which I subscribe and which will be explained below, she concludes : 'The discourse must be conducted in the present tense, and by an identified author' (ibid: 128). This is what I intend to do whenever possible. However, I have not entirely rejected the use of the past when the text seems to call for it. For example, when I recount conversations I held with informants, the present tense just does not work. On the use of grammatical tenses in ethnographic writing, see Davis (1992).
2. The few technical terms I use in this chapter are explained in the next one, entitled 'A Glossary in Disguise'.
3. A five-year civil war ensued, which came to an end when General Mobutu seized power in 1965. The 'march' to independence, and its catastrophic aftermath, must be one of the most debated topics in the human sciences literature on the Belgian Congo/Zaire (as the country was renamed from 1972 to 1997). I refer the interested reader to the following selected works: Slade 1960; Merriam 1961; Lemarchand

1964; Hoskyns 1965; Young 1965; Weiss 1967; Gardinier 1982 and references cited; Stengers 1982; Vanderlinden 1985; Braeckman et al. 1990; Académie Royale des Sciences d'Outre-Mer 1992. See also Bustin (1971), section 'Décolonisation' (vol.I: 57–60) and section 'Suites de la décolonisation' (Vol. II: 13–16), for a bibliography on the subject until 1970.
4. Everybody seems to agree that the Mobutist regime, which emerged in 1965, had disastrous consequences for the Zairian population. In 1980, Gould spoke, amongst other things, of 'near-total breakdown of vital services, military incompetence and repression, mass impoverishment' (Gould 1980: xii; cf Gran 1979). The situation kept deteriorating in the 1980s and 1990s (see for instance Young and Turner 1985; Jacquet 1987; Schatzberg 1988; *Cahiers Marxistes* 1990; *Politique Africaine* 1991; Willame 1991 and 1992; de Villers 1992; Gondola 1997). General Mobutu was ousted in May 1997 by Laurent Kabila. The country was immediately renamed Congo. At time of writing, it is too early to pass a judgment on the new regime, although its refusal to allow UN representatives to investigate alleged massacres of Hutu refugees in the eastern part of the country appears as an ominous sign. It should be noted that the Zairian/Congolese crisis is part of a general crisis in Africa (Bayart 1989; Young 1994).
5. '*Doctrine qui ne considère dans la colonisation que l'intérêt des colonisateurs*'. Note the use of the term '*colonisation*' in this definition.
6. It should be noted that, like any other word, the term '*colonialisme*' is a living one which has been used differently through time. It is interesting that the Petit Robert had opted for the following definition in its 1972 edition: '*Système d'expansion coloniale*'. (Compare with the definition given by the Grand Robert in 1985).
7. Be it in terms of populations, landscapes, production, etc.
8. Thus, I have found recent memoirs by former territorials, published (Dupont 1981 and 1983; Depoorter 1983; Bourgeois 1987; Domont 1988; Willaert 1990; Ghislain 1992; Jacques 1995; Ryckmans 1995) or unpublished (Leroy 1963 to 1977; Augustin s.d. [circa 1985]), and periodicals edited by and for former colonials (such as *Congorudi*) extremely valuable sources for my research, at least as much so as 'historical documents', which nonetheless needed to be called upon for understanding the present memories of colonialism.
9. For a philosphical discussion of the dangers of such a process, see Haarscher (1998).
10. In my view, the most meaningful discussion on reflexivity in anthropology remains that provided by Myerhoff and Ruby (1982). But see also how Hastrup (1995) paves a way to anthropology in a discussion where reflexivity is constantly present, whether explicitly or implicitly.
11. It should be noted that this reflexive approach could theoretically be adopted in respect to the informants whose complex 'self' is also in need of exploration (Cohen 1992). Such a project, however, raises serious difficulties in terms of empirical investigation. Cohen, who recognises this, calls for a more modest, although still very challenging, project, and writes: 'We can use our experience of our selves to contain the anthropologist's temptation to generalise and simplify others' (ibid.: 226). This is a beautiful maxim, which expresses a principle with which I entirely agree, but whose practice I have found extremely difficult to achieve. I am not even sure that I have been thoroughly successful in doing justice to the heterogeneity of the experiences, characters and views which exist among the informants, let alone to the complexity of a single informant!

12. Fabian discusses these in his celebrated work *Time and the Other* (1983).
13. Hastrup (1995, chapter 7) is one anthropologist who acknowledges the violence of our ethnographic practices to our informants. Such acknowledgement seems to be more common among oral historians (see for example Thomson 1990: 81).
14. A similar feeling must guide scholars engaged in analysing what has come to be referred to as 'the colonial discourse' As Nicholas Dirks has remarked: 'So powerful are [colonial] texts and their retellings that colonialism has come to occupy a paradigmatic position in the tropics of discursive power' (1992: 175). He appropriately proceeds to regret that 'it is all too often the case that the historical experience of colonialism – along with the contemporary politics of postcolonialism – gets lost in the elegant new textualism of colonial discourse studies' (ibid.). Homi Bhabha (e.g. 1984; 1986a; 1986b) is one of the prominent figures in this literature (cf Young 1990: chapter 8).
15. I found the work by Johannes Fabian most inspiring. I was thoroughly gripped by his monograph on *Language and Colonial Power* (1986) which appeared just before I embarked on my doctoral research. Since then Fabian has produced more monographs on the Congo/Zaire, equally worth reading (1990a; 1990b; 1996). Wyatt MacGaffey is another important anthropologist of the Congo. I find his explorations of the early encounter between the Africans and the Europeans especially fascinating (MacGaffey 1978 and 1994). For landmark collections on anthropological analyses of colonialism in the last decade, see Cooper and Stoler (1989); Thomas (1992); Pels and Salemink (1994b); *Terrain* (1997). See also relevant headings in the recently edited *Encyclopedia of Africa South of the Sahara* (Middleton 1997).
16. Frederick Cooper has recently noted that, while historical scholarship has started to show the divisions among colonisers and thus to break down monolithic views of colonialism, studies which explore what individual agents of colonialism thought of themselves are still missing (1996: 9). For monographs which look at the colonisers (or Whites) in an interesting way, see Crapanzano 1985; Kennedy 1987; Callaway 1987; Prochaska 1990; Strobel 1991; Schieffelin and Crittenden 1991. See also the seminal essay by Ann Stoler (1989a) on 'Rethinking colonial categories'. Henrika Kuklick (1979) has offered an anthropological study of the British colonial administration in the Gold Coast. While this study has the merit to have been undertaken, it was obviously not influenced by the scholarship which developed in the 1980s. Robert Heussler is another scholar who has studied the British colonial service (1963; 1983; 1987).
17. A central point of Nicholas Thomas's book on *Colonialism's Culture* (1994) is to argue that this literature tends to present colonialism as if it was 'monolithic, uncontested and [always] efficacious'. See also Byrnes (1994: 228).
18. Anthropology has always resorted to personal narratives, even when such an expression was not yet in vogue (for an extensive bibliography, see Langness 1965 and Langness and Frank 1981). Since the 1980s, the social sciences have expressed a renewed interest in the 'life-story' genre, as demonstrated by the following collections: *Annales, Economies, Sociétés, Civilisations* (1980); *Cahiers Internationaux de Sociologie* (1980); Watson and Watson-Franke (1985); *Actes de la recherche en sciences sociales* (1986); Personal Narratives Group (1989). Also worth consulting are the *International Journal of Oral History* and the *Oral History Journal*, replaced since 1992 by the *International Yearbook of Oral History and Life Stories*, and the valuable reader edited by Perks and Thomson (1998). Parallel to this interest in personal narratives, memory has become, in its own right, an object of attention in anthropol-

ogy as in the other social sciences. In anthropology Connerton (1989) can be considered as a landmark. For two recent monographs which make a wonderful use of reminiscences on one hand and personal narratives on the other, see Bahloul (1996) and Caplan (1997). Both these studies acknowledge the reflexivity of the process through which they were produced.

19. Sally Chilver tells me that the same perception lingered on in West African colonial circles (with the exception of the mining sector), until it was finally dissipated by the publication of Lord Hailey's *An African Survey* in 1938, war-time cooperation, and the meetings which took place under the auspices of the Committee for Technical Cooperation in Africa South of the Sahara (personal communication).

That such perception is enduring is confirmed by a recent article on Leopold's Congo which recently appeared in *The Guardian* (13 May 1999). Under the title 'The hidden holocaust', the article discusses the reception in Belgium of a book which claims that ten million people may have died in the Congo Free State (Hochschild 1999). As is reported, the book has infuriated former colonials and been criticized by historians. What is interesting for our purposes is that *The Guardian* would make a story out of the dispute. Feeding on existing British perceptions, the caption by the reproduced picture of Leopold II reads: 'He's reputed to have said, "cut off hands – that's ridiculous. I'd cut off all the rest of them, but not their hands. That's the one thing I need in the Congo"'.

2: A Glossary in Disguise

*T*his book relies on reminiscences by former members of the Belgian colonial service. In turn, these reminiscences make free use of a set of knowledge about the way the colonial service was organised. Especially after the initial interview, my informants were aware that they did not need to explain what the magistrate of police was doing, or the difference between a chiefdom and a sector, or other technicalities of the same kind. I cannot assume, however, that my reader shares this knowledge. The aim of this book is not to describe the colonial service. At the same time, I must put my reader in a position to understand memories of the Belgian Congo by clarifying a few facts about its organisation. The purpose of this chapter is to act as a glossary, i.e. to provide explanations for a number of technical terms. The reader familiar with the Belgian colonial administration or not particularly interested in its details may wish to skip it and return to it if necessary.

The territorial service: creation, ranks and numbers

The *service territorial* (territorial service thereafter)[1] had been established in 1912, i.e. four years after the *reprise* of the Congo by Belgium. The date 1908 marks the end of the personal rule of the King of the Belgians, Leopold II, over the large territory of central Africa. The King had gained sovereignty in Africa by securing recognition of the existence of the 'Congo Free State' by international powers in the 1880s. Due to the international protest, led by the Englishman E.D. Morel, about the abuses of Leopold's regime, the Belgian government reluctanctly took over the Congo, which thus became a colony in the strict sense of the term.[2] The Territoriale (Territoriale), as the service was referred to in common parlance, was created in an effort to redeem the colonial administration from its entanglement in the atrocities which made the Congo Free State infamous. Whether it did represent a breakaway from the previous administration is open to question (Gann and Duignan 1979: 160). It is nevertheless clear that abuses on the scale of those witnessed in the Congo Free State (1885–1908) were not reproduced during the period of the Belgian colony (1908–1960).

At the most general level, the Territoriale's function was to represent the colonial state throughout the colony. The sheer size of the territory to be administered, which represented an area eighty times that of the metropole, made it difficult for the state to maintain effective presence and control. This led to constant redrawing of the administrative map of the colony (de Saint Moulin 1988). The 2,343,930 square kilometres of the colony were divided into six *provinces* (provinces) in 1933. These remained basically unchanged throughout the rest of the colonial period. Each province was divided into *districts* (districts), themselves divided into *territoires* (territories), and further divided into *circonscriptions indigènes* (native circumscriptions). The units of the districts and territories underwent continuous and sometimes major reshuffles, although the principle of the divisions was not altered.

The territorial service was one *service* (service) amongst others (including the agronomic, medical and judiciary services, to list but a few) within the *Administration d'Afrique* (African administration). All civil servants of the African Administration were classified, according to initial salary, into four categories, namely *hauts fonctionnaires* (high functionaries), *fonctionnaires supérieurs* (senior functionaries), *fonctionnaires* (functionaries) and *agents* (officers). Each service encompassed various ranks. Although this is not an official classification, perhaps the easiest way to introduce those within the territorial service is to speak of a territorial presence in the colony at five different levels (see also Table 1).[3] Thus we can talk of the *gouverneur général* (governor-general), the highest administrative colonial authority at the level of the colony and of the *gouverneurs de province* (governors of province) at the level of the province. *Commissaires de district* (district commissaries), responsible for an administrative unit much larger than the 'district commissioner' in the British colonies,[4] and *commissaires de district assistants* (assistant district commissaries) are at the third level, the district. *Administrateurs de*

Table 1: *Administrative divisions and territorial ranks (1947–1960)*

Territorial Division	Rank	Abbreviation (from the French)	Category
Colony	Governor-General	GG	1st: High functionary
Province (6)	Governor of Province	GP	
District (16+)	District Commissary	CD	2nd: Senior functionary
	Assistant District Commissary	CDA	
Territory (110+)	Territorial Administrator	AT	3rd: Functionary
	Principal Assistant Territorial Administrator	ATAP	
(Detached Post)	Assistant Territorial Administrator**	ATA	
	Principal Territorial Officer	Agt Princ.	4th: Officer
	Territorial Officer*	Agt	

** Entry for University graduates   * Entry for humanities degree holders

The territorial service (statute)

The Territoriale (common paralance)

territoire (territorial administrators), *administrateurs de territoire assistants principaux* (principal assistant territorial administrators), a rank officially introduced in 1953 but recognisable in practice before, and *administrateurs de territoire assistants* (territorial assistant administrators) are at the level of the *territory*. Finally, the *agents territoriaux principaux* (principal territorial officers) and *agents territoriaux* (territorial officers) are at the lower level of the territorial hierarchy. The latter were often responsible for a '*poste détaché*' (detached post) within the territory.

In this book I shall only be concerned with the last three levels, which formed what common parlance designated as the Territoriale. Nobody would have said that the governor-general, the governors of provinces, and other higher administrative figures such as the *secrétaire provincial* (provincial secretary) were territorials, even though they legally belonged to the territorial service. In practice the territorials were understood to be those members of the service territorial who belonged to the third and fourth categories (functionaries and officers), as opposed to the first and second ones (high functionaries and senior functionaries).

There were two ranks at which one could enter the Territoriale, namely those of officer and of territorial assistant administrator.[5] A *diplôme d'humanités* (humanities degree), gained after six years of secondary schooling, was required to become an officer. A University degree in any discipline led to joining the service directly as territorial assistant administrator. Candidates to the territorial service had to apply to and be accepted by the Ecole coloniale. The latter was based in Brussels and operated a six-month training course.[6] Only the University graduates with a degree in colonial sciences, and those from the Université Coloniale at Antwerp who were especially trained for the territorial career, were spared this detour through Brussels.[7] The Université Coloniale had been created, for the first three years under the name of Ecole coloniale, in 1920 on the model of the French colonial school (on the latter, see Cohen 1971). It was renamed Institut Universitaire des territoires d'Outre-Mer (INUTOM) in 1949. I shall simply refer to it in this book as the Colonial University.

The graduates from the Colonial University constituted, at least in the 1950s, about 25 percent of the Territoriale.[8] Doctors in law represented around 10 percent of the body. A fair number of these law graduates tended to leave the territorial service after a few years, presumably to turn towards more lucrative and comfortable careers, for instance in the judiciary. Other University graduates accounted for some 7 or 8 percent of the body. All other territorials, thus some 55 to 60 percent of the total, had begun their career with a humanities degree. Most of these men were actually ranked officers or principal officers, two ranks which represented well over 40 percent of the territorial workforce. Former officers were also present at higher ranks, although the higher up on the territorial scale the less represented they became (on all these figures, Dembour 1992a).[9]

The difficult years of the Second World War when no recruitment took place due to the German occupation of Belgium are worth noting. During this period, no recruits could be sent from Belgium, so that territorials in place could not be replaced. Some territorials served seven years with no chance to take the leave in Belgium to which they were theoretically entitled every three years. Those whose career should have come to an end during the War remained in service. The sense of crisis was in no way alleviated by the sudden great intake of new recruits, colloquially known as '*bleus*' (freshers) in 1946. This generation is the one to which the great bulk of my interviewees belong. Referred to as the *relève* (literally the relief), they were brought in to make it possible for the territorials who had been in place during the War to start taking the leave in Belgium to which they had long been entitled. It is generally said that an average of three to four territorials were present in a territory just after the Second World War, with perhaps only one of them enjoying any solid colonial experience. In June 1960 on the eve of independence a territory was often staffed by a dozen or more territorials.

In absolute terms the 1950s indeed saw a steady increase in the number of territorials serving in the Congo and in Ruanda-Urundi.[10] There were just over eleven hundred of them in 1950, sixteen hundred in 1956, and almost nineteen hundred in 1960 (Dembour 1992a).[11] With a sharp increase in the overall number of effectives and thus a continual intake, territorials were mostly very young.

It is generally agreed that the Congo was more densely administered than the other African colonies (Young 1965: 11; Cornevin 1972: 73; Gann and Duignan 1979: 91; von Albertini 1982: 379; Young and Turner 1985: 223). This may well have been the case and could be explained by the presence of officers in the Belgian colonial administration whose 'executive functions' (see below) would probably have been devolved to African intermediaries in other colonies. This would also explain why the Belgians who are said to have looked at the British model of 'indirect policy' for inspiration were more interventionist than their British counterparts. To my knowledge, however, the extent to which the Belgian colonial administration was indeed denser has not been properly studied.[12]

The territorial functions

The Territoriale was said to be the backbone of the colony. Its members represented the State and felt ultimately responsible for 'everything': tax collection, agriculture, transport, justice .... This was the overall feeling even though specialised services had always existed, like justice, or were created at a late stage, like *inspection du travail* (labour control) in the 1950s, and even though not all members of the territorial service were performing the same tasks. The official texts suggest that a division of labour operated according to rank. The senior functionaries (at the level of the district) provided general guidance; the functionaries (at the level of the territory) were considered truly in charge and responsible for the '*politique indigène*' (native policy); the officers (lower level) were deemed competent to perform tasks of 'execution' only (cf the *Vade Mecum* compiled by Gevaerts, 1953 esp.: 140–41 and 7).

The territorial administrator, abbreviated as A.T., was considered to be the cornerstone of the territorial fabric. As one interviewee wrote in answer to a questionnaire where I asked former territorials whether the experience of one function or one place had been particularly enjoyable: 'I have been in charge of a detached post, assistant of A.T., A.T. chief of territory, district commissary. But it was the A.T. chief of territory who was at the centre of everything' (Dembour 1991b: 38). The administrator was indeed ultimately responsible for almost all administrative aspects in his territory. He could lighten his burden, however, by assigning '*besognes matérielles*' (material tasks) to the territorial officers under his authority. The *Vade Mecum* provided a list of such tasks. They concerned the collection of native tax and any other taxes, the census, matters of *état-civil* (i.e. certificates of birth, marriage and death and similar duties), administering the local prison, maintaining transport, guaranteeing fresh food was in sufficient supply, supervising agricultural and road work, taking care of land cases (*dossiers terres*), doing the correspondence and the copying work, etc (Gevaerts 1953: 8). There were three tasks which a functionary could not delegate to an officer: the *conseils de chefferie* (councils of chiefdom), the civil aspect of the '*justice indigène*' (native justice), and the keeping of the native circumscriptions's accounts.

The council of chiefdom

The first function which the Vade Mecum identifies as being in the exclusive remit of a functionary, and thus not allowed to be delegated to an officer, concerns the council of chiefdom. Such councils were seen to provide the link between the State and the population or, phrased more specifically, between the territorials and the African *notables* (dignitaries). Each territory was divided into native circumscriptions. These were of three types: the *chefferie* (chiefdom), the *secteur* (sector) and the *centre extra-coutumier* (extra-customary centre or CEC).[13] The CEC, a legal entity since 1931, regrouped Africans who had left their traditional setting and lived on the outskirts of European posts. These Africans were referred to as '*détribalisés*' (literally detribalised) and were opposed to those who had remained '*coutumiers*', i.e. attached to custom, and who lived in a chiefdom or a sector.[14] The distinction between these two entities had been established by decree of 1933: the chiefdom supposedly represented a purely traditional entity; the sector was created in order to fuse chiefdoms deemed too small to permit an efficient administration.

By nature, the chief of the CEC was 'catapulted' to his position, rather than brought to it by 'custom'. To a lesser extent, the same was recognised to be true of the sector. By contrast, the chief of the chiefdom was deemed to be a purely traditional authority. Hence the colonial canon asserted that he held his legitimacy from 'custom'. He was deemed to be 'recognised' by the territorial authorities, as opposed to 'designated' by them (see Magotte n.d. [1952]).[15] 'Finding' the chiefs (or at least identifying politically acceptable figures), and maintaining and reinforcing (in French '*relever*') their 'authority' and 'prestige' were in all cases key-tasks. The fact that the investiture of the chief was conducted by the district commissary, dressed moreover in white ceremonial uniform instead of the everyday khaki shorts and shirt, illustrates the importance attributed to the task of lending the chief authority.

Contact with the native chiefs was presented as the most fundamental task of the territorial administrators, and always came first in the description of their functions (see for instance decree of 9 July 1923; Gevaerts 1953: 7; Laude 1959: 26). One way to maintain this contact was the council of chiefdom, of which the *Vade Mecum* said: 'It is for the Administrator to convene and preside over the councils of chiefs and dignitaries, and to discuss with them everything which affects the life of the natives' (ibid.: 7). The list of the subjects to be discussed in such meetings reads as follows: 'administration and budget of the chiefdom, hygiene, education, native production, co-operatives, economic works related to food and cash crops, organisation of recruits for the colonial army, works of public interest and private societies, organisation of food supplies for industrial centres, roads and communication, tax rates, etc' (ibid.). What is striking about this list is that all requirements imposed on the colonised population, including the agricultural obligations, the heavily despised army recruitment process, or even the amount of tax to be paid, were first to be the object of a debate in the council of chiefdom. Such an encompassing list points to the necessity for the colonial administration to ensure, at least to some degree, that the people subjected to their domination consented to their policies.

This is not to suggest that the council of chiefdom was a forum of deliberations between equal parties. As an interviewee told me: 'There were discussions, but they did not last for ever. At one stage, we had to act and ensure that the decision imposed from above was executed. There was nothing one could do about it.'[16] Of course, the chief must have been under pressure and cannot be assumed always to have represented the interests of his population. Nonetheless, the council of chiefdom was a crucial instrument in the eyes of the colonial authorities. This is understandable in view of the necessity for the small European administration to rely on African intermediaries for the implementation of its basic colonial policies.[17] Because the council of chiefdom was considered to be a key element in native policy, the *Vade Mecum* presented it as a matter reserved for the administrator (as opposed to the officer).

The judicial organisation

Another function specifically attributed to the administrator was to act as *juge du tribunal de territoire* (judge of the tribunal of territory). This function is best understood within the background of the judicial organisation of the colony, which I shall briefly outline. In my description, I shall concentrate on those courts which are relevant to an understanding of the Territoriale's role in relation to the administration of justice. My description is based on a decree of 1934 which co-ordinated two decrees of the 1920s and which laid down the principles of the judicial framework of the colony until the eve of independence.[18] It will introduce not only the one judicial function reserved to territorial functionaries, but also the other judicial functions performed by territorials.

As in other colonies, there existed a fundamental distinction in the Belgian colonial judicial organisation between the *tribunaux européens* (European tribunals) and the *tribunaux indigènes* (native tribunals).[19] With one exception, these were composed of European and of African judges respectively. (The exception concerns the tribunal of territory which was classified by law among the native tribunals even though the

Table 2: *Judicial Organisation (1934–1958)*

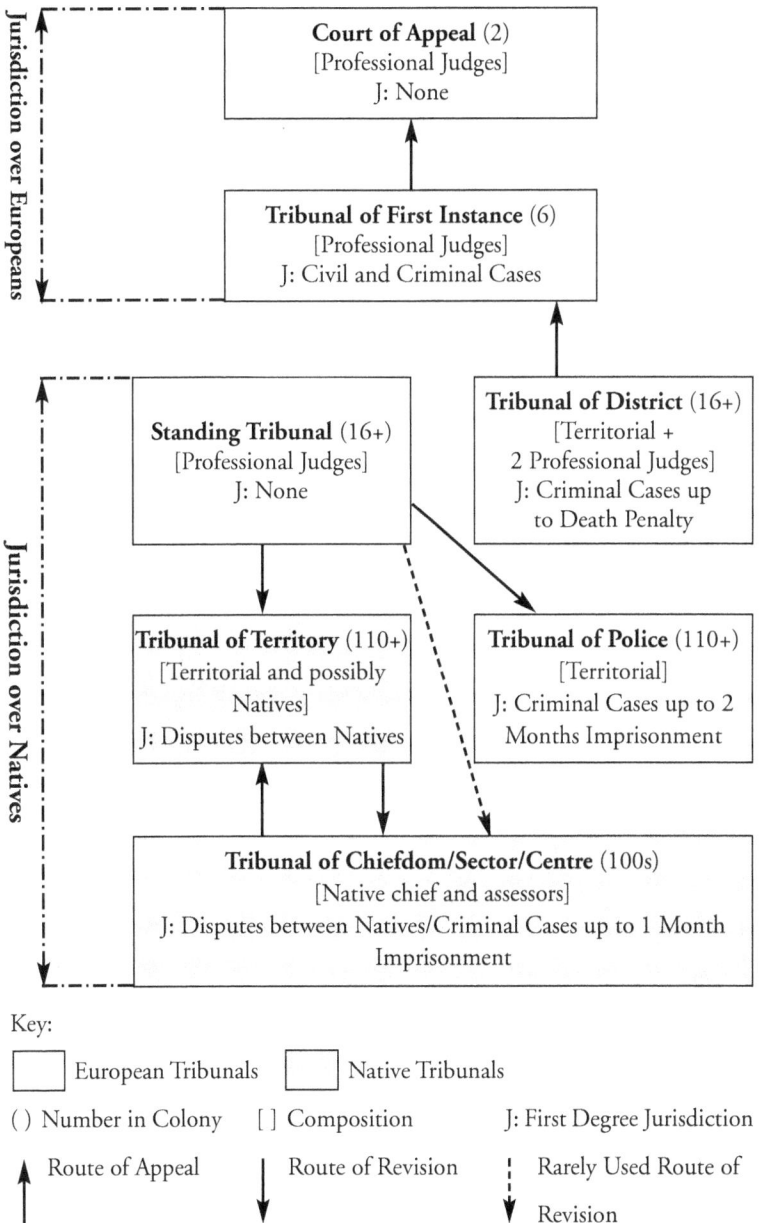

territorial administrator presided over it). It would be an inaccurate portrayal, however, to say that European courts dealt with cases involving Europeans, and native courts with those involving Africans. To present the respective competence of the two sets of courts, one must take into account the distinction classically made in Western law between civil and criminal matters.

As a first approximation let us say that native courts were competent to judge civil cases arising between African parties. The competence of the European tribunals was much broader: it encompassed all cases (whether civil or criminal) involving Europeans as well as criminal cases directed against African defenders. These statements require two qualifications. On one hand, the law had progressively attributed to the native courts competence to pass sentence on Africans for petty offences of an administrative nature. On the other hand, the native courts dealt with what was legally called '*contestations entre indigènes*' (disputes between natives). The term '*contestation*' (dispute) had been chosen to avoid phrasing the jurisdiction of the native courts in terms of either criminal or civil cases, a distinction absent in pre-colonial African law. As a consequence it was possible for a native court to hear a dispute which would have been classified as a criminal offence in a Western legal system. Lack of respect to the chief (interpreted as including disobedience to the administrative obligations the chief imposed as a result of colonial rule) is an example of such a charge: it was not provided for in the penal code, but because it was considered to be a customary infraction it constituted a dispute between natives within the jurisdiction of the native courts.

On the whole, however, the colonial government wanted criminal justice to remain in its own hands. Only in matters which it considered not serious enough to require either an entry in the penal code or a heavy sanction, was it ready to take advantage of the punitive powers of the native courts and to delegate the competence to deal with the offence. In all cases, native courts could not pass sentences higher than one month's imprisonment. Sentences above that had to be imposed by a European court, either the *tribunal de police* (tribunal of police) or the *tribunal de district* (tribunal of district).

There was a tribunal of police in each territory, which was competent to sentence Africans for up to two months of imprisonment. Above this, each district was the seat of a tribunal of district which imposed higher sentences, including the death penalty, on Africans. While the territorial administrators were *juges [au tribunal] de police* (magistrates [to the tribunal] of police) by law, the officers and assistant administrators were generally commissioned magistrates of police after a few months of service. As a consequence, a territory often had as many magistrates of police as territorials working in it. As for the tribunal of district, the district commissary was its legally appointed judge. Nevertheless it was common practice to commission territorial functionaries to this office.

The magistrate of police sat alone according to an expeditious procedure. He sent copies of all his judgments to the *tribunal de parquet* (standing tribunal) for control. Each district was the seat of a standing tribunal, which was composed of *magistrats* (professional judges), i.e. trained lawyers appointed to the judiciary exclusively for the exercise of judicial functions.[20] The most common offences which came before tribunals of police were related to labour law (breaking a labour contract was called 'deserting' and legally sanctioned),[21] agricultural obligations, thefts, common assaults and alcohol (see statistics published in the *Rapports annuels de la colonie*).

The judge of district, whom we have seen was a territorial, sat with two professional judges (the same in practice as those composing the standing tribunal). The tribunal of district was the only court where the Africans were tried by professional judges in the first instance. By contrast Europeans were always tried by such judges: the *tribunal de première instance* (tribunal of first instance), of which there was one in each province and which was exclusively composed of professional judges, was competent to hear the first degree of all civil and criminal cases involving an European. The tribunal of first instance also heard the appeals against the decisions of the tribunal of district. Such appeals, however, were not always possible. By contrast an appeal could always be lodged before the *Cour d'appel* (Court of appeal) against the decisions of the tribunal of first instance relating to a 'European case'. There were two Courts of appeal in the colony: one in Leopoldville, the other in Elisabethville. Such an organisation is of course a reflection of the colour-bar which pertained to all aspects of colonial life (Young 1965: 87–105).[22]

The disputes between Africans, the great majority of which concerned civil matters in the classical Western legal classification, were heard by the native courts. There were four of these: the *tribunal de territoire* (tribunal of territory), the *tribunal de chefferie* (tribunal of chiefdom), the *tribunal de secteur* (tribunal of sector), the *tribunal de centre* (tribunal of centre). The last three directly corresponded to the three (main) statutory native circumscriptions, namely the chiefdom, the sector and the extra-customary centre. The courts attached to these administrative native units were composed of African judges. Supposedly they were following 'traditional' African law both in its procedural and substantive aspects (but see Chanock 1985). The rationale which had presided at the creation of the native courts was that the coloniser should not interfere in the private affairs of the Africans. The native courts were nonetheless subjected to European control through the tribunal of territory, i.e. the fourth native court in the legal nomenclatura, and theoretically the standing tribunal (which in practice had little time to devote to controlling the 'inferior' native courts).

Each territory included one tribunal of territory. Its judges were the territorial administrator and his principal assistant. A judge [to the tribunal] of territory could hear any dispute between natives with the help, if he so required, of *assesseurs indigènes* (native assessors) who were knowledgeable in customary law. In practice, assessors were chosen from among the African judges composing the other native courts of the territory. The tribunal of territory was competent to hear the disputes in first degree. Generally, however, it heard them in second degree. This could occur following two routes. First, a party dissatisfied with the judgment of an 'inferior' native tribunal could draw the attention of the judge of territory, in practice the touring territorial. In this case one talked of '*appel*' (appeal). Alternatively the judge himself could decide that judgments delivered by the (inferior) native courts of his territory needed to be quashed, a conclusion he reached as he read through the books containing the summaries of their judgments. This latter procedure was called '*révision*' (revision). The standing tribunal was responsible for controlling the activities of the tribunal of territory. It exercised this function by inspecting the books of tribunals of territory during touring.

We are now in a position to understand the second function which the territorial administrator could not delegate to a territorial officer. In the words of the *Vade Mecum*: 'It is for the Territorial Administrator to lead and control the activity of the native tribunals, to take cognisance in the tribunal of territory of the appeal or revision of their decisions' (Gevaerts 1953: 7). The reason behind this proviso was that (civil) justice was considered to be at the heart of native policy. The judge of territory was required to make rulings which had implications for the organisation of native society and which were related to matters of potentially great sensitivity to the Africans. Because of this, the function was deemed too important to be left to officers. By contrast, the activity of magistrate of police was considered to be a routine one which did not necessitate especially careful and judicious attention. It only served a disciplinary role – the more so since the prisoners did not see any dishonour in being sent to jail (Dembour 1991a: 83–4). It was thus in the realm of the tasks which could be performed by officers. The 'true' power to punish, however, which is at the heart of the politics of the state, could not be left even to the administrators. Thus, it was dealt with at a higher level, that of the district.

Native accounts

The third function devolved exclusively on the territorial administrators was related to the accounts of the native units. In the words of the *Vade Mecum*: 'It is for him [the Territorial Administrator] to control the revenues and expenses of the native accounts, to lead and control the use of their capital, to check the organisms: health centres, schools, workshops, cooperatives, which they defray' (Gevaerts 1953: 7). The number of organisms listed in the preceding sentence may serve as an indication of the importance of the budgets of native circumscriptions. The management of the native budget in fact represented a crucial factor in the 'development' of the territory. As such it could not have been left to an officer. Major decisions were taken through the allocation of funds. Moreover I am told that *caisses noires* (finances under the counter) existed in every territory. Although their purpose was not so much embezzlement for personal advantage as the stretching of available resources to the maximum possible, the administrator would have insisted on being in control of the account-books.

The distribution of tasks in practice

The three functions which a territorial officer could not perform have now been introduced. The reader may have noticed that the *Vade Mecum* spoke of them as being the attribute of the 'territorial administrator'; it is, however, more accurate to say that they were the province of the territorial functionaries, for the territorial administrator was not alone in assuring the fulfiment of these functions. His principal assistant was entitled to fulfil them too, as well as the other territorial functionaries of the territory, namely the assistant administrators. The young University graduates who joined the service with the rank of assistant were nonetheless performing the same tasks as the officers for at least the first three years.

Some tasks, for instance the actual collection of taxes, were always performed by the officers and the young assistants in charge of a 'detached post'. Other tasks were supposedly executed by officers and functionaries alike. In practice, however, they belonged more to the realm of the former than of the latter. An example of such is provided by the activity of magistrate of police which was more often performed by the officers and assistants than by the administrator and his principal assistant. The same applies to the function of *officier de police judiciaire* (judicial police officer), i.e. to the duty of the officer to report and to investigate offences which come to his attention. All territorials, whatever their ranks, were judicial police officers, and thus under such an obligation. In practice, however, the higher the rank, the more reluctant a particular territorial was to devote time to this function. If circumstances demanded it, the territorial could nevertheless decide to take the investigation of a case into his own hands. A former district commissary, for instance, explained to me how he did so when a European was murdered in his district.

Ranks and functions did not always coincide. The law decreed that function was independent of rank (article 35 of the 1947 statute). As a consequence, a territorial could fulfil functions generally attributed to a rank superior to his own. For instance, when a territorial administrator was leaving, his principal assistant could be asked to take over the functions of territorial administrator, although he did not have this rank. He was then referred to as *A. de T. f.f.* (*faisant fonction*) (acting) and acted as chief of territory. Due to the frequent turn-over of the officers entitled to six-month leave after each tour of three years, such a situation was not unusual. Functions were more important than ranks in the sense that they determined titles, insignia and precedence.

Internal organisation: Transfers, itinerance and control

Territorials were entitled to a six-month leave every three years. Despite the increase in the numbers of territorials through the 1950s, re-allocating the functions which had been fulfilled by a territorial who was departing always remained a Chinese puzzle. In some cases the work could be redistributed among the remaining territorials of the territory, with one thus becoming a *f.f. (acting)*. A subordinate might be called upon to perform the tasks of the departing superior as explained in the previous paragraph. Someone coming back from leave might be sent to fill the post, with a possible intermediate solution in which a territorial fulfilled functions *ad interim*. Failing the above, the only alternative was to order the transfer of a territorial from another territory (thus creating problems of replacement in that territory).

The 'interests of the service' continually commanded transfers, either on return from leave or during a term of office. A territorial could receive an order of transfer at very short notice, without having a say in the matter: orders had to be obeyed. For a territorial to remain in the same territory throughout his career was a thoroughly exceptional situation. (My 'best informant' who entered the territorial service in 1946 as an officer actually did remain in one area; he tells me he only heard of one other territorial in the same position). Most transfers took place within the same district up to the rank of territorial administrator, and within the same province above that. A territorial was rarely posted in more than two provinces in the course of his career.

The relatively rare transfers from one province to another could follow personal requests. One interviewee, for instance, had asked to be posted outside the province of Equateur, renowned for its unhealthy climate, after his two eldest children successively died of malaria in infancy. His request was granted and he was transferred to the Kivu province which enjoyed a moderate climate. The transfer to a different province could also be motivated by political reasons, or act as a disciplinary sanction. Of course transfers also occurred as an honorific reward, following promotion to a rank within the senior functionaries range.

The fact that the great majority of territorials stayed in the same district for a number of years ensured that they were generally acquainted with the societies they were administering. The interviewees nonetheless agree that frequent transfers should not have been allowed to take place in an ideal situation (see also the *Vade Mecum*, Gevaerts 1953: 142). They disrupted the continuity of the administration. They also destroyed any incentive to acquire an in-depth knowledge of the local languages and customs. Too often, I am told, knowledge was limited to the lingua franca and to no more than the principles governing the African social systems of the region rather than the detailed customs of the various groups.

The accepted wisdom was nonetheless that the territorials were 'in direct contact with the African populations' (Tancré-Van Leeuw 1992: 401; see also Scohy 1952: 1–5; but also chapter 6 for a critique of this view). The obligation of touring, a distinct characteristic of the Belgian colonial administration, probably prompted this feeling. Officers were theoretically required to tour their area for twenty days per month, administrators fifteen. The latter figure allowed for the continual presence of a functionary at the *chef-lieu* (headquarters) of the territory, either the chief of territory or his principal assistant. A few territorials did not tour because of the nature of their functions. This was, for instance, the case of the *comptable-gardien de prison* (accountant-jail warden) who was an officer posted at the headquarters of the territory.

The assigned targets in the number of '*jours d'itinérance*' (touring days) were probably rarely met (as annual *Rapports de territoire* I consulted suggest). They nevertheless represented an objective which the territorials had to take seriously, as the private archives of an interviewee indicate. The monthly comments which this (then) territorial assistant administrator received in 1954 from the territorial administrator twice began with the words: 'Residing twenty days a month in native quarters is a target which must be met.'

A day was included for the purpose of the calculation of touring when a territorial had not spent the night in his main habitation (i.e. either in the detached post of which he was in charge or in the headquarters of the territory). If the territorial had travelled back and forth to his principal residence on the same day, it did not count as a 'touring day', whatever the distance covered. After the War, accommodation during tour was generally sought in *gîtes d'étapes* (rest-houses) which had progressively replaced the tent of earlier years. In many cases, the rest-house was just a hut, perhaps slightly larger than the native one. Comfort was variable, but never more than rudimentary. Intensified building efforts resulted in the multiplication of brick constructions, but not in remote places. The latter were thus often for the benefit of the other members of the African Administration who were also travelling, but not to such places. Everything needed during the tour was packed in trunks. Thus there were the *malle-lit, malle-cuisine, malle-bain, malle-bureau* (bed-, kitchen-, bath-, office-trunks) and so on. These various trunks were either carried by Africans or loaded in a van. If she so wished, the wife accompanied her husband on his tour, possibly with their children under school age.

Before the Second World War, journeys had been done on foot or carried on a *tipoye* (hammock). This continued to be the case throughout the 1950s if no roads crossed the regions to be visited. But the car undoubtedly became the favoured means of transportation after the War and, as a result, there was a transformation in the way the tour came to be organised. Before, it had been from village to village, spending a few days in each, in the knowledge that the place would not be revisited perhaps for a few months. With the advent of the car, distances were worked out differently. Visits would be made as various duties necessitated, without long days being spent in one particular place, and allowing more time to be spent at home with the family.[23] Another transformation worth noting is the increased emphasis on paper-work in the post-War period, which also affected the organisation of the tour (cf Quinet 1955: 11). The organisation of the *pièces annuelles* (annual reports) alone kept the territorials busy throughout December and January.

Although they enjoyed a large measure of autonomy, territorials were not entirely free to do as they pleased or to arrange their time as they wished. Priorities set at a high level had to be respected. For each territory, targets (in regard to tax collection, agriculture, the building of constructions and roads ...) were decided each year at the province level on the basis of yearly reports.[24] The district commissary ensured that the realisation of the targets was satisfactorily progressing in the various territories of his district through the year. He instructed the chiefs of territory accordingly, while the latter made sure that the work of the officers and territorial assistant administrators of their territory kept pace with these requirements.

Officers and assistants received monthly instructions from the chief of territory on what their activities should be in the coming month. The form of these instructions depended on the circumstances and the traditions which had developed in different territories. It varied from a detailed plan for each day to a general invitation to continue what had been done so far. Territorials also kept a daily record of their activities in a *journal de route* (road diary). The latter, written up monthly, briefly indicated the places where the territorial had stayed each day (including Sundays), how many kilometres he had travelled and what had been his main activity (there was generally none on Sunday). This was followed by the number of inspections of *C.A.I.* (*caisses auxiliaires indigènes*) (native auxiliary accounts), reviews of native courts records, judgments as magistrate of police and judgments as judge to the tribunal of territory he had done. The road diaries were sent to the chief of territory who forwarded them, together with his own, to the district commissary. Comments on these by the superior were then sent to the subalterns.

This exchange of correspondence represented a form of control, in so far as it provided general information on the activities that had been performed by the territorials. It nonetheless gave no indication of how the territorials performed them or on their conduct in general. Presumably this is the reason why the law insisted on control exercised on the spot. To turn once more to the edicts of the *Vade Mecum*:

> Administrative control both by the District Commissary over the Territorial administrators and by the Territorial administrators over subordinate members of the administration must take place afterwards and on the spot.

Contact in writing between the personnel must be kept to the minimum. It is *in situ* that the chief must check what has been done (Gevaerts 1953: 141–2).

Although the tours accomplished by the functionaries of the territory of course enabled them to perform their specific functions, essentially presiding over the councils of chiefdom and acting as judge to the tribunal of territory, they also served as a means to control the activity of their subordinates (including checking the state of the roads, how the constructions were progressing, which policy was generally maintained in the post). At district level, the senior functionaries were also invited to carry out tours. In their case, the purpose of the tour was not so much the performance of specific functions as the exercise of a general function of control. Rather than their visits being strictly provided for in enacted law or in circulars, it was up to each district commissary and district assistant commissary to decide when and where to go. They planned their tours according to their personal inclination, state of health or interests. The frequency and length of the tours could therefore vary greatly from district to district. The same can be said of the tours undertaken by the professional judges of the standing tribunal.

How effective these controls were remains open to question. Presumably many things could take place without the knowledge of the superior officer. For instance I was told of the case of an officer who was sexually abusing the prisoners of his detached post in a particularly sadistic way. Months passed before the case was reported to, and investigated by, the territorial administrator. As soon as the facts were established the officer was sent back to Belgium and imprisoned. I do not doubt the integrity of the (then) territorial administrator, a law graduate with a deep concern for justice and strong determination in ensuring respect for principles, as many events in his career demonstrate. Had he been better informed, I am sure he would have reacted immediately against the officer whose conduct he would never have condoned. Although this particular story indicates that the control exercised by superiors over subordinates was a real possibility, it also demonstrates that serious loopholes remained.

The territorials were not free to do as they wished, and sanctions of various degrees of gravity were provided for by the statute for undetermined disciplinary offences. They were (in 1947): reprimand, admonishment, loss of half of one's salary for up to fifteen days, transfer, suspension for up to one month, suspension for an indeterminate period, and loss of employment. Of course it was also possible for the administration not to integrate officers in the service after their '*stage*' (first three probationary years). Territorials were certainly aware of limits beyond which they could not go without risk to their career. For an illustration, let us turn again to the private archives of an interviewee.

When the related incident took place in 1954, the interviewee in question had been a territorial assistant administrator for two and a half years. One day a native authority had requested that he intervene to assist in the reintegration into the village of two men who had recently left it. Acting, in his own words, 'in the interest of the service and with the aim of safeguarding the policy against village dispersal', he had sent two policemen to 'exercise moral pressure' on the two men. Instead of moral pressure, the policemen took down the bamboo walls of their new huts and made them prisoners. This was illegal. Following their complaint, a disciplinary action was started against the A.T.A. In consideration of his otherwise excellent work and in view of the fact that his *bonne foi* (good-will) had been betrayed by the action of the policemen, the *Procureur du Roi* (attorney in charge of the prosecution of Europeans) eventually decided to drop the case against him. His chief of territory nevertheless admonished him in the following way: 'I am nonetheless obliged to reproach you. When you address an order to subordinates, do it with precise instructions; seriously examine complaints of this kind before taking any decision.' He also had to pay damages to the two men. More than thirty years later, when I turned the pages of the private archives testifying to this incident, his comments were something like: 'This was serious, very serious. It was no laughing matter. My career could have been ruined.' Whether this is an exaggeration I am not able to say. But what is certain is that fear of sanctions was present, probably increasingly so over the years, and must have acted as a deterrent to many territorials belonging to the generation I interviewed.

Once again, this is not to suggest that abuses never took place. This all too real possibility represented a serious concern for the higher authorities, perhaps particularly so in view of the historical reasons which led to the creation of the territorial service. In 1932, the future Governor-General Ryckmans[25] gave an address to an audience of metropolitan lawyers on the theme '*La loi et l'homme*' (Law and man) where, in very harsh words, he described his colonial experience. To cite just one paragraph representing the tone of the text:

> Is this hypertrophy of the ego a colonial disease? Not at all. The virus exists everywhere, including in Europe. This virus is nothing else but Force – a dangerous, deceiving Force. A Force which ends up weakening because it

first creates blindness; a blindness that negates experience, because it falsifies the lessons of life, because it gives success without merit and allows for mistakes to take place without sanction. A Force which pretends to be wisdom, a Force which loses sight of reason ... But what is colonial is the atmosphere, a cultural hotchpotch which leads to a monstrous proliferation of vanity. After all, few men in Europe enjoy authority without any discussion, power without any safeguard, power without any control. While there! In Bangala or in Kiswahili, one translates 'quia nominor leo' as 'because I am a white man' (Ryckmans 1948: 167).

The text continues with concrete examples of situations which, without ever amounting to criminal offences, illustrate how power could blind territorials against experience and make them lose all sense of judgment. It is to be noted that the author carefully distinguishes between the nature (or effect) of force which is not peculiar to the colonial world, and the social conditions of its expression where the specificity of the colonial situation plays an essential role. He speaks of the colony as a world where authority is not discussed, force not counterbalanced, power not curbed. Perhaps, to get his message across, he chooses words which are especially strong. Nevertheless he touches upon a nerve in the system, well rendered in the French translation of the title of a book dealing with the French colonial administration in Africa: *Empereurs sans sceptre* (Cohen 1973). This title, which literally translates as 'Emperors without sceptres', could equally have applied to other colonial administrations, including the Belgian one.

At the beginning of my research, a friend suggested I should meet the father of her partner for she thought he had been governor of a province in the Congo. When I enquired further, she said she was not actually sure of the title of the functions he had fulfilled, but that she knew he had been responsible for the administration of a very large region. It turned out her 'father-in-law' had finished his Congolese career as a principal assistant territorial administrator. My friend's original lapse must have derived from what her partner had remembered he was told as a child. It is nevertheless significant: an ordinary post, accessible to most middle- and upper-lower-class Belgian men, was presented as the seat of a very important personage. In this case it was the story of a father happy to dazzle his young son by suggesting that he had been administering a territory as big as a Belgian province. But in some minds the 'innocent' presentation of self for the purpose of story-telling could transform itself into fantasy and belief in one's great powers. Thus the dangers identified by Ryckmans might arise.

Territorials were very conscious of the concentration of powers they enjoyed. Little details, such as the fact that they had precedence over the members of the other administrative services of equivalent rank, irrespective of seniority (article 40 of the 1947 statute), reminded them, if at all necessary, of the central importance ascribed to the service to which they belonged. An article entitled '*Tu seras broussard*' (You'll work in the bush'), published in a a popular Belgian magazine just at the end of the War, presented the territorial career in the following terms: 'The whole life in the Congo is based on the territorial administration; this is why we can consider this career as the one which offers the most wonderful work to the colonial' (*Le Moustique*, 29 July 1945, no. 20, 3). Territorials indeed asserted with pride that the Territoriale was the '*épine dorsale*' (backbone) of the colony.

The territorials as a group of Belgian men in a wider society

The reader may have understood from my account that territorials were male. Women were never considered for entry in the territorial service. During the Second World War, when shortage of staff was deeply felt, the help of so-called '*dames auxiliaires volontaires*' (volunteer auxiliary ladies) was sought. My informants emphasise that their assistance was restricted to purely mechanical tasks such as the typing of reports. They were neither remunerated, nor were they *a fortiori* members of the service (on the status of the white woman in the Congo, see Van Leeuw 1987).

It would have been unimaginable for women to be accepted in the ranks of the Territoriale for territorial functions were perceived to be of a distinctly male nature (cf Callaway 1987: 4–8; Kirk-Greene 1991: 62). This is very well rendered by the statement of a former territorial explaining (probably in the late 1970s) that his job had to do, amongst other things, with a 'certain male pride … (yes that's right) to … go and assume a commanding role' (Van Leeuw 1981: 148). The 'yes' in parenthesis indicates the deliberate choice made by the author of using the qualificatory '*mâle*' which is not as commonly used in French as in English and emphasises male nature – almost in a bestial way. Presumably it conveys the sense of perfect legitimacy there was/is in his view in seeing command as a male attribute. The three little words in brackets seem to say: let us call a spade a spade and recognise the nature of the world without making a fuss about it.

There was a feminine presence within the territorial service, but it was a peripheral one. For a long time it had been the unofficial policy to discourage men from bringing their wives to the Congo. A letter dated 1 February 1927, addressed apparently by a doctor to the students of the Colonial University, advised against bringing a wife to the Congo; among undesirable consequences it was mentioned that the tropical climate and colonial conditions of life released female sexuality in an uncontrollable way.[26] A number of territorials were nonetheless married, and with a family, before the Second World War. But it is only after the War that men were commonly arriving in the Congo already married or bringing back a wife after their first or second leave in Belgium. All interviewees agreed that wives, and especially the wife of the chief of territory, were key persons in the post, either facilitating its smooth administration or destroying it by exacerbating tensions. As *'maîtresses de maison'* (hostesses, literally leaders of the house), they fulfilled important social functions, organising numerous parties and hosting travelling guests. In so doing, they influenced the quality of the relations between different branches of the administration and different sectors of the white community.[27]

If women were conspicuous by their absence from the centre of the Territoriale, the Africans were equally relegated to its periphery, although in another way. As with women, this is not to say that they had no role to play in the administration of the colony. Without the help of African *'auxiliaires'* (auxiliaries), a territorial would never have been able to perform the various functions which had been attributed to him. To take the example of tax collection, African *collecteurs principaux*, *délégués* and *subdélégués* (principal, delegated, and sub-delegated collectors) were doing most of the work, although the ultimate responsibility for the collection lay with the officer – or the assistant. Needless to say, the tasks accomplished by the African auxiliaries were exclusively those considered to be of a very subaltern executive nature.

The administration was not only composed of the four categories listed above, but also of three categories, numbered 5 to 7, and reserved exclusively for Africans. Once an auxiliary had been promoted to the fifth category, he had no chance of further advancement. He was barred from entry to the fourth on two grounds: firstly because he could not present the required humanities degree and secondly because he did not fulfill the condition of nationality. The education system of the Congo, segregated and in the hands of the missionaries, resulted for a long time in the lack of equivalence between the degrees received by the Africans in the Congo and those conferred in Belgium. Even in 1953, only two or three individuals could have taken advantage of a humanities degree (Young 1965: 96). The numbers of Africans in such a position significantly increased in the 1950s, reaching four hundred by 1958 (ibid.: 96). At that time the condition of nationality to enter the fourth category of the colonial administration was still imposed – and would be for another year.

Originally, at a time when it was difficult to persuade Belgian recruits to embark for the Congo, the law had omitted, no doubt purposefully, to enact any condition of nationality for entry into the African Administration.[28] As might be expected, members of the latter were nonetheless Europeans. As time passed, and notably in 1933, the nationality of the members of the administration became an object of discussion (Van Leeuw 1981: 20). In 1947, the new statute formally restricted entry into the administration to those in possession of the Belgian – or Luxemburgese – nationality (article 6). In so doing it only endorsed the contemporary practice.

It is not surprising that it was not deemed appropriate for Africans to hold posts of responsibility within the territorial service, for it was generally assumed (although with some exceptions) that the Africans were by nature lacking any sense of initiative and responsibility and that they could not have been trusted with the exercise of territorial functions. Presumably, the latter, including those attributed to the officers, needed to be reserved to a *corps d'élite* (elite body), acting as the representative of Belgium in the colony. Of course, this particular discrimination was consonant with the general colour-bar which pervaded the legal rules (related to education, justice, work, …) and the social practices of the Belgian Congo. Following the movement of the late 1950s towards the relaxation of these segregationist measures, a new statute was finally enacted in January 1959, with the consequence that the territorial service included a few black officers at the time of independence on 30 June 1960.

This chapter has set out to provide the reader with a clear understanding of terms which occur in the book, so as to eliminate the need to elucidate the reminiscences of the interviewees through long footnotes explaining the terms they use. Obviously it does not offer a full introduction to the work, methods and objectives pursued by the Territoriale in the Belgian colony. What is particularly missing in this account is the context of the relationships between the territorials and the population. A few statements cannot do justice to the complex composition of the latter. I shall nevertheless attempt to provide sketches of the European and African colonial groups, after having emphasised that some in the colony, e.g. Asian but also 'coloured', did not fall squarely within this two-fold classification.

The Europeans have traditionally been represented as forming an alliance of interests between three Cs, namely Command, Church and Capital (see, for instance, Young 1965; Markowitz 1973; Kanyinda 1975; Vellut 1981). If we agree for the moment to equate the first branch of the alliance with the territorials and to forget about the other members of the administration, two main groups of European actors on the colonial ground remain – the missionaries on one hand and the employers of the private sector on the other. By the territorials' own generalised accounts, their relations with the former were varied, although on the whole and with a few exceptions, unproblematic.[29] The picture they give of their relationships with the employers is often that of a pestering pressure, at least in posts with a high concentration of settlers around them (such as in many territories of Kivu) or located at the centre of important industrial sites (such as in Katanga). One classical form of pressure was a request to sanction Africans who had 'deserted'. Allegedly these attempts by the employers were only intermittently successful. This is not especially surprising. Vansina has indeed warned against the dangers of seeing the various European groups as simply converging in serving the colonial interests, and has stressed the rivalries which existed between them (1972: 283; see also Stoler 1989a: 135–7). In places where the absence of employers meant that economic activity focused on governmentally-imposed agricultural production, the private sector was still on the scene, for agricultural production ultimately benefited private companies, such as the Cotonco, which bought and re-sold most harvests. Nonetheless, territorials in such regions did not feel they were under great pressure from economic European interests.

While the Europeans of the colony are conveniently broken down into three sectors, the colonial African population defies easy classification. Vellut speaks of a fundamental distinction between the Africans who worked either directly or indirectly for the Europeans and those who made up the 'rural mass' of the 'bashenzi', but he insists on the limits of this distinction (1981: 51). In this, he is followed by Perrings (1979) and Higginson (1988 and 1989) who have both documented how the mine-worker often returned to his village periodically and, to this extent, remained a peasant. Nevertheless, making a distinction between peasants and workers is heuristically useful, and broadly corresponds to that forcefully asserted by the colonials between the rural and the urban African populations, between the '*coutumiers*' (difficult to translate, those who remained attached to custom) on the one hand and the '*détribalisés*' (literally, detribalised) and '*évolués*' (difficult to translate, those who have evolved) on the other.

A variety of Africans served as 'middle-men' between African peasants and workers and Europeans. Such intermediaries were found in the three European sectors identified above. Thus the missionaries employed catechists and nurses; private companies and settlers needed so-called *capitas* to supervise teams of workers; and the administration relied on a series of 'middle-men' amongst whom I have already mentioned the chiefs and tax collectors, but who also comprised policemen, clerks, drivers, capitas, and so on. Another category of middle-men was constituted by the 'boys' who worked in the houses of the Europeans.[30]

My best informant established three categories among the Africans employed by the administration. Firstly there were workers, such as builders, roadmenders, drivers, who were employed by the territory on an *ad hoc* basis and who were paid out of chiefdom accounts. Secondly, there were auxiliaries who were again directly employed by the territory but whose functions were specifically recognised by the statute, such as the policemen, the tribunal clerks, the *moniteurs agricoles* (agricultural instructors). Finally, there were civil servants with a formal education basically corresponding to the Belgian technical humanities, whose employment did not depend on the person of the chief of territory (who 'inherited' them), such as the clerks in charge of keeping some aspects of the account-books and the secretaries who typed reports in French. The *planton* (untranslatable) assumed a particular role. Not mentioned in any statute, he assisted the administrator in all kinds of ways, hopefully becoming his '*homme de confiance*' (literally, trustworthy man).

The above sketches have implicitly dealt with male populations, and excluded women and children. This reflects the prevailing representations of colonial reality, legal or otherwise, in which only men are taken into account. An excellent example of this trend is the fact that it was the *H.A.V.*, or *homme adulte valide* (adult and able-bodied man), who was legally responsible for the obligatory cultivation of crops even though it was common knowledge that it was the African women who were growing food-crops (cf. MacGaffey 1988: 163 and 167; 1991: 34–5).[31] Except in a few situations (including court proceedings), territorials tended not to meet African women in the performance of their functions. 'Absence' from the legal text and from routine contact occasioned by work were echoed in an almost general disregard for African women during the interviews. In turn this book also contains very few references to them. Although this must be deplored, it may well be that scholars need to be specifically interested in the predicament of African women to be in a position to pay attention to their position in society. The same is even more true of children.

Notes

1. The first time I use a technical term, I leave it in French, but I normally offer an English translation in brackets immediately afterwards. It is to this translation that I resort afterwards.
2. On the institutional history of the Congo Free State, see e.g. Slade (1962); Stengers (1963 and 1989); Louis and Stengers (1968); Académie Royale des Sciences d'Outre-Mer (1988). On the 'red-rubber' atrocities of the Leopoldian regime, see Harms (1975) and Vangroenweghe (1986).
3. The intricate details of the history of the administrative organisation of the colony need not detain us (but see Van Leeuw 1981: 25–6). The Minister of Colonies Pierre Wigny introduced a simplified structure in 1947, on which I base my account for the following reasons. Firstly most men I interviewed left for the Congo after 1945 so that there is little point in describing the previous structure. Moreover, the simplified structure of the 1947 reform is recognisable in the earlier and more complex administrative pattern. This is not to deny that the pre-1947 sub-divisions had significant implications for the persons concerned, notably regarding salary and promotion.
4. This is why I have decided not to translate '*commissaire de district*' as 'district commissioner'.
5. The holding of a University *candidature* actually allowed entry to the service at the rank of principal territorial officer. This possibility was rarely used in practice.
6. The duration of the course was progressively increased from eighty days at the creation of the school in 1910 to six months (Van Leeuw 1981: 21).
7. With exceptions such as that at the end of the Second World War when candidates to the territorial service were sent to the Congo without any special training.
8. This represents a lower percentage than is generally assumed. In 1959, Dekoster, a former student of the Colonial University, estimated that the latter produced 90 percent of the territorials (1959: 160). This figure is undoubtedly too high. Even in 1960, only 56 percent of the whole rank of territorial administrators were constituted by graduates of the Colonial University (Dembour 1992a). Nevertheless the myth that almost all territorials were trained at the Colonial University has persisted (see for instance Kestergat 1985: 73; Cornevin 1989: 265).
9. Appendix 1 provides basic career information about the former territorials I cite in this book, including their training. This table makes it clear that my sample of interviewees is disproportionately biased towards Colonial University graduates and lawyers. Out of twenty-five interviewees I cite, twelve were trained at the Colonial University and seven were law graduates. The bias towards Colonial University graduates is explained by their marked tendency to keep in touch with each other, for example through an annual banquet, so that they referred me to friends. In the book, I cite only four territorials who entered the service with a humanities degree or a University candidature, thus as officers. This is of course completely out of line with the fact that officers constituted over 40 percent of the territorial workforce. The former officers I cite, however, are major figures in this book. They include 'Milnaert', 'de Glaise' and 'Peters'.
10. Belgium had occupied Ruanda-Urundi during the First World War and was given in 1923 the mandate to administer the territory by the League of Nations (for the legal details of this history, see Reyntjens 1985: chapters 2 and 3).

11. These figures include territorials temporarily 'detached' to other services and for the performance of specific functions, as well as those on leave; terms of appointment were for three-year tours followed by six-month leaves in Belgium.
12. The authors cited above all rely either on Buell (1928: 466) or on each other to make this assertion, which suggests that more detailed comparison remains to be undertaken before evaluating the respective density of the administration of each colony.
13. There were also a few *cités indigènes*; moreover *communes* were established in 1957 (Beyens 1992).
14. The division of Africans into ethnic groups and tribes has since been criticised by historians and anthropologists as a colonial invention (see e.g. Amselle and M'Bokolo 1985; Verdeaux 1987; Chrétien and Prunier 1989).
15. My best informant accordingly never failed to castigate me for speaking of the 'nomination' of the chiefs of chiefdoms. That there was a difference of emphasis between the three types of circumscriptions and that the colonial administration often put great effort into finding *the* 'legitimate' chief of a chiefdom (arguably, of course, an impossible task) is without doubt. At the same time, it remains that 'recognition' was often a romanticised view of a very different practice, as some colonial authorities were perfectly aware (see, for instance, Kestergat 1985: 77 and 176–8).
16. See Engels and Marks for an interesting collection of essays illustrating 'the continous but uneven association between coercion and consent' in colonial Africa and India (1994: 8).
17. On the necessity of indirect rule for the coloniser in Africa, see Fields (1985). But on the danger of using a single expression ('indirect rule') to cover policies which differed throughout the colonial period, see Vansina (1972).
18. The decree of 26 November 1934 amalgamated the decrees of 9 July 1923 and of 15 April 1926, respectively dealing with European tribunals and with native ones. As part of the reforming move of the late 1950s, a decree dated 8 May 1958, which entered into force on 15 April 1960, abolished the dual criminal system described in this section.
19. For a useful critique of the so-called *régime dualiste* and its progressive abolition in Zaire in the name of 'national integration', see MacGaffey (1982).
20. Note that magistrate (in English) and *magistrat* (in French) are what linguists call faux-amis, i.e. one cannot be translated as the other.
21. Not surprisingly, the subject of 'desertion' figures prominently in monographs dealing with mineworking (Perrings 1979; Higginson 1989).
22. For a critical appraisal of the criminal judicial system, see Dembour 1991a.
23. The discussion of the role of women in the colonies has often turned around the question of whether they reinforced racial prejudices (see for instance Brownfoot 1984; Gartrell 1984; Callaway 1987; Stoler 1989a: 146–9). My sociologically-minded informant, whom I call 'Milnaert' in the text, suggested that the feminine presence widened the gap between Europeans and Africans, not so much through racist prejudices as through the new construction and perception of the home, now decorated in the Western tradition, and to which the territorial returned in the evening. For a text expanding this comment, see Strobel 1991. For a recent collection of studies of Western women in colonial settings, see Chaudhuri and Strobel (1992). For a collection which points to the importance of introducing gender in all

aspects of colonial studies, see the special issue of *Gender and History* on *Gendered colonialisms in African History* edited by Hunt et al. (1996).
24. Vansina (1972) notes the conflictual views which could exist in that respect between members of the administration, especially working at different levels, such as the territory and the province.
25. For his biography, see Vanderlinden 1994.
26. Archives Moriamé, Boîte A, Farde I, Musée Royal d'Afrique centrale, Tervuren.
27. As hinted in the advice given to '*partantes*' (departing women) in the brochure prepared by the Union des femmes du Congo belge et du Ruanda-Urundi (1956: 78–80).
28. See Gann and Duignan for a table of the nationalities of the Congo Free State officials in 1908 (1979: 100).
29. On the relationships between the administration and the missions, see Markowitz (1973).
30. For an insightful study of servants in another part of Africa, see Hansen (1989).
31. In practice, although again not legally, building-work could also be the responsibility of women – and children (Jewsiewicki 1987: 114).

3: MY PROJECT

At a time when anthropology has become aware that there is neither objective knowledge nor neutral observer, it is important to pay attention to the way the position of the anthropologist affects the production of anthropological knowledge. This chapter examines the prejudice which as a leftist student I held against colonialism, how this made me actively seek to appear unthreatening to the former territorials I was interviewing, and how my unexpected but growing respect for them caused my certainties to evaporate, making it increasingly difficult for me to be sure what the Congo was like. This chapter is not meant to deal with my position once and for all. Since the book explores the significance of the relationship between the researcher and her informants to the way we remember or should remember the Belgian Congo, I shall feature thoughout the book.

Original prejudice against colonialism

In this section, I trace the assumptions with which I embarked upon my doctoral research: what did I know about the Belgian Congo, or rather what did I think I knew, and how did this influence the way I approached my topic? Exploring the answers to these questions sheds light on my personal memory of colonialism. However, through the following self-analysis I am trying to grasp the collective memory of my generation, especially those who share my political inclinations. When, then, did I first learn about the Belgian Congo? Impossible to say. Perhaps I have always known that the Belgian Congo existed, even though I could not imagine as a child what this far-away place was like. Three African paintings and two masks hanging in my bedroom testified to the fact that my uncle had lived in the Congo – not that he talked much about the decade he had spent over there. In my childhood, the word 'Congo' could not have evoked many or precise images. Perhaps it was a country where children died of leprosy and whose development we needed to help by giving money to missionaries.

My earliest conscious memory concerning the Congo is a remark by a primary school teacher when I was around eight years old. Standing out amongst the lay staff in the prime of life, this (to us) elderly nun was in charge of a class of about twenty third-graders whom she taught with benevolence. When we had been 'good', Sister Xaviera rewarded us with a story. (Looking back at it, I expect this 'reward' came at fairly regular intervals, probably weekly or fortnightly). She went to fetch a picture from the attic which she installed on an easel to illustrate the story of the day and then she started to talk. I think I can still see her telling us about Clovis, who converted to Christianity in the sixth century because of a promise to his wife Clothilde; the six hundred Franchimontois who paid with their lives in their attempt to free Liège from the Burgundy yoke in the fifteenth century; the King Albert who died climbing between the two World Wars, and other landmarks of our national past. One day she explained that King Leopold II had given the Belgians a very large piece of land in the middle of Africa with all that it contained, including its people. She asked us what greater gift our King could have given us than actual people, created in God's image. I was impressed: indeed no greater gift was possible, and only the King could have given it. Did Sister Xaviera proceed to explain that there was something not quite right about this gift? Would this explain why I also seem to remember having been slightly puzzled: if I had been born at the time the King made the gift to the Belgians, what would I have done with someone I owned? The nun must have talked about independence, which had taken place less than ten years before. Independence, however, does not seem to have struck my imagination. I only remember being told in this class of the great gift of the King to his country.

Much later I learnt, of course, that such a gift never took place: Belgium took over the Congo in 1908 following international pressure in the face of the abuses of the Leopoldian regime (Stengers 1963; 1989: 168–78). The myth nevertheless persists in Belgium that Leopold gave the Belgians the Congo in his will. When I entered University in 1980,

I do not think I would have queried this. What I would have objected to, however, was the idea of giving, or for that matter of having, a colony. As a young student, I saw myself as belonging to the Left. Breaking with the conservative tradition dominant in my family, my first vote had been for the Socialist party. I had also decided against studying at the Catholic University of Louvain, where most of my classmates seemed to have congregated. I went to the Free University of Brussels instead, a university which prides itself for being founded on the principle of *libre examen* (value-free examination). I welcomed the rejection of dogma it entailed (although in time I became critical of the unrefined conception of the scientific fact on which it rests). One of the three 'adopted' prisoners of the Amnesty International group I joined on the University campus was Zairian. He had just been relegated for having founded in 1981, along with twelve other dissidents, the Union for Democracy and Social Progress (which remained the most significant party of opposition in the 1980s and 1990s). A fellow student told me that the Belgians had invented the administrative sanction of relegation during the colonial period. By implication, were not the Belgians ultimately responsible for the relegation of 'our' prisoner? In my mind, it was clear that there was a connection between Belgian colonial and neo-colonial practice and the problems that afflicted Zaire. I did not know much about colonialism, I just associated it with exploitation and held the Western world responsible for the terrible situation in which the Third World found itself (a position analysed by Bruckner 1987). For example, I was happy to chant slogans denouncing the evil of colonialism in student demonstrations against measures that made it more difficult for African students to gain access to Belgian Universities.

My first acquaintance with the 'reality' of the Belgian Congo came as Professor Jacques Vanderlinden asked me to write a paper on punishment during the Belgian colonial period. In the fifth and final year of my law studies at the University of Brussels, I had had the privilege of following his courses on comparative law and on African law. Aware of my interest in these subjects, he had encouraged and made it possible for me to go to Oxford to study social anthropology. He was then the General Secretary of the Jean Bodin Society for comparative institutional history. In this function, he was in charge of organising a Congress held in Barcelona on the theme of 'Punishment' in June 1987. One of his intellectual ambitions was to counteract the European bias which characterised most of the work of the Society. Either he was particularly keen to have someone writing something about the Belgian colonial tradition, or he wanted to give a promising graduate student the opportunity to participate in an international conference. Whatever the case, he invited me to present a paper on 'La peine durant la colonisation belge'. What I found during this early piece of research reinforced the little I knew about colonialism, and my prejudice against it.

My paper documented the discrimination which pervaded punishment in all its aspects, formalised as a series of questions Vanderlinden had asked the participants of the conference to examine. These were: who was to be punished? The answer I found and gave was: (generally) the native. Who decided to punish? (Generally) the European, most often a member of the administration in the case of African defendants but always a professional judge in the case of Europeans. According to which method? Some unheard of in contemporary Belgium such as capital punishment and flogging of Africans. In which way? Using severity where Africans were concerned but moderation with Europeans. These cursory answers require elaborate qualifications which can be found in the published article (Dembour 1991a). I emphasised the paternalism that characterised Belgian colonialism, inclined to consider the Africans as children to be reared (cf Brausch 1957; Malengreau 1950). I also stressed the disciplinary function of imprisonment which was used frequently and for short periods to teach the natives how 'to behave', which meant to pay their taxes, to attend to the obligatory crops, to build the roads and so forth.

It would not be too strong to say that I was disgusted by the system I was describing. However, I remember also being puzzled by reading about accusations of witchcraft that led to innocent victims dying. These stories made me wonder whether the authors I was reading had a point when they talked of the benefits of colonialism. Still, I found much of the prose I was reading, mainly articles written by lawyers during the colonial period, unashamedly racist. Let me take one example (which indicated that discrimination had become an object of debate in the 1950s, a point which probably escaped me):

> If Whites and Blacks ever appear before the same tribunal to answer similar facts, any difference either in the nature or the seriousness of the penalty will be even more obvious. For, whether we like it or not, the same penalty used against a native and a White undoubtedly produces very different effects. The native has a different conception of the penal offence than the White and, most importantly, he reacts differently towards the inflicted penalty' (Cornil 1953 : 36).

In this passage, the author recognised that different sanctions were used in relation to Europeans and Africans. He objected to the same tribunal judging both groups on the grounds that such differences would be less easily concealed. The justification he implicitly offered for the system in place was the effect the penalty provoked, or perhaps failed to provoke, amongst the Africans, as opposed to the Europeans. The author did not elaborate on how different this reaction presumably was. However, the literature I read was full of remarks about Africans who did not understand the principle of punishment, did not feel ashamed about having been in jail (thinking instead that this experience constituted a good reference in European circles), did not feel physical pain in the same way as Europeans did, needed to have their imagination struck by appropriately severe punishments, etc. These must have been the kind of sentiments that informed the statement found in the passage quoted above. While the practice of using imprisonment as a reference (reported ibid : 37) made me smile, I found the other suggestions pathetic. In the margin of the photocopy I took of the quoted passage, I wrote 'What!'. This single word, written in capital letters with a very bold exclamation mark, must have expressed my absolute indignation.

Of course, Cornil's observation on the different ways Africans and Europeans reacted to a certain penalty may have been factually correct. The racism I felt pervaded his text may have pertained not so much to him as a person as to the system upon which he was commenting and of which he was part. That did not make it more acceptable to me or the fellow student friend who was helping me type my paper. I remember that we could not believe our eyes as we were looking at the material I was discussing in the paper. This was terrible, worse than what we generally knew about colonialism, so blatantly racist, and all there before our eyes. Retrospectively, I consider our reactions naive in their failure to put the sentences we were reading in context. But what is important is that such was my memory of colonialism when I embarked on my doctoral research. This memory, which I share with many others,[1] could not help but influence the way I conceived of my research project.

Seeking to appear unthreatening

I had not planned to write a doctoral dissertation on the Belgian Congo. When I heard that the Belgian Fonds national de la recherche scientifique had accepted to fund me to work on a doctorate on 'Punishment in Africa' in the law department of the Université Libre de Bruxelles, I asked whether I could work on a doctorate in social anthropology at the

University of Oxford instead. The Fonds raised no objection, putting me in the rare position of being funded but having no defined area of research. I asked Michael Gilsenan to act as my supervisor at Oxford and suggested two ideas for research. One, which followed an old dream of living with nomads in the Sahara, we never discussed. The other was to continue on the work I had started for the Barcelona conference. This is how, very much by chance, the development of the colonial legal system in the Belgian Congo became the official area of study for my doctoral research, although I soon decided to focus on the territorial perception of law and colonial experience more generally. The prejudice I held against colonialism could not but taint the way I approached the men I met in the course of my research. In particular, it was impossible for me to be open to my interviewees. If I did so, I feared they would refuse to speak to me, putting an end to my research project before it even got properly started.

My parents must have remarked that one of my uncles had been working in the Congolese administration. As an anthropologist, I felt I could not 'just' study texts but needed to find people on whom to practise some kind of participant-observation. My uncle provided an entry away from archives and I arranged to go and visit him (without anticipating that this visit would mark a turning point in the focus of my research). My mother, aware of my stance against colonialism, anticipated that the encounter I planned with my uncle would turn into a useless conflict with hurt feelings on both sides. I tried to reassure her, saying that I was going to listen and not to discuss. She was only half-convinced, but the fight she feared never happened. I was absolutely determined to adopt an attitude that did not risk interrupting the flow of information I wanted to elicit from my potential informants.

It is generally said that I look a few years younger than I am, which means I barely appeared to be over twenty when I started my research. This, coupled with my link to the University and other details such as not possessing a car, contributed to place me in the student category (a status I did not formally hold in Belgium). I obviously belong to the female gender. Such a combination, I felt, could be useful in producing an unthreatening image and I nurtured the image of the young female student as I hoped it would encourage the interviewees to talk to me. To be taken for a young student would spare me the delicate task of having to explain where I was coming from intellectually and where I envisaged I was heading with my research. Indeed, only two interviewees (including 'Milnaert' who became my 'best informant') began the interview by asking me with which sources I was working and what aims I had in mind. The great majority of the interviewees did not ask any questions about the project I presented in a slightly diluted form (see below) in my letter of introduction. I assumed the role of the young student who knew nothing (or not too much)[2] and was to be taught, and did not blink but dutifully listened when, on two occasions, the people I visited presented me with a plan of my thesis, which they had prepared in advance of our meeting. (One of them was 'de Glaise' whom I shall shortly introduce). Presumably they expected their words to find their way into my study, almost verbatim. This, I thought, could turn into an advantage: providing me with the bare bones of what they wished to see going down onto the public record and giving me the chance to check their presentation for simplifications and omissions.

I was hoping for my interlocutors to talk and talk, without reservations. The fact that I was a young woman and they were senior men with full careers behind them could hopefully assist in opening the floodgates: perhaps they would wish to dazzle me, as has been reported by other researchers.[3] They indeed sought to dazzle me, or perhaps it is just me who was fascinated by their accounts. The diversity of their functions, the responsibilities seemingly resting on one person, and the often apparently genuine interest in a different way of life amazed and impressed me. However, I also wanted to hear about the other side of the story, i.e. the violence I had no doubt pertained to the colonial situation in all of its aspects. In regard to these issues, I feared that the interviewees would play on the possible naivity of the young student I was perceived to be, especially since I had no irrefutable evidence with which to confront the interviewees to force them to acknowledge violent acts. Fortunately, some did 'talk'.

One such was 'de Glaise'. An ususual character, he submerged me with anecdotes which to me demonstrated his complete lack of respect towards the Africans, but to him must have demonstrated his glaring power. Quoting him from my notes: 'My wife was always telling me that I would end up being murdered. I answered her by comparing myself to a tamer of wild beasts who, as long as he is sure of himself, runs no risk'. 'de Glaise' also illustrated the impartial character of Congolese justice by resorting to the following story (which I again reconstruct from my notes):

> One day, in order to show the chief's son that his position was not going to bring him favourable treatment, I sentenced him and, to stress the point, I told him that from now on, I was going to regard him as a goat. Thus, when

I was passing him, he had to go on all fours and greet me with a bleat. Shortly afterwards, a Hungarian Professor in psychiatry happened to travel through my post. I told him I had come across a case which could be of interest to him : a chief's son had taken a conviction so badly that, from that day onwards, he had begun to act as a goat. The Professor was very interested indeed and we went to visit the man. The latter was so afraid when he saw us heading in his direction that he began to browse on the grass. He was really taking himself for a goat! Later on, I explained the whole story to the Professor; he was furious (Laughs).

Part of my strategy to appear unthreatening was to give the impression to my interlocutors that I went along with what they were saying. Thus, when 'de Glaise' interrupted the telling of his story to laugh, which he did frequently, I laughed along with him, however uncomfortable this felt. Most often, however, the twist this strategy required was far more innocuous. It involved, for example, adopting their vocabulary. Thus I talked of *indigènes* (natives) and *HAV* (*homme adulte et valide;* adult and able-bodied man) as they did. The morality of such tactics, which aimed at concealing from my interviewees who I was (i.e. what I really thought), could appear questionable. Before discussing this issue, I shall discuss the way I introduced myself and sought to appear unthreatening in my letters of introduction.

I shall take as an example the letter which introduced me to most of the territorials I met in the course of my research (which was dated December 1987). It began with the name of Claire Van Leeuw, a history graduate who had written her graduate thesis on the Territoriale and who had been generous enough to send me a long list of addresses she had collected during her research. Omitting her name would of course have led my addressees to wonder how I had got their details. Including it, however, could give my addressees the impression that I was following in the tracks of my predecessor – a 'young female student'. Van Leeuw's thesis, meticulously researched as it was, seemed to have taken the statements of her interviewees at face value and to have left out the more embarrassing statements, opinions or anecdotes inevitably heard in the course of a study of this kind.

The letter further included a brief presentation of my status. I indicated that I had studied law at the Université Libre de Bruxelles and social anthropology at the University of Oxford. Although I could hardly have invented another curriculum vitae, I could have chosen to present it differently. For instance, I did not mention who my supervisors were in order to avoid the name of Professor Vanderlinden who had appeared on a number of occasions on T.V. programmes about the Belgian Congo, for I did not want to take the risk of referring to a figure of whom my adressees might have a negative impression. I was thus consciously putting forward some pieces of information and playing down others. (I was probably not doing this to the best effect: a number of interviewees found it puzzling that I was studying in England; they wondered why, and asked me to be cautious in view of what they regarded as the unjustified British campaign against Leopold II's regime. However naive these fears may sound, the limited historical British consciousness about the Belgian Congo lends them some credit).

The letter finally presented my research as the study of law in its actual application. In so doing, I emphasised the descriptive and factual aspects of my research, while playing down more general and value-loaded questions. Such phrasing corresponded to my primary interests at that time. As I knew hardly anything about the practice of law in the Congo, I thought my efforts should concentrate on that area. Later questions revolving more around the conception of law held by territorials were presented in introductory letters.[4] Nevertheless, I never blatantly disclosed to the interviewees my central area of concern, which was the ways they legitimated their presence in the Congo; that I reserved for academic circles.[5] With the aim of gaining their cooperation I was attempting to make my work appear more 'neutral' than it was.[6]

All anthropologists must face the question of how to explain their project to their informants, what to disclose and how frank to be about it. Jean-Paul Dumont recalls that when his informants asked him 'what do you want?', he used to answer 'to learn your language'. He comments: 'Being a half-truth, it was a half-lie (language was only a tool), but I could live with it' (1978: 43–4). Arguably my position was one degree further remote from genuineness than his, in the sense that I then imagined that I would wish to use what my informants had told me to build up a (true) analysis of the territorial reality at the antipode of the image they would have expected me to present. In other words I anticipated to use their words against them – and their self-respectful image. Was it justifiable? It had to be, if identifying and understanding colonial mechanisms was a worthy pursuit. The options were either to take it (a not-too-straightforward attitude) or to leave it (the field).

I have stressed how important it was for me to appear unthreatening to my interviewees. This is because I felt that somehow I *did* represent a threat to them. But the interviews partly changed me; as a result, my original strategy and the moral qualms to which it gave rise almost became a non-issue. At the beginning I was concerned to know if my tactics fell under a scientific attitude of non-provocation, or under that of a betrayal of trust. What happened is that a number of relationships developed. I have said above how I mimicked 'de Glaise''s laughter, but this does not mean that I always strictly followed the attitude of my interlocutor. Of course, I was resolved to avoid open confrontation – which could only have brought the conversation to an abrupt end and was therefore useless, but I did not always feel bound to refrain from expressing my opinions. On the contrary, because I did not wish to leave the interviewees with expectations about my work which I knew I could not sustain, I generally tried to unveil my 'real' aims, or simply my doubts, at the end of the interview and even more so when I was going back to the same person. The fact that I was participating in a relationship where one is not just a role but a person led to this 'natural' disclosure.

Of all the relationships that developed between researcher and interviewees, one stands out. This is the one with 'Milnaert', a former territorial officer who has read more sociology, history and philosophy than I have. We spent many days, from morning to night, discussing his colonial experience, and furthered this exchange through a long correspondance. 'Milneart' has read and commented upon all that I have written on Belgian colonialism. His voice appears recurrently in this book. Our relationship is characterised neither by non-provocation nor trust, but by willingness to continue a dialogue on a subject in which we are both interested. In this case, the tactics I have used to approach the interviewees are not a moral problem. We are so far beyond them that they become irrelevant.

In search of the real Congo

I would never have thought that 'Milnaert' would become my 'best informant' when I left his house on the evening of 18 April 1988. He was the nineteenth former territorial I had met and I was experiencing what Daniel Bertaux (1981) has called the phenomenon of saturation: I (wrongly) felt that I had already heard from other interviewees what 'Milnaert' had been telling me that day. I was also slightly exasperated by the feeling of 'everything-was-nice-and-beautiful-in-the-Congo' which I felt came out of the interview. Whatever problems I had asked 'Milnaert' about (concerning territorials' relationship with the judges, difficulties in getting imposed tasks executed or in maintaining the so-called public order …), he had flatly denied that such problems had affected him. For example, I had asked how many people he had had to send to jail for failing to pay their taxes. His answer had been that he could not imagine having imposed one hundred such condemnations in the fourteen years of his territorial career. I was not ready to believe him. I supposed the reality of the Congo to be a nasty one and, with 'Milnaert', I had not managed to get what I was after. I found the interview disappointing. I was concerned that he was 'holding back' the most important pieces of information, which I still conceived to be related to illegalities, brutalities, and oppression. Could he be another 'de Glaise', simply one who was hiding behind a mask of 'everything was nice and beautiful in the Congo'? If I could not open myself up to my informants because of my prejudices, I could not trust them either.

I could not hear, and certainly could not accept at face-value, what 'Milneart' was telling me. When I look back at my notes today, however, I am more ready to do this. 'Milneart' recognised that his experience might have been a particularly fortunate one. This he attributed to a number of factors, including the following three. First, he had been posted in the same territory throughout his territorial career, from 1946 to 1960; this exceptional situation had meant that he had been able to resort less and less to coercion and that he had got to know the language of the place and the people with whom he was working better and better. Secondly, he felt that the populations of his region were open (*ouvertes*), a characteristic which he suggested might be linked to the fact that they had been experiencing the beginning of an empire before being colonised by the Belgians. Thirdly he pointed out that his territory had been one of the major seats of the agricultural *paysannat* project in the Congo – which meant, amongst other things, that people in his region had money and paid their taxes without difficulty. He stressed that the peasants always participated in this project of their own will, although enlisting their cooperation sometimes required long negotiations. But I was doubtful of all that he was telling me.

Take for example his last remark; the emphasis on negotiations fell in line with the way he generally presented his relationship with the Africans. Let me give three examples. At one stage, he reprimanded me for comparing the Africans to children and said that they had taught him 'everything'. At another, he recalled how his conversations with the natives had been interesting right from the beginning. Later still, he commented that the power of the native chief was – almost – more legitimate than his, for the native chief was a personage in society, and he was not.

His words did not seem to acknowledge the subordination inherent in the relationship between coloniser and colonised. I noted at one point that some territorials had committed abuses and had been sent back to Belgium. His reply was that the Africans knew the European hierarchy and complained in case of abuse. 'Everything nice and beautiful again', I thought. To me, the interview with 'de Glaise' rang more true. Now, however, I can see that the stories 'de Glaise' told me, including that of the man-turned-into-a-goat recounted above, show that 'de Glaise' was cruel. Moreover, I believe that cruelty was fairly exceptional in the Congo which most of my interviewees experienced, i.e. that which followed the Second World War. Let me discuss each of these propositions in turn.

The social scientist Véronique Nahoum-Grappe (1996) has distinguished cruelty from violence. Cruelty, she suggests, is committed for its own sake, with nothing to stop its excesses, by an aggressor in a position of advantage, in a context of impunity. By contrast, violence is committed as a means to an end, thus stopping when the aim is achieved, by the more *and* by the less powerful, even when the project underlying its rationale is not guaranteed to be successful. Cruelty aims at hurting the person primarily in her moral and social rather than physical aspects, demeaning her in her own eyes, and ultimately leading her to regret to have been born. This must apply to the African who was forced to be a goat. Speaking of torture, Nahoum-Grappe notes: 'The once threatening enemy ... is now in agreement on the most minute point (and) implores ...' (ibid.: 282) – our man eating the grass. She explains that cruelty always calls for more cruelty, having 'no other content than its own outbidding' (ibid.: 290). She also talks of the accompanying laugh (ibid.: 304) – which 'de Glaise' did not omit. Nahoum-Grappe's penetrating analyis can help us to understand the reality of the Congo: power and violence (symbolic if not physical) was ubiquitous but cruelty was not, although that does not mean it was altogether absent.

As we were talking about the former territorials we had met, Van Leeuw remarked that 'de Glaise' was *un fou* (a mad man), to whom she had given no place in her University thesis. I can only agree with her that he was out of line with the other interviewees.[7] Indeed, I have only come across one other story in the same vein as that of the goat. It concerns a territorial who ordered a village supervisor to sit on his hat and sing 'cluck, cluck, cluck' until he laid an egg; the reason for this punishment was that the supervisor had failed to bring the territorial some eggs, as was the practice at the arrival of a European official in a village (Augustin n.d. [circa 1985]: 126). This story appears in the unpublished memoirs of Paul Augustin, who had heard it from the men in the village of Kibati, territory of Walikale, where he was posted for five years in the mid-1950s. Augustin says that his predecessor, whom he suggests might have been supervising the rubber collection just before the Kitawala revolt,[8] had the reputation of being 'makari', which means 'terrifying'. The very fact that this person was known to be terrifying indicates that his colleagues were not – or not to the same extent. The stories of the goat and of the egg do not represent a main trend. I do not think, however, that this is a good enough reason to dismiss them as extraordinary and therefore insignificant.[9] They show that sadism existed in the Congo.

Considering the powers enjoyed by any one territorial and the impossibility for the superiors to exercise a close control over their subordinates, the opposite would be surprising. As I have noted above, it is the nature of cruelty to express itself when it is safe, i.e. when impunity can be expected. There must be many stories of sadism that we shall never hear. This happens everywhere, of course. However, it must have been especially so in the Congo, as Ryckmans noted in the text where he talked of the 'dangerous force'. While sadistic attitudes must have been more commonly expressed in the colony than in the metropole (to a degree which cannot be accurately estimated), they were nonetheless the exception rather than the norm, certainly after the Second World War.[10] Cruelty was not part of the intention of the system; if anything the system was actively looking at eliminating it. This at least is what the pervasive territorial concern for the rule of law suggests.

Over and over again the interviewees talked to me about the rule of law. This does not mean that territorials always respected the law. In chapter 5, I shall present material which indicates that some did not, especially in certain fields. Nonetheless the rule of law was a recurrent theme throughout the interviews. Let me start by reporting what 'Milnaert' had to say about it. During our first interview, he had commented that he had had the impression of bringing not so much a higher justice (as I suggested) as a regulatory one. He elaborated by explaining that written rules represented the limits to territorial action and that the intention was always to follow the law, which the territorials indeed held in great respect. He repeated the same idea more than a year later in his answers to a written questionnaire. To quote him:

> For the territorials law was a protection. I think that the territorials, true executors of the law, respected the texts and acted outside the limits fixed by law as rarely as possible (which does not mean that there were no blunders and no

attempts to circumvent the law, etc …). I have always been scared by the perspective of illegality, less because of the possible sanctions than because of my feeling that to go beyond the law was to risk arbitrariness, personal fantasy, tyranny, the abuse of a power which was lent to me (Dembour 1991b: 54).

I received these words with some incredulity.

E.P. Thompson (1977) has convincingly argued that, even from a Marxist perspective, the rule of law can be seen to further the interests of the weak rather than just acting as a masking ideology exclusively serving the interests of the privileged few. This celebrated conclusion notwithstanding, I remained more inclined to conceive of the rule of law in the Belgian Congo as a means to legitimate, rather than to prevent, violence. The rule of law could legitimate violence in a number of ways. To me, 'Peters', whom 'Milnaert' had recommended that I meet so that I could hear about an experience different from his, epitomised one: stretching the law to include as much violence as possible within its confines. Like 'Milnaert', 'Peters' had left for the Congo soon after the War (in January 1948) and had started his colonial career as a territorial officer. 'Peters', however, had been posted in a 'backward' region of the Sankuru district, where there was 'close to nothing'. As a result, the Africans had to be forced to grow cotton to have money to pay their tax. During the interview, 'Peters' indeed insisted on the importance he attached to the execution of the legally imposed work (*travaux d'ordre économique*). He also talked of his respect for the law. I shall quote him at some length:[11]

> It was out of the question to register a lower return compared to that of the previous years; quantitative results had to be good. Thus, we could not afford to be lax and to let someone go through the meshes of the net. Each HAV [adult and able-bodied man] had to clear thirty-six *ares*[12] a year. The agricultural monitors determined where the good places were. We used a system of rotation which differed from region to region according to the ground and the climate. Where I was, it was as follows: manioc in the first year, rice in the second, cotton in the third, nuts in the fourth, manioc again in the fifth, and then back to the forest. Agronomists acted as judicial police officers and could send me those who had not been working well with a statement to this effect.
>
> I was strict in my condemnations. In his report, the professional judge [of the standing tribunal] noted that I always gave the maximum penalty (seven days for the offences which we are talking about). This I felt was justified as I had warned them of what to expect. Although I was strict, I always applied the law. In fact I cannot remember a judge ever revising one of my judgments. But then I never went anywhere without my code.

I preferred to send the defaulter to jail rather than to impose a fine. There was no point in taking away from them their last penny (*sou*). Moreover, other members of the clan would have paid for the culprit who would then have failed to draw any moral lesson from the condemnation. The punishment would have affected the wrong persons. With imprisonment, it was a different matter. This was especially so since, with me, seven days of jail meant seven times four strokes of the whip. I always managed to find a [legal] excuse to give the whip to the prisoners. Maybe you find this shocking, but it was like that. At the beginning one is shocked, but then you get used to it.

You talk of someone who told you that he decided, following the remark by a judge that he could not continue to inflict the maximum penalty, to put people in jail for three days (without this appearing anywhere). You say that he then wrote a judgment where he inflicted a penalty of four days only (thus still reaching in practice the maximum of seven days). I can tell you that the elders would never have tolerated such a practice. The rules were *formelles* [both formal and strict]. The courses we followed at Brussels for six months were very clear on this topic: we were impregnated with it – perhaps because of Leopold II, even though I cannot believe that hands were ever cut.

You ask whether I liked being magistrate of police. My answer is yes. All that I have done, I have done with enthusiasm and pleasure. For us, to work was to serve. When I arrived in 1948, I was astounded. Materially, the Congo was undoubtedly a success. I could not help thinking: 'How much work they have done before us!' We had also been told that we had to learn to know, and that this was to love. Perhaps I especially had this mentality as I had been a boy-scout.

'Peters' did not particurlarly like the text I constructed from our interview (which is much longer than the quotation I have given here). Although he admitted having said what I had written, he felt it was too *cru* (rough, coarse) and lacking in nuances. Indeed the impression which can come out of it is that he is satisfied with himself, faithful in the overall colonising project and blind to the taking away of freedom and the harshness colonialism entailed. As for the rule of law, he made sure that he remained within its confines, but he nonetheless used it in what appears to be as oppressive a way as possible. He claims that the men he sent to jail were disciplined every day with four strokes of the whip, the maximum provided for penitentiary offences in 1951. While this may have been an exaggeration due to his being carried away by his own discourse (in front of a young female student?), it remains the case that he apparently ordered strokes of the whip regularly, without any second thoughts – except at the beginning when, like many of his colleagues, he recalls having been shocked. In his opinion, all that he did, including the way he used his legal powers, he ultimately did for the Africans' own good. What I retained from this interview was that 'Peters' may well have respected the letter of the law, but certainly not its spirit; he stretched it to its outer limits to make room for practices which even he had found shocking, at least to start with. In other words, the rule of law was a means to practice violence with impunity, although apparently not to satisfy personal inclinations towards sadism as I argued was the case for 'de Glaise'.

The precision with which the interviewees remembered legal provisions they had not used for thirty years is astounding. Such memory can only be explained by the fact that they either did apply the rules or at least were careful to be seen to apply them. Whatever the case (and one individual need not have acted in exactly the same way as another), they all had to pay attention to the law. But was the law any good (just) or was it exploitative? I of course was inclined to think the latter. As a result, I found the absence of critique and personal reflection by the interviewees towards legal provisions both revealing and horrifying. 'Peters', cited above, is a good example of this trend. 'Peletier', who left for the Congo in 1947 as a graduate of the Colonial University and was posted in the northeastern part of the country, is another. He remarked about coercion: 'Yes, we sometimes resorted to coercion. The law is the law. I cannot fail to coerce someone to pay his tax as the law requires for the tax to be paid.'

In December 1989, about a year after this interview, I was watching on television the film *Un amour en Allemagne* by Wajda (1983). The hero was a prisoner of war who was working in a farm run by a German couple in the early 1940s. I could not help reaching for a pen when the husband expressed indignation at the fact that the law prevented the non-German hero to eat at the same table as him, and his wife reacted: 'I do not make the law; I only know it exists.' What interested me in this statement is that the woman relied on law to avoid having to justify her own attitude. Just like my interviewees, I thought. But to what extent does the comparison hold? And when can we say that we have understood what a situation is all about?

A matter of interpretation

I drew other comparisons between Nazi Germany and the Congo, notably concerning the meaning of 'occupation', a word which cropped up more than once during the interviews. When 'Milnaert' realised as he read the first draft of my thesis that I was equating the job of the territorials with blatant forms of oppression, he wrote back:

> Here is a country which is admittedly under 'occupation' by foreigners who impose their law and to some extent their culture. These foreigners, however, respect the law they enact, guarantee good material conditions through an administration that is far from overwhelming (fifteen hundred persons). The administration has to account for its actions, wishes to be benevolent, and participates in projects which are not negligible. You qualify this system as oppressive. You do this while you are contemporaneous with situations of nazi, soviet, dictatorial and anarchical states, where law is violated and citizens imprisoned day after day. For both types of situations, only one word comes to your mind (oppression). Isn't this a strange contortion of thought? … (Mind you, my own grandchildren believe that they experience daily oppression in the family and at school!).

I now wish to question how appropriate it is always to be drawn back, as I have been, towards comparing the colonial and the Nazi regimes. Uncertainties on analytical, moral and empirical grounds all converge towards this central interrogation.

When I started the interviews, I assumed that the interviewees would seek to hide 'the truth' about their past. I accordingly pictured my task as making them confess the unspeakable. Fortunately a few of them, including 'de Glaise', did not need any encouragement on my part to keep telling anecdotes in which repression, illegalities, arbitrariness or prejudice against the Africans played a major part. In these cases, I left the interview with a feeling of jubilation as if 'I had it'. Most of the interviewees, however, were giving me accounts of the Congo where everything was 'nice and beautiful'. When I mentioned that another person had told me such-and-such, they would often respond that they had never experienced that themselves – rarely adding, however, that such a thing was inconceivable and could not have happened. In my mind this added up to a discourse that lent itself to another kind of unmasking. If interviewees did not want to tell me 'the truth of the Congo', I was going to examine how they presented their functions in order to legitimise their colonial action, forgetting and playing up some elements, according to a strategy of which they were not necessarily themselves aware.

It became increasingly clear, however, that a negative value-judgment implicitly underlaid my concern with legitimation. Such concern meant that I was assuming either that power would be denied and would thus fail to reveal itself as such, or alternatively that its exercise would call for justification when it could not be denied. Thus I took it that power was 'bad' and put my informants in the position of the 'baddies'. The desire for an 'egalitarian' society exempt from relations of power and a concomitant aversion for hierarchy (Dumont 1979: vii) prompted me to classify the coloniser, i.e. the dominant in the colonial relationship, into a category which 'by nature' attracted moral blame. But as McLachlan argues in an excellent article (1981), power in itself is neither 'bad' nor 'good'. The interviews woke me up to the objectionable foundation to the analysis I was originally proposing to undertake. I was meeting men who very often appeared warm, generous and honest. They were opening their doors and their memories to me, and then I would betray the trust that implicitly underlaid the interview by explaining how they legitimated their colonial action? This was a morally uncomfortable position to adopt. Who was I to condemn them? More crucially, was it warranted on empirical grounds?

Many territorials did not live up (or should I say down) to the implicitly negative image my concern with legitimation presumed. It was obvious that going into the bush was not compatible with a stay-at-home mentality, and the longing for exoticism (shared by many anthropologists) was going hand-in-hand with a certain openness.[13] Territorials were, and remain to this day, people with manifold interests. I have already mentioned that 'Milnaert' reads more sociology than I do; many of his former colleagues follow courses at the University, either for the retired or as regular students. One interviewee was setting up an industry in Rwanda (this was before the genocide) where handicapped people built and sold ovens which cut the consumption of the country's scarce wood; another, then in his seventies, agreed to go back to Zaire in 1990 to assess a development project. I could give more examples testifying to their diverse interests. Their material achievements, expressed through the number of roads, bridges, dispensaries and so on which they constructed, also bore witness to their energy, skills and ingenuity. But, most important of all, what disturbed my preconceptions was that morally I did not see how I could dare to condemn them and their past functions, especially those men who appeared to me to live a life governed by moral integrity. This included 'Milnaert', 'Parmentier' (who quit his career in Belgium as a lawyer in disgust at the unfair purging process which took place immediately after the war) and others.

Gilsenan warned me as I was telling him how 'Peters' had received me with a big smile: 'Himmler (or did Gilsenan mention another SS?) also smiled'. Gilsenan's intention was probably to remind me that a smile, as such, did not mean anything. Anyone can smile, and anyone can commit atrocities. Hannah Arendt (1964) has tried to explain who Eichman was in a book which is subtitled 'A report on the banality of evil'; Christopher Browning (1992) has described the 'ordinary men' who took part in 1942 in the execution of the 'final solution' in Poland. The shock these men experienced the first time they had to round up and kill all the Jews living in a village (apart from one hundred abled-bodied men sent to a work camp) reminds me of the shock my interviewees almost invariably recalled at their first encounter with the whip. So here I am again with a pernicious comparison with Nazi Germany. It is pernicious not only because the horror of the events described in Arendt and Browning's books is definitely not of a scale which is applicable to the territorial practice, but also because the last proviso does not annihilate the suggestion that there was something horrific about the Congo even though it did not contemplate a genocide. But can we suggest that?

Where are the facts? This is a question which has haunted me. The only honest answer is: I do not know. When a former territorial was talking to me, I could not help being concerned with trying to assess whether the story I was being told represented a fair account of what had actually happened: did the event really happen, when, where, in the presence of whom, with which consequences? But the vanity of the enterprise never failed to strike as soon as I was revising my notes or transcribing the tape of our conversations. It was plain that I would never be able to 'really' know how a particular event occurred or how representative it was of general practice.[14] Of course the thirty (or more) years' gap which separated the event from its recollection meant that memory could not but have done its work of distortion (chapter 5). But a detour through the archives could not help much, for they were characterised by the same, unescapable, fragmentation as the words of the interviewees. What I would find in the archives would be written from a particular perspective and would fail to answer the question of the representativeness of the facts thus reported. More importantly, I do not think that having been there at the time would have solved my problem. I cannot help thinking that there are no 'hard' facts, for ultimately it is all a matter of interpretation.

Let me take the example of the whip. A number of facts are irrefutable: it was used as a punishment for breach of penitentiary discipline and the law provided for how many strokes could be inflicted. The territorial ordered the sanction which an African soldier implemented on the prisoner who lay down on the ground debagged; this took place in the morning, immediately after the salute to the flag. The most important question is not answerable, however. It is the value-judgment: 'is this horrific?' I am not sure that the answer is 'yes'. In the article which I have written on the topic, I ask that we consider the possibility that the meaning then attached to the practice is not synonymous with instinctive feelings we have today that it was either cruel or barbaric, or both. By raising this possibility, I may appear open-minded. But this is so only in a limited sense. Perhaps this is even a deception, for choosing to write about the topic of the whip (rather than, say, the infrastructure which the Congo enjoyed at the time of independence) not only indicates where my inclinations are but also affects the contribution of knowledge I offer. No facts exist independently from value-judgments, however implicit these are.

The first week I started to revise the thesis which became this book, I realised that I had enough material to write a book on law in the Belgian Congo. The possible chapters came to my mind with ease: chapter 1 would set the institutional frame, chapter 2 could examine the annual statistics of justice, another would discuss customary law, yet another would look at the law practised by and for the Europeans, the final one would need to address the multifarious aspects of the question: 'what is law?' Had I written this thesis/book, the chapters may not have turned out to be those I have just suggested, but what is clear is that the book would have been very different from the one which you are reading now. Most anthropologists first write an ethnography; the most reflexive amongst them then come to reflect on what led them to this ethnography (Pratt 1986: 3; Okely and Callaway 1992: xi). For me, things happened the other way around. I first needed to sort out my feelings.

Perhaps this is because, in a world which had taught me to think in such a way, I had mistakenly conceived of colonial domination as a despicable evil, without qualifying the very term 'domination'. I now despair with Nahoum-Grappe that 'the great theoretical productions in the social sciences have broadened the content of the word "violence" until it came to designate any implicit, virtual, imaginable power relationship' (1996: 299). I now wish to make distinctions: 'Milnaert' is not 'de Glaise' – both are equally exceptional – and the Belgian Congo was not Nazi Germany. It may be that the most powerful way to show this would have been to document the 'structures' of the Belgian Congo rather than to have been concerned with how I felt about the Belgian Congo. But the thing is: I could not write even the first line of this other book, so that what I wish to share with the reader of this book are my fundamental doubts, rather than certainties about a reality of fairly limited scope.

My Project

This chapter started with a description of early memories of the Belgian Congo and my first encounter with its 'reality' through the research of an academic paper on colonial punishment. This description was included in an attempt to situate who I was at the beginning of my research project. In the second section of the chapter, I explained that my leftist inclinations and anti-colonial stance made me feel it was imperative that I appear unthreatening to my interviewees. I was hoping that the image of the young female student upon which I could rely would be an advantage in this respect and I also resorted to a number of soft tactics. All of these originally presented me with a moral dilemma, but I was happy not directly to confront it. The practice of research supposedly justified the adoption of these tactics. Interestingly, the more I proceeded with the research, the more their morality became a non-issue. This was expecially true of my relationship with 'Milnaert', with whom I had and shall probably continue to have long, open, and inconclusive discussions. The third section opened with the remark that I had not anticipated 'Milnaert' becoming my best informant. If anything, I had been irritated by the feeling of 'everything was nice and beautiful' which I had (wrongly) felt emerged from what he was telling me during our first interview. This was at a time when I was still convinced that remarks pointing to illegalities, oppression and blatant racism were the only ones which accurately captured the reality of the Congo. I do not think so anymore. Of course, expressions of cruelty may have flourished and remained unchecked in many instances, some reflected in the interviews I conducted, for example with 'de Glaise'. But the Belgian colonial system was not intentionally cruel, as suggested by the attention which the territorials had to pay to the rule of law. The last words are nonetheless problematic, for the rule of law does not guarantee the elimination of violence. What was the reality of the Congo? This question, I argued in section four, cannot be directly tackled. Over and over again, I have been inclined to compare the reality of the Belgian Congo with that of Nazi Germany. But what justifies such comparison? I was also concerned with the way the territorials legitimated their colonial experience. This implicitly put them in the role of the 'baddies'. But what justified such negative presumption about them on my part? What I have are not so much facts, for these are partial, as uncertainties. Recounting these uncertainties can be illuminating, but I need the following chapters to explain why and how.

Notes

1. As revealed by the opening words of the first chapter of Nicholas Thomas' *Colonialism's Culture* (1994). They refer to a discussion on a radio breakfast programme which invoked colonialism and its horrors without making any effort at capturing specific realities (: 11). While the programme took place in Australia, it could have happened anywhere. Thomas notes in his introduction that there is a kind of pervasive 'public anger' from liberals and radicals in the West towards colonialism and neo-colonialism (: 1–2).
2. My fourth interviewee was the father of a cousin's friend. As soon as I arrived, he asked me whether I knew of a thesis completed by a student in history on the Territoriale. On my negative answer, he sent me home with Claire Van Leeuw's thesis (1981), commenting that what I intended to study had already been done. This shows, if need be, that the image the researcher projects of herself is not without consequences. In this case appearing not knowledgeable enough had led to the irremediable failure of getting the interview going. By contrast, one interviewee commented a few months later that I already knew all there was to be known.
3. Ghiglione and Matalon (1978: 68) note that the combination of a young female interviewer facing male interviewees whose job is characterised by a strongly masculine public image generally works well.
4. For instance, I wrote on 8 November 1988 to a former territorial whom I had not yet met: 'I started a doctoral thesis a year ago … on the territorial administration of the Belgian Congo and law: what place did justice have in the work of the administrators, what did they think of the judiciary, the laws of the Belgian Congo, why did they respect law in some cases but not in others, did they think law and justice had a role in the civilising mission, and other questions along similar lines.'
5. As illustrated by the following passage in a letter I sent to a specialist of the Congo on 29 January 1988 to solicit advice on my research: '… Like colonisation, law can be seen in two different and contradicting ways. It can be seen as predominantly oppressive … or it can be seen as justice brought to the people. Law is neither just one or the other but is a mixture of all kinds of things. How did persons having to work with law perceive and practise law? How far did law help to set up and legitimise the colonial system? With what contradictions? Resolved in which ways?'
6. And more neutral than I think anthropological research can ever be. This was particularly clear in my case because I could not escape the question of how to present myself to my interviewees in view of my topic and prejudices.
7. The way 'de Glaise''s study (the only room I saw in his flat) was decorated is worth noting. The walls were covered with pictures of (European) men in uniforms dating from the colonial period, a *chicote* was still lying on the window sill, a leopard skin was spread on the floor. It was as if he had never moved out of a colonial setting and had continued to live in a colonial atmosphere. This impression was never so strong in other houses into which I was introduced. Even when African objects were displayed, they were integrated into a European decor. And indeed, many houses hardly had any reminders of the colonial period directly striking to the eye.
8. On this revolt, see Lovens 1974. On acts of resistance in the Congo, see Vellut 1987.
9. The more so because 'de Glaise''s territorial career was a very successful one. He talked to me of nineteen enquiries which the administration and judiciary had

started against him, but which never led to any sanction. On the contrary, he became assistant district commissary in less than twenty years, which points to a remarkable promotion through the ranks by comparison with the career of other officers. For example, by 1960, none of the territorial officers who had joined the Territoriale in 1946 had achieved the rank of assistant district commissary; ten of them had become territorial administrators; ninety (principal or simple) assistant territorial administrators; and fifty-six were still (either principal or simple) territorial officers (Dembour 1992a: 180).

10. Cf the view expressed by Engels and Marks (1994) as far as the British Empire was concerned.
11. I have rearranged his words into one continuous text, thus skipping large passages and my questions, and also sometimes changing the order of his remarks.
12. The '*are*' is a land-measurement unit of one hundred square metres.
13. Of course ethnographic interests can be impressive. But they reveal nothing in themselves about the humane or violent nature of the person who holds them. Patricia Hayes (1996) beautifully points this out in her analysis of 'Cocky' Hahn, an important figure of the Namibian colonial administration in the first half of the century.
14. Failing to address this last question is what arguably weakens Hayes' analysis of 'Cocky' Hahn, mentioned in the previous footnote.

4: Their Expectations

*I*n chapter 3, I explained that I thought I needed to be very careful in the way I presented myself if I was to persuade enough former colonials to participate in my research project. Retrospectively, my fears seem unfounded. In contrast to the reluctance I was expecting, I encountered considerable eagerness to help me with the research. Social scientists who collect life-stories have often commented on the ease with which they find individuals who are ready to tell them about their lives. Confirmation of this trend in this case is interesting for formal colonials do not generally talk about the Congo anymore, except amongst themselves. Why then were they so eager to talk to me? This chapter seeks to explore their motivations, aspirations and assumptions. While it is essential to analyse the frame of mind in which the researcher approaches her research project, it is equally important to operate the same kind of decoding vis-à-vis the agenda of her informants.

Muted voices

In the spring of 1989, I sent a written questionnaire of thirty-three questions to the thirty-four former territorials I had met so far.[1] Through this questionnaire, I was hoping to be able to collect their views on domination, a word which I did not dare to use during the interviews. The constitution of this taboo was very much of my own making. As the twenty sets of answers I received indicate, my interviewees have no problem with tackling questions that explicitly refer to domination. My own perspective on colonialism had nonetheless led me to feel that I needed to include innocuous questions if I was not to turn them away from answering what I thought was a very sensitive questionnaire. The first question asked them whether their Congolese experience represented the best time in their life, something many of them had said during the interviews. The second question asked what had led them to enter the Territoriale. This was followed by a series of questions which attempted to elucidate what they liked and did not like about their job. Question 9 asked how their territorial experience affected their life after independence. This led to a question about the image held by the average Belgian on the Territoriale and to another about T.V. programmes on the Congo contemporary to the questionnaire. Question 13 asked whether they still talked about their territorial experience today. It is the answers to these last three questions that I wish to consider here, for they poignantly render the atmosphere of misunderstanding which the territorials feel surrounds them.

First to summarise these answers: all respondents agreed that the average Belgian holds, if not a negative, then a misconceived idea of what the territorial job entailed; twelve spoke of T.V. programmes exclusively in negative terms; thirteen remarked that they still occasionally talk about the Congo but only with some people, generally former colonials and family members, while a few simply answered question 13 negatively. A closer examination of the content of these answers reveals how much they are interconnected. Let me start with question 13. A number of respondents made remarks to the effect that, if they do not talk about the Congo any more, it is because the Congo is now a thing of the past which has lost its interest for everyone except those who were directly involved in it (Dembour 1991b: 13, 53, 67, 103). This could be taken to reflect a common experience in a society which is more turned towards the present and the future than the past. But this does not seem to be the whole story, for many respondents hint that their avoidance of the subject is due to their awareness that it would not help to talk about the Congo.

One of them writes: 'I avoid talking about it to the *Belgicains*. As a matter of fact, when the topic comes up by chance, *they* are the ones who explain "the case" to me. In principle I only talk about it with other colonials' (ibid: 115). I have not found the term Belgicain in any dictionary but it is clear that its suffix indicates pejorative overtones of small-mindedness. In contemporary Belgium it is used to designate either Belgians who adopt an anti-federalist political perspective or Zairians (now Congolese) who have never been to Zaire (now Congo). The colonials, who can probably be credited with having invented the term, used it to refer to Belgians whose horizon finished at the Belgian frontiers and had no understanding of the African experience. To return to the answers to question 13, another former territorial reports: 'I only rarely speak about it ... When the children ask a question, I answer them. Whether they believe me or not, I do not care' (ibid: 74). The full sense of the last remark appears when put in parallel with the answer by the same person to the question about the T.V. programmes: 'The average Belgian believes what the T.V. tells him, and that is it. After the French Professor Guillaumin, a polemicist, appeared on T.V programmes about Leopold II, I was even told by family relatives: "Anyway he knows more about the subject than you do." Here is your average Belgian: "This brandy is excellent, my dear, I heard it being praised by someone who saw it being tasted"' (ibid: 74). This accusation, directed at a professional historian perceived as polemical and inexperienced, is in line with the criticisms which almost all respondents addressed towards T.V. programmes on the Congo. The most forceful phrases used to characterise the programmes include: 'biased and inadequate', 'shamefully incompetent', 'on the whole perniciously deceptive', 'disgraceful' (ibid, respectively: 16, 18, 38, 96). It is clear that former territorials hold the media partly responsible for maintaining the lack of understanding which they feel surrounds them to this day. As one says: 'The average Belgian does not know anything about the Territoriale. He is aware neither of the diversity of the activities to be fulfilled, nor of the ambit of the territorial responsibilities, nor of the kind of life that territorials led. If he has an image of the profession, it will remain a negative one until he is enlightened and the details of the job are explained to him' (ibid: 79).

It must be stressed, however, that the problem is not new. One respondent for example observes: 'I have the impression that even my brothers and sister do not really know what my job consisted of, even though I talked to them a lot about it.' He goes on to explain in a few sentences the various responsibilities of the territorial and concludes that the average Belgian had no idea of what the job entailed (ibid: 96; see also: 12, 25, 42, 79, 109, 114 which echo this answer). Of course, it is not uncommon for family or friends to be unaware of the situation in which one of their members lives. What is different in this case, however, is that prejudice seems to have accompanied such ignorance. To quote a respondent: 'The average Belgian hardly knew the colonial. According to him, the colonial worked a minimum, enjoyed a fat salary, lived like a king surrounded by servants whom he paid or not and who more or less held the status of slaves. The image of the colonial in Belgium was a very negative one' (ibid: 86; see also pp. 52 and 114 for similar anwers).

Let us try to unravel the bitterness which is apparent from these answers. To do this, we can start by commenting upon the image of the territorial that the 'average' Belgian held during the colonial period. In those days, the territorials would probably have accepted that people in Belgium were never going to realise exactly what their work consisted of and accept that it was a demanding one. Civil servants in the Congo were entitled to a six-month leave, which they had to take, after each period of three years of service.[2] At a time when paid leave had not yet been legally introduced in Belgium, this could only foster feelings of envy towards apparently idle and rich colonials. It was not rare for young single men who had accumulated savings during their stay in the Congo to be able to lead an extravagant and ostentatious life-style. For territorials with a young family, the leave could occasion tremendous difficulties and costs, especially in terms of housing and children's education. Even in such cases, the family and neighbours tended only to see the large American car, which was bought (in the 1950s) to cope a few months later with the rough roads of the Congo. The misunderstanding was nonetheless devoid of serious consequences; perhaps it was even enjoyable at a certain level. Certainly it was not the cause of the bitterness which I encountered at the end of the 1980s. To explain the latter, we must turn to the way the territorials were received in Belgium after independence, which they feel still affects the way they are perceived today.

As more than one interviewee commented, from having always been colonials, they suddenly became colonialists in 1960 (ibid: 74 and 96; see also Brausch 1961: 61). This happened at a time when the international political climate was evolving, as demonstrated by the adoption of the U.N. Declaration on the granting of independence to colonial states. When colonials returned to Belgium in the weeks following the independence on 30 June 1960, unprepared and sometimes in dramatic circumstances, they did not feel welcome. At best, they were met with indifference. The attitude of Belgian officialdom was certainly a terrible blow for them. Instead of the promised reintegration, they found that they were expected to take examinations and to begin again at the bottom of the administrative hierarchy in order to enter the Belgian administration. An interviewee with a law degree recalled how his brother, pursuing a career as a judge in Belgium, told him on his return that he could not expect, and should not be given, priority for vacant posts in the Belgian judiciary. Returnees also experienced mistrust or outright hostility. 'Peletier' told me that he decided to take an unqualified job so as to avoid having to say he was returning from the Congo in succeeding applications. The daughter of 'Michel', who had been brought up in the Congo and returned to Belgium in 1960 at the age of twenty-four, told me she was so harrassed by her colleagues about having been a colonial that the director of the company which employed her assembled all the employees and ordered everybody not to mention the matter of the Congo ever again. But the stigma of having been a former colonial should not be exaggerated: stories of employers who were so impressed by the qualities of a former territorial that they just wanted to hire more of them also abound. Nevertheless, it remains that the overall feeling among former colonials about this period is that the world was turning its back on them.

The hostility that former colonials attracted was generated by the infamy with which colonialism was increasingly considered. Everything that so far had been regarded as an achievement now appeared to have contributed to the evil oppression of the Africans for the benefit of the coloniser. Many interviewees reflected upon this transformation with acrimony or simply disillusion. One remarked: 'Twenty years ago, what we had achieved in the Congo was said to be astounding ... Now [it is said that] we have done no good whatsoever' (ibid: 102; see chapter 7 for a further analysis of the significance of this remark). As those external to the colonial regime became more stringent and all-encompassing in their attacks, so former colonials sought to defend their actions, one could almost say against their best judgment. An extreme polarisation of positions occurred on each side of the debate. To illustrate this, I shall examine the writings of Crawford Young and Fernand Grévisse. Needless to say, I could have examined those of other authors.

Crawford Young is a leading political scientist on the Congo. His first major work, *Politics in the Congo* (1965), rightly remains a highly-praised classic. Its first part consists of a well-documented discussion of Belgian colonial policies. (The second part of the book deals with post-independence Congo). The survey is well-organised, concise and precise. What Young, or presumably the Africans, thought of the system appears occasionally throughout the work. For instance, the agricultural officer is said to have been 'most familiar, and most unpopular' (ibid: 11) in a chapter entitled 'Behemoth'. The picture presented to the reader is clearly not favourable to the colonial administration. Nonetheless polemical discussions and value-judgments on colonial policies are conspicuously absent. The tone is descriptive, and in line with the introduction where Young had announced that he would 'deal with the Belgian effort to engineer the Congolese polity. This will treat the evolving vision of the future terminal goal of colonial policy and the successive policies adopted to give effect to these objectives, culminating in the "*pari congolais*"' (ibid.: 8–9).[3] Twenty years later Young's tone has completely changed. The *Rise and Decline of the Zairian State* (co-authored with Thomas Turner, 1985) opens with the reproduction and discussion of 'Colonie belge', a painting by the Zairian painter Tshibumba representing an African soldier whipping an African prisoner under the supervision of a territorial.[4] In the words of the authors: 'Dominating the center of the canvas is the African soldier, coercive backbone of the state. Colonie belge depicts the soldier in a pose which vividly communicates the strength and brutality of the system' (ibid.: 3). A discussion follows on the nature of the colonial state in Africa which points to a memory of colonialism that emphasises the oppression of the colonial system. We are a long way away from the 'low-key' account of 1965.

As Fernand Grévisse's writings illustrate, a similar though opposite hardening of position is noticeable among those inclined to take a stance that favours the colonial administration. When he was assistant district commissary, Grévisse wrote a memoir entitled 'La grande pitié des juridictions indigènes', which was published in 1949 by the Institut Royal Colonial Belge. Heated discussions in various territories followed its publication.[5] The text indeed contained some very harsh words on the Territoriale. For example Grévisse stated: 'The *relève* has brought to the Congo a respectful number of young men who are first and foremost concerned with their comfort, who consider the bush to be hell, are ready to do anything to get out of the territorial service, manifest little curiosity and even less interest in local problems, and fail to express sufficiently deep or actual feelings for the native' (ibid: 6). He substantiated this statement with remarks such as: 'Too many territorials display a frightening ignorance of the customs of the people they administer' (ibid.: 42). When Raymond Verdier (1985) argued that colonial officers had not only ignored, but also destroyed customary law in (French) Africa, Grévisse referred to his 1949 memoir to 'reestablish the truth' which was now that: 'The territorial elite did its utmost to penetrate and apply customary law with the attention and respect required' (1984: 421).

This is not what the 1949 memoir suggested. The apparent contradiction can only be explained by Grévisse's change of perspective. In the 1940s the assistant district commissary offered criticisms from within a system to which he belonged and which he sought to improve. In the 1980s such criticisms and/or improvements no longer had any raison d'être. What had become crucial for the former territorial was to reply to a hostile world, taking in this particular instance the form of an article by an academic. What Grévisse remembered and resurrected in this new context was the faith and dedication which characterised his work and that of his colleagues of the territorial 'elite'. In his view, the publication of his 1949 memoir perfectly testified to this attitude. He referred the reader to it, probably without going back, and without feeling the need to go back, to a text whose very existence supposedly amply demonstrated his point.

The colonial regime had always generated important criticisms from within its ranks.[6] The retrospective criticisms that the colonial regime attracted after independence were of a different kind, however. They arose from outside the criticised system, conceded no positive aspect in what had been done and, last but not least, accused the work of the colonials of being the source of the problems experienced by the Africans after independence. This last feature is crucial, and enduring. A picture of Laurent Kabila who succeeded General Mobutu as head of state in May 1997, attracted the following caption in the *Guardian* of 1 July 1997: 'Congo leader Laurent Kabila ... [made] an independence speech [in Kinshasa yesterday] calling on developed countries to contribute to the reconstruction of his country. He said they must repay colonialism's debt.'

This idea that colonial powers owe a debt to the Third World is not new. It was at the centre of the crisis which developed between Belgium and Zaire as I was in the middle of conducting my interviews. The crisis originated in November 1988 when the Belgian Prime Minister promised Zaire that Belgium would remit part of its debt. Members of the Belgian government reacted critically. So did the Belgian press which pointed out the oppression and mismanagement of the Mobutu regime. The Zairian government counter-attacked. The whole affair degenerated in what came to be referred to as the '*contentieux belgo-zaïrois*' ('belgo-zairian dispute') (cf Willame 1988). Although economic at root, the dispute came to include an appraisal of Belgian action in its former colony and the discussion of a possible moral debt owed by Belgium to Zaire in the light of colonial misdeeds.[7] It was the occasion for the media to reassess the Belgian colonial past. They did so in a way that confirmed former colonials in their belief, or should I say knowledge, that the world neither knows nor understands them.

The intensity of their feelings is well illustrated by the July 1989 issue of *Congorudi*, a periodical published by former colonials. The contributors to this issue give full vent to their indignation at the way the media are treating them. Their resentment is especially directed at three media items which cut across the major political divides found in (French-speaking) Belgium: from the right to the centre-left, from the catholic to the atheist intelligentsia. These items are: a *carte blanche* (kind of leading comment from someone external to the newspaper) published on 12 January 1989 by *Le Soir*; a two-page report published on 4 April 1989 in *La Libre Belgique*, the other single most important daily newspaper in French-speaking Belgium; and a T.V. programme produced on R.T.L. on 4 April 1989. The Marxist historian Benoît Verhaegen signed the *carte blanche*, entitled: 'Zaire: debts and creditors'; the historian Jean-Luc Vellut from the Catholic University of Brussels is quoted in the *La Libre Belgique* report, entitled 'The diverse and deep roots of the belgo-zairian dispute'; Jacques Vanderlinden from the Free University of Brussels was among the experts who participated in the R.T.L. programme, entitled 'A colonisation in black and white'. Former colonials could only be reminded that the entire spectrum of society was taking a stance against them.

They reacted vehemently. I shall quote a former territorial whose indignation was directed not at any of the items mentioned above, but at Colette Braeckman, the regular correspondent on Zaire to *Le Soir*. Maurice Lenain wrote her an 'open letter' where he criticised her for the way she had represented the colonials over the years in the most widely-read newspaper in the Belgian capital. His elegant but caustic tone is well-captured in the opening words:

> For years now, you have been filling the columns of *Le Soir* with your haughty spirit of condemnation against the paternalist Belgian government in Africa and its representatives, the colonial officers. If we are to believe what you write, we have been nothing but disgraceful, profit-thirsty slave-traders, perpetually wielding a whip over the backs of those wretched Blacks, dazed by blows and exhausted by forced labour, those miserable slaves, chained to the chariot of Profit (ours of course) (*Congorudi*, July 1989, 8).

These words eloquently suggest that Braeckman has recurrently presented her readers with a negative image of the colonials. But it is important to note that Lenain only expresses his interpretation of the journalist's reports; he does not quote her. In the rest of the letter, he proceeds first to ask the journalist whether she has helped the Congolese as the colonials (the territorials and also the health workers, doctors and technicians) have done, and then to criticise her for enjoying a comfortable desk job rather than lending a hand to technical aid teams in Africa.

It presents the sound economic infrastructure bequeathed at independence as the 'present of a wonderful Father Christmas'. According to Lenain, Braeckman has been 'judging', 'denigrating', 'attacking' the colonials 'in their dignity'.[8]

These words certainly express the way former colonials generally feel towards the media. In my view, they are too vehement, if not misdirected: Braeckman would probably readily recognise the (paternalist) dedication of many colonials described at some length by Lenain and the material development that had taken place in the colony under the Belgian administration. But it is as if Braeckman's consistently critical stance towards colonialism, as a political principle governing relations between states and between people, made her permanently suspicious and even dishonest in the eyes of Lenain – who concludes his letter: 'We were not the agents of imperialism, as you know perfectly well!' Irreconcilable moral and epistemological principles underline Braeckman's and Lenain's analyses of the 'colonial situation' (to borrow the term coined by Balandier in 1951). The journalist's assumption is that the phenomenon of colonialism is ultimately a political and moral evil. Lenain, by contrast, would object even to the use of the term 'colonialism' and would obstinately stick to that of *'colonisation'*: like his former colleagues, he does not think that a pejorative 'ism' needs to be added to a term which adequately renders the idea of the material construction in which he collaborated. The former territorial and the journalist's respective underlying assumptions, and thus conclusions, are so far apart that communication between them is virtually impossible.

The other articles contained in the July 1989 issue of *Congorudi* exemplify further how the debate surrounding colonialism is characterised by opposed discourses and discussions working at cross-purposes. Let me take just one more example, which is related to Verhaegen's *carte blanche* of 12 January 1989. In this short article, Verhaegen commented upon the belgo-zairian dispute by seeking to outline the balance-sheet which existed between the former metropole and its ex-colony. To quote the words especially related to the colonial period experienced by the interviewees:

> ... The debt also arises out of the Belgian colonial administration having imposed the cultivation of crops in a way which routinely attracted corporal punishment; repressed – often violently – social and religious movements; denied political rights until the eve of independence; limited school education; infused daily contacts with racism and apartheid; practised administrative and judicial arbitrariness. ... On the positive side, there is all that made the Congo a 'model colony', as marked by the universal exhibition of 1958 in Brussels.

Verhaegen then advises:

> Neither the negative nor the positive should be exaggerated. Nor should they be separated. Most important of all, the different periods should not be amalgamated and the atrocities of the Leopoldian regime should certainly not be attributed to the Belgian coloniser of 1950.

These sound pieces of advice did not calm the fury of the former colonials. By spelling out the liabilities of the colonial regime without doing the same kind of exercise in respect of its credit side, Verhaegen did not achieve the balance former colonials expected. As in the case of Braeckman, his underlying assumptions were clear to the former colonials who found him irritating, if not dangerous. They read his text as an 'outrageous' piece. In the opinion of one, it is something so 'enormous' that, were it not for the credence a historian and University lecturer might receive and the possibly disastrous consequences of the article, one would just feel like ignoring it (Sacré 1989: 7–8).

Marcel Sacré, who had worked for various companies in the Congo, sent a letter of protest to *Le Soir*. The editor of *Congorudi*, which published the letter in its July 1989 issue, explained that the daily had acknowledged the receipt of the letter but had failed to publish it and to take any notice of its content. The lack of attention by the media to their reactions infuriates the former colonials. They feel they have no voice. A respondent to my questionnaire observed: 'After the [T.V.] programme of 2 February [1989], I wrote to the RTBF. I failed to receive even an acknowledgement, nothing. There exists no right of reply to these T.V. programmes. So they can say anything they like' (Dembour 1991b: 74). One respondent to the questionnaire commented that he did not watch the T.V. programmes on the Congo any more, except sometimes for the scenic views, but then he cut the sound (ibid: 96). This frustration at not managing to have their experience put across and to be publicly heard is what leads me to suggest that the former colonials are 'muted' (cf Ardener 1975). The awareness that they are being seen as colonialists, with all the negative assumptions which the term carries in the dominant world-view, must affect the way former colonials talk or do not talk about the Congo.

The chance to be recognised by the outside world

Some time in 1990, a student enquired at the University of Brussels whether my thesis would be available and when. She was very keen to read my work because she knew that I had interviewed her grandfather.

She wanted to learn about his life in the Congo, but he would not talk to her about it. I was most surprised to hear this as her grandfather had immediately responded to the letter I had sent him in December 1987 to say: 'I am fully available to try to give you as much information as possible and seek to help you the best I can.' Politeness did not require him or his former colleagues to answer my call. If the addressees had wished, they could easily have escaped the burden of a collaboration in a polite but unequivocal way. But they did not. At times, eagerness even transpired from their positive answers. For instance one wrote: 'I'll help you the best I can, recalling memories of the most enriching years in my life, for I felt a vocational call to be an Administrator since I was about twelve-years-old'. The spouse of the addressee (or possibly a child of his) often regretted when her husband (or father) was unable to offer his contribution. For example, I received the following reply: '[My ninety-nine-year-old husband] told me as he read your letter: "It comes too late". But if we can be of any help, it will be with great pleasure.' Another spouse wrote: 'I am sorry I must inform you that my husband died almost two years ago. I am all the more sorry as I am sure he would have wanted to be of help to you.' There is a sense in which it is almost as if the potential interviewees had been waiting for an interviewer to come and record their recollections.[9]

Former colonials generally think that they deserve better recognition from 'History'. They share a feeling that their '*oeuvre*', a word best translated in this context as achievements, should be documented before it is too late. In the light of what has been said in the previous section, this should come as no surprise. What is less expected, however, is that they should have trusted that cooperating with me would help them in this endeavour. I had anticipated that prospective interviewees would enquire about my views on colonialism and about the aims of my thesis before agreeing to meet me. Such preliminary quizzing never occurred, except possibly in a very mild way in one case. On receipt of my letter of December 1987, 'Jamiolle' wrote: 'It is not too late to study the way in which those who were attached to the actual application of justice accomplished their task, provided the issue is examined in nothing but an objective way'. I phoned 'Jamiolle' and tried to explain that I did not believe in objectivity but only in honesty. I added that I was not sure that our views were reconcilable. He was not very interested in my explanations and we fixed the appointment for an interview.

When I expressed gratefulness at the welcome with which I was uniformly received, some interviewees linked it with hospitality, a principle which I was told governed life in the Congo and distinguished colonial society from the metropolitan, narrow-minded, belgicain one. In the Congo, a white passer-by was invariably welcome; even if the house was empty, Europeans knew they could come in and help themselves to beer in the fridge. Having guests was one of the few available entertainments, and social life was more developed than in Belgium. Especially in the bush – for 'in town, it was a completely different matter' – people helped each other spontaneously. But all was not harmonious in the European communities of the small posts,[10] and this sense of sociability and solidarity cannot simply have guided practice automatically for years. It certainly cannot fully explain why people opened their doors to me thirty years later, even if it may have played a role.

Interviewers have often been delighted to find that individuals were ready to talk to them, even on topics that the former thought very sensitive to the latter (Denzin 1989). In a society like ours which emphasises 'confessions' (Foucault 1976: 78–84), it may be that people only need a listening interlocutor to begin to tell their life-stories (Bertaux 1980: 206; Poirier et al. 1983: 148). This requires the interviewee to be convinced that his life is worth telling, which is not always the case (Lequin and Métral 1980; Gilsenan 1986; Tonkin 1992: 133). We can foresee, however, that this was not a problem for my addressees. Nonetheless, it is clear that they could have tried to find whether I was the kind of interlocutor to whom they wished to talk. Why did they not? Perhaps this question is better rephrased in the following way: whom did they think I was?

Most of them probably assumed that I was a well-intentioned and/or neutral student, two qualities they would often see as being equivalent (see below). 'Adam', for example, offered to give me documents after my uncle mentioned to him that one of his nieces was doing a study on the Territoriale. A few days after the two met, he wrote to my uncle a letter in which he wondered 'which first-hand or honest sources and documents this little niece can rely upon' to do her work and offered to give me his own private archives. The image of the 'little' niece is interesting. It implies that the researcher is young, perhaps even immature, and suggests that she is both new to the matter and uncorrupted by the outside world. It must have comforted 'Adam' in the thought (or hope?) that I had begun my research devoid of any presuppositions, as the ideal scientific canon requires. Later, we shall see that in 'Adam''s scheme, provided I was properly tipped, I could only come up with the right conclusions; objectivity would lead me to praise the colonial administration.

All prospective interviewees need not have shared this representation of the researcher. I doubt that I could have been a 'little' inoffensive student for 'd'Ave et d'Ove'. 'd'Ave et d'Ove' was the father of the partner of a good friend of mine who had been active in anarchist circles since she was eighteen years old. He could only presume that like his son and (would-be) daughter-in-law, I was far from convinced of the benefits of colonialism. Instead of objecting to an interview, he is the one who insisted, through my friend, that he was willing to meet me. Talking to me must have appeared to him as a better tactic than leaving me alone to interpret books and documents which I might misunderstand. For him, the interview must have represented the opportunity to put his perspective across, even if he could not be sure what I would make of it.

'd'Ave et d'Ove' indeed began the interview by telling me that he first wanted to tell me one or two things – after that he would answer my questions. The first anecdote he reported fitted the scheme I was expecting. He told me that, in the early 1950s, an African chief had lamented to him the decline of prestige amongst the Whites. To make himself understood, the chief explained to 'd'Ave et d'Ove', then a young territorial, how a branch had hit the eye of a territorial who was travelling in a tipoye before the War; all carriers had been flogged on arrival at destination. For the chief, the story illustrated how the Whites should behave but, unfortunately, did so less and less. The reason why 'd'Ave et d'Ove' opened the interview with this story is presumably because he suspected that prestige, indeed a frequent theme in the colonial discourse (see chapter 6), would be something that would shock me in colonial narratives. He wanted to make sure I knew the Africans themselves were requesting the Europeans to behave with prestige, and thus emphasised one crucial aspect of the phenomenon of prestige he feared might escape me.

The interviewees who did not know me may have contemplated the possibility that I was not sharing their views. In this case they were apparently ready to interpret the fact I took the time to listen to them for long hours as proof of my willingness to depart from the hostility of the outside world. 'Duruisseau', who had been a judge in the colony, told me: 'Had you been a journalist, I would not have invited you to come.' His view was that journalists only want to hear a few things which confirm the opinions they already hold. By agreeing to come in the morning and spend the whole day in his house, I had demonstrated that I was ready to learn about the colonials' point of view. 'Colman' who helped me with documentation on more than one occasion, made a similar remark. After one year of exchanging correspondence and phonecalls, I was visiting him at his house to collect yet another document. As the conversation turned to the organisation of his time in the Congo (not an especially sensitive topic) I asked whether I could tape him. 'Colman' showed some hesitation and then added: 'All right, if you wish, you are not a journalist.'

For those who received my letter of introduction, I must have appeared as someone interested in the colonial past, though not associated with the journalists they dislike so much. To them, my sudden appearance in their lives may have constituted a chance they felt they should not turn away: perhaps my study would help begin to reestablish the truth and counteract the negative image from which they suffer. Indeed it is not just to me that the interviewees were talking during the interviews. 'Even the most solitary autobiographical monologue still represents an attempt at communication which implies the phantasm of an interlocutor' (Ferrarrotti 1983: 52). Some writers are very much aware of their potential audience. Paul Augustin, for example, wrote his memoirs as a former territorial against the 'detractors of the colonial *œuvre*'; he dedicated the manuscript to his descendants,[11] wishing that they would benefit 'from the example of one of theirs, away in unfavourable climates in order to fulfill various tasks requiring a faculty of adaptation' (n.d.: 4–5). As for the interviewees, they must have hoped for the presence of an interlocutor who was not just the individual researcher. Through me, they must have tried to reach and address the outside world.

The objective witness

I mentioned in the previous section how 'Adam' had offered me his private archives through my uncle. His letter to 'Bertrand' points to the divide he feels separates the former colonials from the world which surrounds them. It is worth quoting at some length – even if this entails repeating its beginning:

> I wonder which first-hand or honest sources and documents this little niece can rely upon. ... I think I have some very valuable documentation in my cupboards. I had myself thought of using it for a study for the 'vindication and illustration of the Belgian colonial *épopée*' (it is time to call a spade a spade), but it would remain a sermon by a 'colonialist'. ... Therefore it would be much better for someone of the 'second generation' to do it, but tipped to the proper source ... Someone young will be read by her generation, and true history will take over.

Through his use of language, 'Adam' hints over and over again at the difficult situation in which former colonials find themselves when they face, as it were, the world: by referring to the potential shortage of honest documentation; by specifying that a study by him would be read as a sermon by a colonialist; by giving the study he did not write the title of '*épopée*', a word literally translated in English as 'epic' but which can lose its mythical character in French to refer to a succession of historical events of heroic and lofty character (Petit Robert 1982), thus implicitly calling through its grandiose connotations for a recognition of the colonial achievements, in his view long overdue; by implying that true history is in need of recovery. The quoted extract makes it clear how crucial it can be for former territorials to put forward an image of the Congo which will counteract the one emerging from the Belgian media. In view of the vested interests of my informants, one could doubt the value of their testimony. I shall argue in this section, however, that the concept of history which informs their statements is such that we can trust that most of them attempted to stick to the role of the objective witness when they talked to me.

Deceit as a non-issue

There is a tendency in Western societies, reflected in the constitution of institutions such as museums and archives libraries and in academic disciplines such as archaelogy, history and sometimes anthropology, to preserve the past *qua* past – rather than to see it as unfolding in the present. According to this conception, the past is always at risk of vanishing forever, and it must be 'preserved' before it disappears. To rescue the past envisaged in such a way, testimonies are needed, and for the latter to be valuable, they need to be objective. The interviewees, who often commented that it was high time if not too late for their memories to be collected, share this particular conception of the past. Of course they are interested in being recognised as important actors in the colonial enterprise, the achievements of which they admire; but they also endorse the view that the role of the witness is to give objective and reliable information so that the past can live on. I may have been a young student and the scope of my study may have been limited in terms of both its subject matter and its audience; they nonetheless took their role seriously. The concept of history prevalent in our society made them very conscious that the information they were giving me should be impartial, correct and comprehensive.

This concept explains why 'Milnaert' was so keen for me to hear about a territorial experience different from his and sent me to 'Peters'. As I have already said, 'Peters' talked quite openly about quasi-illegal practices during our meeting. For example, he stated: 'To me, seven days in jail meant seven times four strokes of the whip'; on my probing, he added: 'It is always possible to find excuses if you look for them hard enough.' One could be tempted to attribute the carefree way with which 'Peters' talked about his severity and possible abuses of the law to the way 'Milneart' had presented me. As 'Milnaert' was fixing an appointment for me with 'Peters' over the phone, from the living room where I was sitting I could overhear him saying: 'And there is no point in fooling her about anything – the whip and all those things, she knows about them.' A more convincing explanation for 'Peters'' attitude, however, is that the historical genre we implicitly adopted required that we talked of both the negative and the positive aspects of the territorial experience.[12]

I say this because 'Peters' is not the only interviewee, far from it, who refrained from giving me as positive an image of the Congo as possible. Let me give three additional examples. During my three-day visit in August 1987 to 'Bertrand' who thus became my first informant, 'Bertrand' brought up subjects which are difficult not to qualify as sensitive. For instance he explained how people were recruited to the colonial army. Each territorial was informed of the number of men he had to send to the army. One way or another, he had to manage to find his quota of men, who had to be young and vigorous. Most of these, however, fiercely resisted recruitment; they fled and hid in the forest. The territorial was forced to organise their pursuit and to bring them back to the village with a rope around the neck.[13] 'Bertrand' specified that this was the practice in the first years of his service in the Congo (which he took up in 1951), but that it became easier to find army recruits as time passed by, notably because of the advantages soldiers obtained such as the construction of a brick-built house on their return to the village after three terms of seven years. 'Bertrand' did not try to justify the practice, nor did he comment upon it at length. He simply said: 'We did not like to do this. It was *vraiment embêtant* (a real drag).'[14] My second example comes from 'Milnaert'. As he was driving me back to the railway station after our first interview, he asked me how it was that I had not raised the subject of the whip, which he thought would have been within the scope of my interests. Of course it was; I simply had thought, quite wrongly, that he was not the type of person with whom I could raise this kind of issue. At the station, he told me how disgusted he had been the first time he had witnessed an African being flogged and how he had wondered whether the Belgians were taking over the role of the Gestapo – in a land where he was arriving just after the Second World War. For a third example, we can turn to the interview with 'd'Ave et d'Ove', which I already explained had started with the story of a chief who had complained that Europeans increasingly failed to act with sufficient prestige. The second anecdote 'd'Ave et d'Ove' told me was related to the imprisonment of an African in the late 1950s when unrest was feared. 'd'Ave et d'Ove' explained that he had based the judgment of condemnation on the legislation relating to armed bands, even though the act was hardly applicable to the facts of the case. In other words, he continued, what he wanted was to have the African in jail, and the act provided the rather poor excuse for this. Although the anecdote is situated in the exceptional pre-independence period, 'd'Ave et d'Ove' made it clear that he experienced a confusion of justice and politics throughout all his years in the Congo. Examples of this kind, where interviewees discuss topics which do not present the colonial administration in the best possible light and do so without my prompting, could be multiplied.

In one case, the interviewee seems to have done this because he did not realise that what he was telling me was within the scope of my research. I am thinking of 'de Glaise'. When I arrived at his house, 'de Glaise' told me he would first recount his career, after which he would answer my questions. This presentation took up the whole morning and pointed to a rather quick ascent: having entered the territorial service as an officer in 1940, 'de Glaise' finished his territorial career in 1960 as assistant district commissary. 'de Glaise' appeared to be very keen to expand on the seventeen disciplinary and two judicial proceedings to which (he told me) he had been subjected and which (he alleged) had all been interrupted after the personal intervention of Governor-General Ryckmans, whose wife he presented as a close friend of his own mother-in-law.[15] One of the judicial proceedings involved a slap in the face which 'de Glaise' said he had given to a Portuguese tradesman who was using a scale out of balance.[16] I was surprised that the incident had been deemed serious enough to warrant the instigation of judicial proceedings. It suddenly became clear, however, that the man had been carried away on a stretcher with a few teeth missing and that the slap had been a potent punch. Immediately after giving me this clue, 'de Glaise' added: 'But you're not interested in this kind of thing for your study, are you?' Until then, I had been returning to the story for it put, as I then still expected, physical violence and illegality at the centre of the reality of the Congo; 'de Glaise', who presumably enjoyed the opportunity to play the tough guy and to stress his connections with the Ryckmans family, had been happily following me in my interest. After his question about the scope of my research, however, I decided to leave the story of the 'slap' alone. This did not seem to me to lead him to be more cautious, for he continued to tell me stories which I felt were in the same vein. I have already mentioned the story of the chief's son whom he requested behave like a goat and his self-comparison to a tamer of wild beasts. But, as I have already said, 'de Glaise' appears to have been an exceptional figure.

'Peters' expressed some second thoughts about what he had told me. When I presented him with a written account of our interview,[17] he did not like it. He was concerned that his testimony might further prejudice the image of Belgian colonialism, particularly since I was doing my doctorate in a country where he knew this image to be essentially negative.[18] Nevertheless, he did not ask me not to use the account I had prepared (an injunction which he would in any case have had no power to enforce). He simply remarked: 'It is too late. Now I've said it and you've heard it. You cannot behave as if you had not heard it.' Despite these words (and 'Milnaert''s introduction discussed above), my feeling is that 'Peters' would have repeated his original statements even if he had been given the chance to start our first interview from scratch again, because he would simply have accepted to share with the researcher the recollections of his colonial experience and would have done so as these came to his mind.

The question could nonetheless be raised as to whether other interviewees would have tried to deceive me. Even if this was the case (and it certainly can never be ruled out),[19] I do not think this would be a problem, for it is hardly possible that a whole group of informants would have elected to fabricate in the same way the facts they were telling me. My concern was with general patterns and trends, and I am bound to have heard, at least from some interviewees, about the existence of practices which were reasonably common. Moreover, as I have already said, the interviewees seem to have been concerned with accuracy: they wanted to be as objective as possible in the way they rendered the facts of the Congo. But what is a fact, and how does one render it?

Different kinds of facts

The term 'fact' has a large and differentiated range of meanings. Consider for example the Congolese judicial system. One could describe it from a variety of perspectives, including a black-letter law one, a practical one and an evaluative one. The first perspective would lead to a description of the system in terms of legal provisions and could for example explain which judge was competent to pass which sentences; the second perspective could seek to describe who actually became judge among all the possible candidates to that function; and the third could give rise to a general appreciation, such as: 'Congolese justice was fair and even-handed as the natives knew and appreciated.' All statements made under those different umbrellas of course represent objective facts for those who utter them, including the most evaluative one. Now how does one manage to render these different kinds of facts, especially to someone who has no first-hand experience of the reality which is discussed? Each interviewee had his own way of attempting to do this. I shall look at the style of three of them. To anticipate the discussion which follows, I shall say that 'Vastenakel' was trying to be literal and to-the-point, 'Dehon' to render an atmosphere, and 'Milnaert' to offer an all-encompassing sociological analysis.

'Vastenakel' was very careful to make statements which were correct and could be taken at face-value. Such was his concern that he sent me a letter the day after our first meeting to rectify two mistakes he had made the previous afternoon. To quote his letter:

> In respect to my activities as judge of the tribunal of territory, which I carried out on Saturday afternoons to rule upon … disputes involving one or more soldiers of the colonial army at the Watsa Camp, I told you by mistake, for which I beg your pardon, that I delivered up to ten judgments in one afternoon. It is between two and four judgments which I gave, depending on the importance and seriousness of the cases (mostly about adultery, bridewealth payment, filiation, theft, actual bodily harm, debts …) and depending on the number of witnesses I had to hear. As for the second question, I talked to you about the repression of the cultivation, possession, consumption and sale … of Indian hemp by the tribunal of police; in doing so I mistakenly associated this drug to cocaine, while I should have talked of hashish (letter of 2 April 1988).

'Vastenakel' obviously aimed at precision in this letter. He was very careful to be 'administratively' correct. In the last sentence, for instance, he was not content just to mention that hemp was prohibited, but talked of the repression of its cultivation, possession, consumption and sale. The insertion of the three points of suspension possibly indicate that he thought his listing might not be exhaustive. 'Vastenakel' indeed omitted one sector, but only one – transportation.[20] Such meticulousness may be the residue of his training: territorials were required to draw up penal charges in the exact words provided by the law. If they did not, the judge of the standing tribunal in charge of the control of their activity as magistrate of police would have remarked negatively on their judgments. Nevertheless, the accuracy of 'Vastenakel"s 'positive' account is striking, especially after so many years.

The information provided by 'Vastenakel' in the extract quoted above attempts to be faithful to a technical description of the colonial experience. The facts reported are of the same nature as those found in printed documents such as legal codes. For a different kind of description, we can turn to 'Dehon'. I shall quote him extensively (following closely the transcript of a tape):

> – ... In 1936, when I arrived as administrator-candidate, I did not have the right to condemn as I was not yet magistrate of police. ... Now, I was instructed to do the census in the Ankutchu chiefdom. And there I must confess that I took the chief Lukale under my wing, i.e. I acted through him. ... I came to be in agreement, and more than this, with him. In other words, I was exercising pressure. I was telling him: 'Your village is dirty. I am going to do something about it, which your people won't like.'

This passage is better understood in the light of another which came later in the interview (the dashes indicate the alternation between 'Dehon''s interventions and mine):

> – ... When I had to do the census, either people came or they did not. One had to make them come.
> – How did you force them to come?
> – A firmer, more coercive attitude was needed, for example by intervening and speaking to the village chief. I would tell him: 'OK, so many people are still missing. You tell me they are away. I want to see them. There is no way out, my census is not finished. Hm, by the way, I went to see your village – let us leave aside the problem of the census – well, you know that the law requires it to be cleared for fifty metres, this has not been done. Don't force me to intervene once more, clear your village, do what is required, come to an agreement with me, then everything will be fine.' The chief is not stupid. He has seen the undergrowth before I have. He thus thinks: 'If I start with him, he is going to look at everything in detail. He is also going to check the spring. If he wishes, it is clean; but if he wishes, it is not. The same goes for the way things are behind the village. If the grass is high like this, he can either say that it is bushy, or say that it is a lawn and that everything is perfect.'

Now going back to the passage I first quoted, it continued:

... The maintenance of roads is another example. In this respect, I ended up by telling him (after two years or at the end of my three years): 'Lukale, the traders and transporters inform me that there is a problem with the road at such and such a place. Make sure it is repaired, or I will go there myself.' And he made sure it was repaired. This is how far it went. It was my way and it was his way. And this is how we managed.
– And with such agreements, did you ever consciously have to act against the law?
– Of course. We did this at our own risk. When I was going to see the fields with Lukale, still in 1936, 37, 38, we were going together and I acted as if I was taking the decisions ...
– It was not you who took the decisions?
– Of course not, it could not be me, because it was not within my remit.[21] It was the chief who had to take the decision. He was responsible for the native tribunals. *He* was the President of the tribunal of chiefdom, but *I* was the one who directed the tribunal. So, I used to go with him ... to visit the fields ... with the agricultural assistant who had visited them before and who used to say: 'So and so has not yet done anything while he should already be at such or such a stage.' At that moment, I was looking at the chief: 'You must do something.' The chief put on his air, and often he gave four strokes of the whip there and then. ... But who had given the strokes of the whip? Who had ordered them?
– Formally the chief, but in reality it was you
– Exactly
– Your superiors knew ...
– Within the territorial ranks, this was not a problem
– And what about the judges?
– Here is where things could have become problematic.

In this account, without me asking him to do so, 'Dehon' dated the events he was recounting. He also gave the name of the place and of the chief whom he had in mind as he talked. An attempt to recount such precise details was very rare among the interviewees. 'Dehon''s style was also distinctive in that he always used imaginary dialogues to help me understand what he was talking about. Of course 'Dehon' did not intend the exchange of words he reported with the chief Lukale to be taken as a literal reproduction of the conversation he once might have had with him. Rather, he wanted me to get a sense of the general atmosphere in which he worked. The effect of the dialogue was indeed powerful: the tone of the voice (unfortunately lost in the transcript), the repetition of some ideas and the current of thought expressed the relationship between the (lower rank) territorial and the chief in a way a dry and static description could not. Although somewhat fictionalised, these anecdotes undoubtedly sought accuracy.

Like 'Vastenakel' and 'Dehon', 'Milnaert' was also seeking to ensure that I understood precisely what the reality of the Congo was like, but he did this through yet a different means. The extract I shall quote to give a sense of his style, is selected from notes he wrote to himself before setting out to answer my written questionnaire – an exercise that in itself demonstrates a high concern for recalling, replacing, re-understanding 'reality' before beginning to talk about it. Rightly thinking that these notes arranged around various themes could interest me, 'Milnaert' appended them to his answers to the questionnaire. One section consisted in a discussion of segregation. I shall quote it in full to expose the various levels 'Milneart' encompassed in his analysis. (I have placed 'Milnaert's footnotes, numbered 1 to 3, directly after his main text to distinguish them from my own footnotes).

> Mrs Clair[22] says that the Europeans have ignored African 'culture' and that, in any case, they treated it with contempt. But the A.T. had to know (devait connaître), otherwise, how could he have managed the chiefdoms established on the basis of customary inquiries or presided over the tribunal of territory? The missionaries also had an extensive knowledge, and it was an old missionary who gave me the key to the *U-Znla*. The knowledge of the other members of the administration was more 'focused' and the settler, who was usually an employer, knew the Blacks (with notable exceptions) only as workers. But I have never heard of customs being held in contempt. On the contrary, the European has a Rousseau-like side to him which led him to value the [African] systems of social protection (such as kinship solidarity, friendship reinforced by debt, the bridewealth protecting the married girl …). The idea of a simple, peaceful, relatively undemanding society, (apparently) that of the 'Noble Savage', was often evoked as a lost ideal.
>
> Nevertheless, there was a clear segregation between the two communities based on race, which existed at all levels. I noticed it when I first arrived, but was no more shocked than an officer who takes charge of a platoon and finds it appropriate that other ranks are kept at some distance. I suppose that a great number of issues are involved: the obvious cultural gap, the social distance between superior and subordinate, the arrogance of those who have the keys to a particular world, reinforced by the submissive attitudes of the others, and the spirit of domination … probably too, in a vague and sub-conscious way, a sense of the vulnerability of European privilege faced with an enormous mass of people only temporarily quiet … More generally, it is possible that our Indo-European culture cannot help but divide society into different classes (Dumézil). Colonial society was itself hierarchically and tightly

divided (1). Perhaps men need to define barriers to organise themselves and the colour of the skin is the easiest barrier to recognise. I also imagine that the European brought with him a ninteenth-century sociology (with its division of the world into two classes), which he reproduced in Africa (2).

Around 1956, one of the 'clerks' of the territory became a territorial agent.[23] We liked him a lot and were ready to help him getting himself established as much as we could. However, there was absolutely no question of him becoming integrated into European society.

By contrast, a young Black who had studied journalism in Belgium, came to our territory, because he was interested in our agricultural project. We treated him as a European. I visited the region with him, and shared with him my accommodation and meals without any problems.

Thus the barrier was at the same time strong and fragile (3), and also conscious. As I had recently discovered Moreno, I suggested to my clerk Th., who was a remarkable mimic, to put on a 'role play'. He played before a large assembly of Blacks. He first 'ridiculed' the faults of the Blacks (with great success) and then those of the Whites (with enormous success). All the Whites found that the performance was relevant and helped to break down the barrier.

Note: Have I told you the story of Thourdoulin who asks me for a book to borrow? I take him to my study and leave him alone. He selects *Recherche de la vérité* by Malebranche. ... Inquiry ... He strongly believes (as most Blacks do) that we have a secret which enables us to command even natural forces. He had hoped that Malebranche would give him something of that secret. In fact, he read the book with great interest, especially the chapters on sensory illusions: the illusory quality of appearances.

Missionaries had eroded the segregation. They had Black colleagues who had gone to secondary schools and studied theology. These Black priests lived in the same community as the fathers, but without much harmony.[24]

The '*évolués*' suffered the worst of the segregation. The Europeans despised their (blundering) mimicking efforts. When the Black employees met at the 'Club' of the extra-customary centre of our territory, they attributed themselves titles such as AT, C de D [district commissary], Director, etcetera.

Segregation must have been extremely visible and humiliating in town, the more so since there the European could know absolutely nothing about the Black and his attitudes, had no contact with him, did not speak the language, etc.

Segregation had a more 'fatherly' aspect in the bush. When we were discussing something involving the construction of a bridge, cultivation or customs, one 'forgot' about race – on both sides I think.

(1) But, in the 'Club', there was more or less an absolute equality as long as one was white or of mixed blood and accepted.
(2) I remember my first encounter with a factory in 1961. I was shocked to see how the workers were treated. (The same strict order was given in the

subjunctive form in the Congo, according to the level of politeness which one wanted to achieve). The difference? I would go so far as to say that in Europe, the worker was reduced to the level of a mere tool. In Africa, we could not escape a certain feeling that the Africans were 'free men' (there were only free men in the clans) – perhaps this was due to the fact that the tasks were not highly technical.

(3) Frail: ambiguous, difficult to describe. During the RTL programme,[25] [it was reported that] European youngsters 'played' with Black companions and that 'the parents would not have objected to the development of friendships ...'. My own children had particular relationships of trust and affection with the boys (which included exchanging food). In 1960, the Belgian parachutists were in the district. The UN replaced them with troops from Mali. The young Black commander introduced himself to us (we saw him as an intruder). We accepted him as soon as he spoke French slang words (he was a *Saint-Cyrien*).[26]

These notes, not written for the purpose of quotation, are impressive in their efforts to delineate reality. 'Milnaert' tries to define how segregation was operating in the Congo. He begins by rejecting a simplistic view that segregation went together with a complete ignorance of and/or failure to appreciate African culture. He recognises the fact that segregation existed and immediately adds that it was not shocking, providing a comparison with another setting (that of the lieutenant in charge of a platoon). He then proceeds to examine the possible causes for segregation, moving from those particular to the colonial situation (such as the cultural gap between the groups of the Whites and the Blacks) to social ones peculiar to the Western society (such as a nineteenth-century division of society into two classes). After that, he tries to convey, using examples drawn from his personal experience, how segregation manifested itself and what it meant in practice. To do this he contrasts different cases (the territorial agent and the journalist; the situation in town and in the bush), which enables him to bring nuances to the presentation. It appears that, for 'Milnaert', thinking and attempting to sort out the colonial experience intellectually was part of the task of giving an 'accurate' testimony. As he explained to me later, his goal was not as much to reach literal accuracy and Truth with a capital T ('*la Vérité avec un grand V*') in which he said he did not believe), as to grasp something ('*saisir quelque chose*').

The quotations from 'Vastenakel''s letter, 'Dehon''s interview and 'Milnaert''s notes-to-himself demonstrate the variety of 'facts' to be found in the interviews which were all made of a mixture of elements combining, albeit in various proportions, technical information, personal anecdotes, and general considerations. Some of these facts more readily fell under a false/true dichotomy than others, thus allowing for corrections of the kind brought in by 'Vastenakel'. With a description such as 'Dehon''s, the concrete details, despite their presence, lose some of their importance. There was a feeling that what I had to get right was the atmosphere. With 'Milnaert' the case is different again. The sense there was that he and I were engaged in a long-term and open-ended discussion, for which the word 'correction' hardly applied. Although concrete points were important, what was really at stake was an understanding of the colonial experience in its widest sense.

True history will not take over

So far in this chapter, we have seen that the interviewees object to the work of journalists and historians who are contemptuous of anything colonial. To help counteract the image emerging from this arena, they were ready to help me in my project and endorsed the role of the objective witness demanded by a conception which regards history as the accurate recording of the past. I now wish to pay attention to the view, expressed by some of them, that an honest researcher could only produce a study that would vindicate them. Such a view originally put me in an uncomfortable position, for I felt I would not be able to meet my interviewees' expectations. To my relief, however, it turned out that these expectations were quite varied, so that I need not disappoint all my informants to the same degree.

As he was showing me to the door at the end of our first interview, 'Michel' heartily shook my hand and said: '*Vous me plaisez beaucoup.*' There were no sexual overtones in this expression of delight which, in other circumstances, could have meant 'I fancy you'. His daughter (then in her fifties) and myself nonetheless exchanged a knowing smile. We were probably smiling as much at the ambiguity of the remark as at the pleasure of seeing that the old man was happy. Once out of the door, however, the statement left me uneasy. The ninety-year-old was confident that I was preparing a worthy study, in his own acceptance of the term; I knew that he would have been upset, had he realised half of what was going on in my mind. What was I to make of that? The dilemma arose again and again. One example is when my uncle transmitted me 'Adam''s letter. The reference it contained to the 'defence and illustration of the Belgian colonial *épopée*' made it clear that 'Adam''s perspective had very little in common with mine. He had specified in a post-script that the documents were not for sale but free of charge 'to help towards a piece of work which he would have wished to accomplish himself'. His project, to ensure that true history would take over, was obviously one to which I did not subscribe. I felt the best I could do in the circumstances was to refrain from pursuing his offer to give me his documents.

Fortunately, former colonials were not all as extreme as 'Adam' in their desire to promote the defence of colonialism. This I learned early in my research from 'Dehon''s reaction to the paper I had prepared on punishment in the Congo. The paper in no way resembled an appraisal of the 'heroic action' of the Belgians in their colony and I had not dared to mention its existence to my interviewees. 'Dehon', whom I did not know, came across it as he was doing editorial work for the Law department at the Free University of Brussels. He introduced himself to me, and I invited him to comment on the paper. Somewhat to my amazement, 'Dehon' did not object to what I had written. Far from wishing to correct me, he expanded on my statements in some fourteen pages, providing illustrations, details, or explanations. On the basis of this successful experience, I decided to ask 'Milneart' for his reaction. The tape I received in return was a terrible blow. 'Milnaert' was pointing out my mistakes and misinterpretations aggressively, or so I felt. Half-listening to the corrosive remarks, I was devastated. My new certainty was that a relationhip I had experienced as promising had come to an end. Going back to 'Milnaert', however, I realised that I was wrong. I had listened to the tape without having the paper before my eyes, and the comments had seemed more numerous and drastic than they actually were. Also the tone had not been aggressive: 'Milneart' had been asked for his opinion and he was giving it, without compliance but without hostility either – perhaps just with a slight irritation here and there. Having expressed his way of looking at things, he encouraged me also to solicit the opinion of 'Parmentier' under whom he had worked in the Congo and whom he greatly respected.

I did not wish to take the risk of possibly breaking a relationship with an informant, a situation I still feared, but I had little choice and sent the paper. 'Parmentier' read it carefully and invited me to come to his house to discuss it, which we did for five hours. He had marked the passages which, in his view, were incorrect, needed clarification, or to which he wished to add something. A few times, he read a passage aloud and, when finished, concluded that there was nothing wrong in it although he would not have personally chosen my formulation. Only once did he tell me that my leftist stance was unjustified and compared my style to that of a renowned historian of the Congo for whom he had no esteem. As I was departing I asked him how he could accept a paper like mine, for it was obvious that he did not like my general philosophy and often found my presentation harsh or inadequate. He answered that he appreciated my efforts to document the subject and that he realised how difficult it was to understand what colonialism was about thirty years after it had come to an end. We went through the same kind of exercise after he read my thesis. Although not enthused by my approach, 'Parmentier' respected my work.

Perhaps to a lesser extent, the same applies to 'Peletier', whose warm house, musical sensitivity and ease of expression had charmed me right from the first interview. In the perspective of a thesis based on seven people, I had picked him as a good representative of the group of the Colonial University graduates and abstracted from our conversations ten pages which rendered 'his' life-story as a territorial. As we met to go over my reconstruction, I was afraid of giving him the impression that my work would present the territorial experience in a way which closely adopted the interviewees' points of view. I thus made it clear that I did not intend my thesis to be just that. He exclaimed: 'You are thoroughly free to think what you wish. Nero believed he was a great benefactor to Rome even after he had set the city on fire. The same is true of Al Capone in the U.S. I have my ideas; you have yours.' In these terms, almost too strong to be taken at face-value, 'Peletier' implied that he did not expect me to embrace or reproduce his 'truth'. The letter he sent me after starting to read my thesis (he was too appalled to complete the reading) suggested otherwise. He was expressing, in no uncertain terms, his surprise and disappointment at what he saw as my partiality (cf chapter 8). Nonetheless, following my reply, he wrote again to say that he was happy to meet me and discuss the text further. He may have found it difficult to accept my point of view, but he did not choose to stop the dialogue.

Such an attitude, however ambivalent, modulates the expectations, illustrated through 'Michel''s remark and 'Adam''s letter, that I first believed territorials held towards my work. I had feared that former colonials would expect the history of the Belgian Congo I would write to possess a grand character. Many did not. 'Milneart', for example, specifically told me that he was offended by such an idea. For him, what is required is a study which documents the reality in all its aspects – good and bad; this in turn necessitates from the researcher an attitude that is open and, in this sense, sympathetic to former colonials, rather than one which is contemptous and therefore closed towards their mixed experience. We shall see in chapter 7 that he thinks I failed to adopt such an approach. For the moment, however, what I wish to stress is that 'Milnaert' was not interested in a rosy account which would turn former territorials into angels.

With, say 'Adam' at one end of the spectrum and 'Dehon' at the other, former territorials are not in agreement on what a 'true history' of the Belgian Congo would consist of – hence their frequent irritation at what a former colleague has published or said on T.V. I doubt, however, that many realise that they fail to share a group view on what needs to be said about the Congo (or possibly even happened there). Most probably presume that their view corresponds to that of the others. Because they do not doubt that their truth *is* the only one, they also believe, I think, that I can only come to share their views as long as I am objective, because I would then see that they are right. Not until they read my written work do they have to confront the fact that my background is so different from theirs that I might never come to share their perspective at all. Judging from the experiences I reported, they accept that there is little they can do about this. This is particularly clear in the case of 'Peters'. As we were discussing the use I would make of the statements he had made during our first meeting, he told me: 'I do not doubt that you will make good use of this material in your own understanding of the term. But what you believe to be a "good use" may well fail to correspond with what I would understand that to be.' 'Peters' had obviously realised that the final product was in my own hands; ultimately all the interviewees have to accept this basic fact. I think they do this in good grace, which is not to deny that most may wish I had written a different book.

This chapter, concerned with the how and why of the interviewees' involvement in the research project, assessed the bias former territorials might unavoidably have brought along with them, but also the contribution they were able to make. The first section of the chapter focused on the atmosphere of misunderstanding which former colonials feel surrounds them. They say the world turned its back on them in 1960, never to change its mind. To them, the anti-colonialist stance adopted by most media and academic scholarship today is characteristic of the one-sided view in which the outside world holds them. This dominant stance arguably leaves them muted – without a voice. Their longing for public and historical recognition may explain why they were eager to talk to me, as explained in the second section of the chapter. Whether or not they took me for a young and innocent female student, through me, they could hope for their voice to reach the outside world. This was all the more so since I appeared willing to listen to what they had to say for long hours. Their vested interests in my project could lead one to dismiss their testimony as of little value. The third section of the chapter argued otherwise. I noted that the view of history as the objective preservation of the past, which is prevalent in our society, compelled the interviewees to talk about both the positive and the negative aspects of their territorial experience. I went on to remark that each interviewee did this in his own personal style. To illustrate the variety I encountered, I contrasted three types of accounts. One was an attempt to delineate the reality of the Congo through a positivistic account to be taken literally; another resorted to imaginery dialogues which aimed at setting the recalled scene and atmosphere; yet another sought to provide sociological insights through an all-encompassing reflexion. While the interviewees do not have one single opinion about the Congo (which they experienced in different ways), they do not share exactly the same expectations about my work either. This was discussed in the last section of the chapter. For example, my best informant was not interested in my producing the rosy account that my uncle's friend may have dreamt of when he was talking of the Belgian colonial *épopée*. I observed that, this variety of expectations notwithstanding, most interviewees would probably have preferred me to write another book. In spite of this, none have said they wanted to bring our dialogue to a close. This is crucial for, as I have said in the introduction, I consider an on-going dialogue to be at the heart of the anthropological project. This is not to say that the dialogues in which we were engaged were straightforward, as the whole book, but especially the next chapter, demonstrates. Such dialogues, however, are worth pursuing if we are to try to make anthropological sense of our lives.

NOTES

1. I have transcribed the questionnaire and the answers, with some comments, in a manuscript entitled 'Vues actuelles d'anciens territoriaux sur leurs fonctions passées au Congo', a copy of which is held by the History Section of the Musée Royal d'Afrique Centrale, Tervueren (Dembour 1991b). The translated questionnaire is reproduced in Appendix 2 of this book.
2. For an analysis of the sociological significance of these obligatory 'recuperative' visits to temperate climates, taken supposedly for health reasons, see Kennedy (1987, chapter 6, especially: 116).

3. The '*pari congolais*' has come to designate the sudden decision to grant independence to the Congolese, with the hope (*pari* – bet) that it could work despite lack of preparation.
4. On this series of paintings, see Szombati-Fabian and Fabian (1976); Fabian (1996). For a critique of their use in the academic literature, see Dembour (1992b).
5. See, for example, the Moriamé archives at the Musée Royal d'Afrique Centrale, Tervueren.
6. *Dettes de Guerre* edited by the lawyer Antoine Rubbens (1945) comes to mind as an example.
7. Relationships between the two countries returned to 'normal' in the summer of 1989 when a cooperation agreement was signed (de Villers 1990). This, however, proved a short-lived lull as another important diplomatic crisis developed between the two countries in May 1990, soon after General Mobutu announced the end of the one-party rule. According to the Belgian media, more than sixty students were killed in Lubumbashi by the army on the night of 2 May 1990; the Zairian government acknowledged one death. The Belgian media coverage of the massacre (on which see Jewsiewicki 1991) led to the expulsion of the Belgian technical assistants from Zaire in July 1990. It took the dismissal of General Mobutu for the possibility of restoring Belgian cooperation in the country to be seriously raised. Talks to that effect started in the summer of 1997 with Laurent Kabila's government.
8. It should be noted that Braeckman was no more highly regarded by the Zairian government which refused her a visa to enter Zaire and sued her in court after her reports on the events of Lubumbashi in the spring of 1990.
9. I only received two outright refusals for collaboration in the course of my research. One was from someone who had been a judge in the Congo for twenty months in the years 1926 to 1928. He reported that his experience had been horrific due to the unbelievable state in which the local judiciary was. All my attempts to convince him to give me an interview failed. The other refusal was from a territorial who had acted as judge to the tribunal of district. In this function, he had been led, under pressure, to condemn to death an African charged with the murder of a European. One of his former colleagues informed me that this memory was too disturbing for him to agree to talk with me on the topic of colonial law and justice. By its very nature, his experience must have been exceptional. Not all territorials were judges to the tribunal of district and, even if they were, death sentencing became less and less common over the years (Dembour 1991a: 81).
10. For evidence of tensions, see for example the Moriamé archives; see also the novels by Cornélus (1954) and Daye (1928).
11. This emphasis on 'recording for posterity' does not seem to be peculiar to the former colonials. The correspondants to the Mass Observation project have been noted to perceive themselves as ordinary people who write for posterity (Barton *et al.* 1993). See also Myerhoff (1982: 116–7).
12. On the structuring role of genre in oral accounts, see Tonkin (1992: chapter 3).
13. Such were the means of recruitment into the army that Africans compared enrolment, of which they arguably eventually benefited, to the slavery trade of the earlier years (Vansina 1972: 282–3; Smith 1976: 4 and 20; Samarin 1989: 46–9 and 57).
14. 'Milnaert', reading a draft of this chapter, agreed with the latter expression in the following terms: '*Embêtant* (a drag), this is the exact term. I had to do the same thing. But I knew that the guy would come back after six months with his uniform, would

be boasting and would express his satisfaction at having found this life. He would be well taken care of, well fed, etc. In brief, it did not give me any moral problem. But it *was* a drag.' See also André Ryckmans, quoted in Kestergat (1985: 76–7).
15. Because the personal files of members of the administration are not open to the public, I was unable to check 'de Glaise''s account.
16. On the Portuguese population in the Congo, see Vellut (1991).
17. This was not a usual practice on my part. I had done it because I had been thinking of presenting seven life-stories in my thesis and was seeking the assent and comments from the persons I had decided to include.
18. His fear partly rested on the fact that Britain is the country of the 'Liverpudlian merchants', largely held in Belgium responsible for having started an unwarranted campaign against Leopold II. While this campaign was thoroughly justified, the unnuanced way in which the Belgian Congo is viewed in Britain is not.
19. The most striking example of deceit I am aware of is the one that the social scientist Garfinkel suffered. He had interviewed for thirty-five hours spread over a period of months a person who had been born as a boy and had had an operation to become female when she was nineteen-year-old. Throughout the interviews, she had denied having taken estrogens to facilitate her sex-change. Years later, Garfinkel realised that she had (reported in Denzin 1989: 38). For the reasons given in the main text, I do not think this disturbing experience is absolutely relevant to my study.
20. Cf. *Ordonnance-loi* of 10 March 1917: '*La culture, la vente, le transport et la détention du chanvre à fumer sont interdits. La même interdiction s'applique à l'usage de ce chanvre, soit en le fumant, soit en le consommant de toute autre manière.*' According to many interviewees, hemp was a real problem, which concerned pockets of '*réfractaires*' who did not pay the tax and lived wild in the forest (see also Turnbull 1984: 156). In the 1950s, however, there were never more than 2,323 sentences reported in relation to hemp in the *Rapports annuels de la colonie*. This is well under the number of sentences reported under other items including all the other ones in the section '*Législation à caractère spécial*' – relating to labour, agriculture, hemp, hygiene and residence.
21. This implies that 'Dehon' was not a commissioned magistrate of police at the time.
22. Clair wrote a book after she travelled in the Congo between 1945 and 1948.
23. The statute which allowed Africans to become territorial officers was promulgated in January 1959. 'Milnaert' must be talking of a practice which tended to give more responsibilities to the African clerks.
24. Cf Markowitz (1973: 116–9).
25. 'Milneart' is referring to the T.V. programme of 5 April 1987 mentioned above.
26. The words in parentheses indicate that the commander had been educated in a prestigious institution as St-Cyr is the French military academy.

5: Our Dialogues

*T*he last two chapters have highlighted the existence of a hiatus between the research project I had planned and the study the interviewees were hoping I would produce. The present chapter follows from this approach in that it seeks to examine the ways in which this gap created spaces for misunderstandings during or after the interviews. While the previous chapters were concerned with the general background of the interviews – their historical setting as it were – this one is concerned with the way the interviews developed *per se*. I examine a number of methodological aspects, including the effect of the guarantee of anonymity, the question of who speaks about what when, and the way memory works. These factors illustrate that the dialogues are not about giving and receiving straightforward information in a neutral and objective way, but are dynamically produced according to processes which impose limitations on what can be said and understood.

Significant modalities

A vast amount of anthropological literature tends to suggest that a body of material is a body of material is a body of material. Of course, most anthropologists know that things are more complicated than this, but they rarely discuss in their writings the way their material was produced. In this section, I pay attention to the guarantee of anonymity, the time and place of the interviews and the recording of our conversations,[1] for they all had an impact I had not suspected. In other words, they do not constitute mundane modalities which just fix the external conditions of the interview and can then be forgotten. Their influence both on the development of the interview and on the research process more generally is thus worth assessing.

The guarantee of anonymity

Following my pressing questions on the coercive means used by new recruits who were not yet magistrates of police, 'Wilkin' implicitly admitted to the practice of illegal flogging. He added with a smile: 'But this should remain between you and me' (*Mais ça, il ne faut pas le dire*). I understood him to intend this remark more as a joking comment on the divide between those in the know and the naive 'others' than as a literal injunction for me not to mention the irregularity in my work; after all, our preceding dialogue made it clear that he was not the source of a new piece of information. Did the anonymity I guaranteed my interviewees as a matter of course nonetheless encourage him to talk about this sensitive issue? Although this is exactly the kind of remark I was hoping the guarantee of anonymity would foster, I doubt it. Let me explain how I had anticipated the guarantee would work before discussing how I think it worked in practice.

An anonymous territorial pointed out in an article published in 1951 that there was a '"wriggle your way out of the red" style of economy which required [territorials] to resort to barely regular tricks' (*'une économie de "tire-ton-plan" qui exige[ait] des astuces très peu régulières'*) (*Problèmes d'Afrique Centrale* 1951: 154). I was interested in this statement which could suggest that a multitude of practices were going on which were either on the verge of illegality or truly illegal. One example of such a practice which I heard from an interviewee involved putting Africans in jail for a longer time than the actual sentence indicated on the judgment of police. 'Verbrugge' explained to me that he began to do this after the judge of the standing tribunal requested him to stop giving the maximum penalty, i.e. seven days, for all the infractions related to crop cultivation. 'Verbrugge' agreed with the judge on the principle that a sentencing scale should ideally have existed according to which the penalty should reflect the seriousness of the infraction. In other words, he recognised that someone who had begun to do some work in the fields deserved a shorter sentence than someone who had done absolutely nothing; but he was also convinced that a jail sentence of less than seven days was useless. As a result, he felt that he had no choice but to sentence light offenders in the same way as heavy ones until and unless the maximum penalty for offences related to obligatory cultivation was legally raised above seven days. While doing this, he had to satisfy the judge that he had reduced some of his sentences. These double and contradictory goals he achieved through the trick of sending the defaulter to jail and waiting three or four days before writing the judgment. The result was that the sentence actually served by the Africans, i.e. seven days, did not correspond to the sentence which appeared on the paper, i.e. four or three days. The discrepancy escaped the notice of both the Africans and the judge: the former because they were used to seven-day sentences and did not realise they had a matter for complaint to the Judiciary; the latter because his control over the activity of the magistrate of police was almost exclusively based on the reading of the judgments of police the territorial (obligatorily) sent him.

To what extent did the guarantee of anonymity help 'Verbrugge' to recount this spurious practice? It is difficult to give a definitive answer to this question. 'Verbrugge' told me that he would never have dreamt of discussing such '*ficelles du métier*' (tricks of the trade) with his father who was a judge in the Congo. At a cocktail-party in Belgium twenty years later, however, he met the judge who had told him to reduce some sentences and explained to him the trick he had been resorting to when he was a territorial. (The judge was apparently infuriated by the story, which suggests that he had been genuinely unaware of the practice). With the years, 'Verbrugge' had clearly become more open about a practice which was of no consequence to him and his career anymore. Telling a story in a specific and restricted social setting, however, does not amount to agreeing to the story being published under one's name.

Although I cannot rule out that the guarantee may have helped 'Verbrugge' to tell me the story, I think it rarely played such a role. My hope had been that anonymity would encourage the interviewees to speak about the illegal and violent practices central to my original image of the Congo. However, this image did not correspond to the reality, which is that the territorial routine most often followed the legal and administrative rules and that illegalities were on the whole related to one of two fields: accountancy or flogging. The consistent testimony of the interviewees, who did not consult each other before talking to me, is very clear in this respect. On one hand I was told that '*caisses noires*' (fiddled accounts) were universal, implying that administrators wrote false entries in the accounting books – for example salaries of road-builders which had in fact not been paid. On the other hand many interviewees admitted having ordered strokes of the whip outside the strict legal framework which provided that territorials could do this only in respect of African prisoners and only for breaches of penitentiary discipline (Dembour 1992b); they quite often mentioned having ordered flogging outside this context, either when they were not yet commissioned magistrates of police and were thus prevented from sending anybody to jail in the first place, or when the urgency of the situation demanded it. For example, 'Dehon' once justified the recourse to illegal whipping by the imminence of famine, which allegedly required the mobilisation of as many people as possible to work in the fields as quickly as possible. In all these cases, territorials did not think their behaviour was morally reprehensible. Territorials did not 'cook the books' for their own embezzlement: the extra money served to execute work which had not formally been planned – for instance an additional room to a building. As for flogging, it was the situation which required the territorials to inflict it in a way which was formally illegal, but they saw nothing wrong in the practice itself. Of course they were aware that some people, and especially the judges, did not share their views on the matter. This, however, did not make them all reluctant to tackle the subject of illegal actions with me – and with the larger audience behind me.

Nowadays, some former territorials are very open about their personal involvement in illegal practices of the kind described above. For example, Augustin recounts in his memoirs a visit to a leper colony which had remained out of European control for many years (n.d.: 28–9). He first describes the lack of respect with which he was received. Then he explains that the policeman who was with him, in order to demonstrate where the authority lay, ordered a leper to lie down and administered some strokes of the whip. The phrasing does not give any hint that he had no right to do so, but the illegality would be clear to anybody familiar with colonial law. The attitude of 'Praet' illustrates even more strikingly how some interviewees were ready publicly to recognise their involvement in such practices. 'Praet' had mentioned during our interview that he sometimes ordered whipping outside the legal framework. When I wrote to him to ask whether I could cite him on this in a text to be published, he replied he had no objection. By contrast 'Jamiolle' certainly would never have accepted such 'publicity'. When I mentioned the practice of illegal flogging in a letter to him, he assumed I had heard about it from Van Leeuw – to whom he must have confessed it. He was very cross with her and told me: 'She betrayed me.' He did not seem to believe me when I said not she, but other interviewees, had talked to me about this practice (which suggests that, in contrast to 'cooking the books', illegal flogging was not universal).

The guarantee of anonymity must have been a deciding factor for some interviewees in accepting to participate in my research project. I cannot imagine that 'Jamiolle' would ever have considered meeting me without it. This is not so much because it made him free to talk about the ubiquitous violent and illegal events which inhabited my imagination, as because he wanted to maintain the privacy of the interview. Over and over again, he mentioned that he did not want the interview to be seized upon by family relatives, friends or acquaintances and to force him in a useless debate about the Congo. Anonymity, however, may have been less of a guarantee than an imposition on other interviewees (cf Szombati-Fabian and Fabian 1976: 19, note 13).[2] A friend of mine pointed this out as she saw me preparing the manuscript in which I was reproducing the answers I had received to the questionnaire. On her suggestion I gave the respondents the choice between being named and remaining anonymous. Only seven out of twenty opted for anonymity. The reasons for their choice in one direction or the other are not easily tracked down. Those who decided to be named may have wanted to claim the authorship of their text and to be recognised as the subject of the experience they reported. But this cannot be assumed always to be the case. When I phoned 'd'Ave et d'Ove' who had omitted to indicate his preference, he told me it was probably easier and better for me if everybody agreed to be named.[3] After I told him that it did not matter and that the choice was really his, he opted for anonymity.

Contrary to my original assumptions, 'd'Ave et d'Ove' cannot have decided upon anonymity because he was the source of 'horrendous revelations'. Nor could it be because he retrospectively rejected colonialism and did not want to publicise his previous involvement with it. Although he stated that he 'now questioned the very principle of colonialism', he also remarked that the territorials 'had no reason to entertain any guilt feelings' with regard to their previous functions – a remark which I read as an implicit answer to the negative image of colonialism now circulating in Belgian society rather than as the expression of any moral discomfort which 'd'Ave et d'Ove' would have tried to repress. 'Milnaert' was the respondent most careful in maintaining his anonymity. He removed from his answers to the questionnaire all specifications of location and date which could have identified him in the text I had prepared for publication. Why anonymity was so important to him is difficult to say. Perhaps as a scholar does not wish a draft paper to be widely circulated, he did not think his answers represented the definite conclusion of what he had to say about his colonial experience; perhaps he did not have enough confidence in the value of his reflections; or perhaps it was just a question of modesty. He himself offered the following explanation after having read the draft of this chapter: 'I hate to be put in the forefront and I hate the notion of individuals.' By contrast, 'Parmentier' reminded me after having read my thesis how he had specifically told me that he would have preferred for me to lift his anonymity. The fact that I did not feel able to respect this clearly-expressed wish makes it clear how much the so-called guarantee of anonymity works at least as much to my advantage as to that of my interviewees.

Lifting the anonymity of those of my interviewees who would have opted for such a solution would have required going back to each informant and asking him individually what he wanted me to do with his name. This would have raised great difficulties. Informed consent (especially to be named) could only be given after the individual concerned had read the text of the book and had a clear idea of what image I presented of him. This would have implied a very cumbersome procedure of deciding when the draft was sufficiently final to start the process, in some cases tracing individuals with whom I had lost contact, and in all cases waiting for the answers and revising the text accordingly before publication could go ahead. This would have caused considerable inconvenience, although not of an insuperable kind. More importantly, a decision on the part of a particular interviewee to be named could have impeded me in subsequent work if I decided to analyse his words in a different and perhaps less favourable light. In fact, I experienced this very difficulty when I was quoting in this book respondents who were named in the questionnaire: at least one of them cannot like what I say about him in the book. In order to avoid coming across this difficulty again in the future, I have decided to 'preserve' the anonymity of the whole group, without giving any individual any say in the matter.

This solution carries some inelegances, for I do not designate in this book the respondents to my questionnaire as I did in the manuscript which reproduced their answers; also some people appear in this work both under their real name and under a pseudonym, for example Lenain who wrote the open lettre to Colette Braeckman and Augustin, the author of the unpublished memoirs I have quoted a few times. The advantages of a solution which treats all interviewees consistently in the same text and in a way which gives me greater freedom of analysis in the future seems to me to outweigh these disadvantages. Of course, this means that, in the last analysis and with a few exceptions, anonymity is to my benefit rather than that of the interviewees; it represents less a guarantee for their own gain than a solution of convenience for me. Rather than giving the interviewees freedom to talk, the primary object of anonymity may well be to give the researcher freedom to write.

The time and place of the interviews

The interviewees generally received me in their homes. It never occurred to me not to volunteer to do the travelling necessary to meet them.[4] Quite apart from the fact that I would have been embarrassed to meet them in my student room, I felt that deference for people much older than me commanded that arrangement. I was certainly not going to object to it as I was hoping that it would open up the possibility for me to gain some insights into their family life, personal interests, and social position. The interviewees who were still professionally active, however, normally suggested that we met at their place of work, unless I was socially acquainted with them in which case they invited me to their house. Invariably occupying higher ranks (either in the private or in the public sector), they received me in their office. Frequent interruptions, in the form of phone calls or third persons coming in, made it impossible to have a smooth conversation and reminded me of time pressure. In the office I was forced to endorse the role of the competent expert who came with a specific agenda and knew exactly what she wanted to cover, for although the interviewee was ready to answer my questions, he had no time to waste. By contrast, the atmosphere at home was more relaxed, and this generated the opportunity for longer and more encompassing conversations.

Professionally active interviewees were not willing to devote their free time to my research (except if I was a family relative or a friend). 'Praet's attitude perfectly encapsulates the sharp distinction they made between office and leisure hours, with the time of the interview belonging to the former. An ambassador temporarily posted in Belgium, 'Praet' received me twice in his office to answer my questions on the colonial administration of law and justice. At the end of the second interview, he mentioned that he had a few family photograph albums on the Congo and he invited me to come to his house after I had expressed an interest in seeing them. I was hoping that this visit would represent the opportunity to hold a more relaxed interview. When I arrived, we indeed sat and exchanged a few comments on my research. But after less than ten minutes he conducted me to the study where the albums were kept and told me I could look at them as long as I wished and could take out any picture for reproduction; he himself went to watch Wimbledon on T.V. When I reappeared he was not interested in checking or commenting on what I had taken. I had come for my job, and he was facilitating it as much as he could. But he was not ready to set aside a few hours of his week-end for a conversation about his colonial past. This does not mean that 'Praet' and the other professionally active interviewees were fundamentally less interested in my work. They too referred to their colonial experience as the most beautiful period of their life and shared the disgust of their colleagues towards the media's misrepresentation of colonialism. Had the interviews taken place ten years later when they were retired, my guess is that they too would readily have opened the doors of their houses to me.[5]

While interviews in the office never extended beyond two hours, those taking place in the house of the interviewee were of various lengths. In the morning, they tended to be short, with the midday meal signalling their interruption (generally after about two hours).[6] Those in the afternoon were generally longer (between three and five hours). Five interviewees specifically invited me to arrive in the morning so that I could have dinner with them (in the middle of the day in Belgium). They all lived far away from Brussels (on a Belgian scale) which seems to indicate that politeness for the travelling interviewee motivated, in part at least, their invitation. 'Duruisseau', a former judge, had nevertheless specifically told me that my topic necessitated long hours of discussion. By contrast, two interviewees who were living in Brussels had another appointment in the afternoon they received me; they obviously thought that one hour was sufficient time to go over my topic.

In the house, we sat either in arm-chairs or at a table. The seating arrangement, which I obviously left to my host, somewhat reflected how the interviewee viewed the interview: as a general introduction to their colonial lives or as a piece of work with a definite focus. Sitting at a table (or at a desk) had the tangible effect of discouraging silences and of preventing the spouse from intervening. Without necessarily signalling a contrasted practice, sitting in arm-chairs nevertheless permitted a different attitude, for it did not constrain the conversation around a specifically defined project: silences were more easily borne, long anecdotes and general comments were often included, the spouse was freer to intervene (which she often did at one stage or another). I vividly experienced the contrast between the two types of interviews at the 'Michels'. Our four meetings always followed the same pattern. I arrived in the (late) morning and 'Michel' took me to his study; the door of the room was shut as we were 'working', the women of the house ('Michel''s wife and daughter) clearly excluded from the 'serious' interview. During that time I was 'playing' the interviewer. ('Michel''s by-then poor memory and difficulty of elocution did not make this exercise the most interesting part of our meetings, except for the fact that he every so often fetched valuable documents from the closet behind him). After an hour or a little bit more, the women appeared and invited us to move to the living-room for the aperitif before dinner. This marked a complete shift in the conversation. 'Work' was forgotten and the women took over the conversation. The latter, although not exclusively about the Congo, regularly came back to it. 'Mrs Michel', an excellent storyteller with a vivid memory, probably never guessed that I considered her to be one of my best informants.

Not surprisingly, interviews conducted in comfortable arm-chairs tended to be longer than those during which one worked at a table.[7] All but one of the interviewees who invited me to come for the interview in the morning chose to sit at a table. Maybe rather than the result of a pure coincidence, a correlation exists between morning interview (which can hardly last more than two hours), a focused research and a 'desk-work'. Although not so consistently, the tendency in the afternoon was nevertheless to sit in arm-chairs, which gave the opportunity of longer, and more 'chatty', conversations. In turn, these arrangements may be seen as the reflection of an implicit, more or less open-ended, conception of the research by the interviewees.

The record of the interview

All my interviewees must have been expecting me to record their statements. For a long time, I took notes of what they were saying, for I imagined the tape-recorder to be too intrusive and too focused a tool to qualify as a 'truly' anthropological method. The wife of an elderly man who had been an important figure in the Congolese judiciary, however, summoned me to arrive at her house with a tape-recorder. I bought the most innocuous little device for that occasion. Ironically, there was little to record from the ninety-nine-year-old former judge, although his great age may explain his wife's determination that his words should be saved for posterity. Having bought a machine, I nonetheless decided to experiment with it, which led me to discover its advantages and disadvantages.

The interviewees did not generally object when I asked whether I could tape them. However, some did. 'Milneart' finally gave in to it after

I mistakenly referred in a letter to a broken arm he had never had, but which I suggested had not prevented him from continuing to fulfil his territorial functions despite the pain and inconvenience it gave him.[8] As for 'Parmentier', he never agreed to be tape-recorded as he was convinced that awareness of the machine would disturb his ability to think and talk. A study has indeed suggested that members of the higher social classes tend to give more accurate answers in the absence of a tape-recorder (reported in Ghiglione and Matalon 1978: 43). Although this study is admittedly dated, it cannot be denied that the tape-recorder has a presence of its own. I was certainly always aware that it was on, and the interviewees never failed to tell me to switch it off when we were interrupted, for example by a phone-call.

The oral historian Paul Thompson argues that the use of a tape-recorder can foster the collection of confidential facts after the machine has been switched off (1988: 204). This, however, equally applies to note-taking. I have already said how 'Milneart' talked to me about the whip when he drove me back to the train-station. Not so much a confidential piece of information as a remark on my research, it could only have been given after we had dropped our roles as interviewer and interviewee. Indeed the conversations I had with the interviewees when the supposedly formal part of the interview was over generally moved to areas that were not directly related to the administration of colonial law and justice – but to family life, the African concubines the Europeans kept, social life, the return to Belgium after independence, the situation in Zaire at the time of the interviews, the last banquet with former fellow-students of the Colonial University, and so on.

Tape-recording had one big advantage over note-taking. When I took notes, the pace of my writing dictated the pace of the conversation: my interlocutor tended to wait for me to have finished writing before proceeding with his story or comments, and I was too busy scribbling his words to be able to engage with him and even look at him.[9] In this sense, the tape-recorder undoubtedly freed the conversation. It also presented an enormous disadvantage, however, and this is the time it takes to transcribe a taped conversation: on average it took me ten hours to transcribe one hour of tape, a rate which does not appear to be exceptional.[10] I soon decided it was not worth recording interviewees I met for the first time: they generally told me things I already knew and I could always direct them towards stories I especially wanted to have on exact record in subsequent interviews (cf Ellen 1984: 236).

The terms of the dialogue

The very first interviews, with my uncle and the fathers of two friends, gave me an idea of the topics which I could tackle with former colonial officers. The themes I identified from these early conversations as worth pursuing with other former territorials had mainly to do with the territorial functions, the administration of justice, the respect for law, the relations between various colonial groups and the meaning of the civilising mission. My aim was to go through these themes with a new interviewee as naturally as possible. In other words, it was more important for me to follow the trend of my interlocutor's speech than constantly to force issues into the conversation. As a result, a single interview rarely covered the whole of the field which I had defined in a series of keywords on the A4 piece of paper which I kept in front of me during the interviews. The aim of this section is to show that the question of which topics were raised by whom was always the subject of a negotiation, either subtle or not-so-subtle, between me and my interlocutor.

My conversations with 'Dehon' provide a good example of how I was hoping the interviews to develop. Because 'Dehon' was talkative, it was easy just to mention a topic and let him talk about it. I only needed to pick up here and there on a particular remark he had made in order to go through the themes I had identified on my A4 paper. We can turn to the extract reproduced above for an illustration of this process (above: 87–8). At one stage I ask for a further explanation of something he has raised (cf 'How did you force them to come?'). Later I encourage him to take a direction which interests me (cf 'Your superiors knew …'). In this extract, 'Dehon' does most of the talking, but I am regularly interrupting him, if briefly, to make sure that the topic of discussion is covered in the way that interests me, not just him. Thus, both of us participate in contructing the image of the Congo that is emerging from the interview.

Although most interviews were the product of the interaction between the interviewee and the interviewer rather than the latter or the former overwhelmingly controlling their development, there were exceptions. I already mentioned that some of my interlocutors were so old that they could hardly produce articulate speech, almost leaving me to talk alone. Interviews with apparently healthy men sometimes also failed to take off. With 'Robert', I was left to build the entire structure of the interview. When 'Robert' elaborated on the 'yes' or 'no' with which he had met my question, this never consisted in more than two sentences. Not surprisingly I got nothing from this interview but confirmation of facts I already knew. The interview with 'Fontor' developed on a similar line, although not so excessively. 'Fontor' was ready to answer my questions, and did so diligently, but he was not inclined to associate ideas freely around the topic and talk at any length. This may be due to the way he regarded his days in the Congo. He felt no nostalgia towards them and even expressed surprise that anyone would still concern herself with it – rather than the delight I usually encountered. For him, the past was gone. To return to an expression I used before, he was happy to endorse the role of the objective witness, but I had to let him know what information I wanted. The interview, which took place in his office, did not last much more than an hour.

At the exact opposite of this attitude stand the interviews with 'Delporte' and 'Jamiolle'. Both of them took the interview entirely in their own hands, or so it seemed to me. After providing a general colonial history beginning at the time of Leopold II, 'Delporte' skipped over his twenty territorial years from the mid-1920s to the end of the War, and lectured me for a few hours on the political and social situation which existed in the Congo in the 1950s, reading aloud large sections of articles of the 1950s periodical *Problèmes d'Afrique centrale* and of the *Middleheim* book, edited by former students of the Colonial University in 1987 (Fondation Royale … 1987). 'Jamiolle' had prepared one-and-a-half pages of notes on what he took to be the subject of my research in anticipation of our meeting. When I arrived, he told me to sit in his heavily-furnished study and to listen without taking notes for he said all that I needed to know was on the paper he was going to give me at the end of the interview.

These two interviews highlighted the points the interviewees found important for my research. 'Jamiolle', who entered the Territoriale with a law degree, is now a judge in a Belgian superior court. He was concerned that my study should recognise the colonial efforts towards the construction of a true legal system in Africa. To quote the conclusion of his paper: 'I therefore think that – if you leave out blunders – "objective" law was continuously applied. … Your study would be useless if it did not underline the attempts … to establish the preponderance of a basic legal system in Africa.' The interview was valuable in that it opened a window onto the perception which a former territorial held of the Congo. At the same time, I could not help finding it frustrating. 'Jamiolle' deemed his personal experience to be irrelevant to the principles and general issues upon which he thought the study should be based. 'Delporte' followed him in this. Both refused to answer the questions, which I inserted with difficulty in their speeches, on what their career had entailed for them in practice. To add insult to injury, 'Jamiolle' generally treated me in a patronising way, addressing me with the French '*tu*' and interrupting his 'lesson' by remarks such as: 'Is that understood? Let us go on then.' 'Delporte' too obviously regarded me as a student to be taught, although he did not refuse my interventions in the same peremptory way as did 'Jamiolle'; he just evaded the topics I raised by answering my questions in a few words. I controlled the underlying anger I felt at not being treated as a responsible researcher in order to avoid interrupting the flow of information. In both cases, we parted on seemingly excellent terms.

Some interviewees may possibly have found *me* irritating. Not surprisingly none raised formal complaints. But there were times when tensions seemed to be simmering near to the surface of overtly civilised conversations during which polite interchange was maintained. This I particularly felt with 'Dehon' who showed signs of exasperation at some of my interruptions. In these cases, he normally finished what he had in mind and turned afterwards to my concerns. Our conversations would then continue in what generally appeared to be a smooth manner. However, no two interviewees are alike. 'Milnaert' remarked at the end of one of our latest meetings, previous to which I had sent him a letter with a series of queries, that he much preferred this kind of focused dialogue to our first ones where he thought I did not ask enough questions. While I probably interrupted 'Dehon' too often for his own taste, I did not come into the conversation enough for 'Milnaert''s. Who is or should be in control of the dialogue is an issue constantly negotiated by the interviewer and the interviewee; it is never resolved once and for all.[11]

As the interviewee and the interviewer are negotiating as to who is getting to talk when, they are simultaneously searching for topics they both agree are worthwhile and safe to be discussed during the interview. There were topics that I felt confident to raise with some, but not all, interviewees (e.g. the absence of questions on the whip during my first interview with 'Milnaert'). Other topics which interested me, such as the place of the *ménagère* or African concubine (cf chapter 6) and family matters, did not find their way onto my aide-mémoire. Questions related to them could admittedly have surprised the interviewees to whom I had announced a research project focusing on the administration of law and justice; but more importantly, my own uneasiness in discussing sexual matters with senior men and in intruding into what I considered to be the private sphere of their life made it barely possible for me to raise these topics (which the interviewees or their wives nonetheless sometimes spontaneously raised, especially after the 'formal' interview was over). Another example of auto-censure concerns the term 'domination' which I did not dare pronounce even after I realised, from the written answers I received to the questionnaire, that it was *I* who felt uncomfortable with it – not the interviewees.

As for the interviewees, some topics never seemed to attract their interest. They never expanded, for example, on my questions about their experience in town; they clearly preferred to talk about the bush, even though most had lived in both settings (cf chapter 6). They must also have had their own reticences in discussing some matters. These reticences need not have corresponded to mine, and it is difficult for me to decipher which topics *they* found sensitive and avoided. At times, I nonetheless could feel an uneasiness on their part. An example of such hesitation occurred when 'Dehon' used circumlocutions and stammered over the story of a judge who had had an homosexual relationship with his servant. More dramatically, one interviewee seemed to be on the verge of breaking into tears as he recalled a conversation with a native which led him to question the benefits of colonialism. He commented that the implications of the episode had been terrible for him and, after a heavy silence, I switched topic.

This highly emotional moment did not, and could not conceivably have taken place during our first interview. With time interviewee and interviewer opened up to each other, probably most often without consciously realising it. This is not to suggest that we attained complete disclosure. On the contrary, the examples I have given indicate that both the interviewees and I tackled some topics that we regarded as extremely significant gingerly, if at all.

The value of memory

More than one former colonial had warned me that I should not expect too much of their testimony because after such a long time they had forgotten everything – or so they thought. They were the first to be surprised at how much they could remember. However, this does not mean that the wealth of their recollections can be taken at face-value as depicting what the Congo was like. Although memory is generally associated with the past, such a conception fails to acknowledge that memory is at least as much about the present as it is about the past. In this section, I shall show that memory arises from the very enmeshing of past and present. It is therefore vain to seek completely to disentangle one from the other. Memory is not static but a working process. It is neither mere fantasy nor reliable testimony. While it tells us something about the past, its primary function is to make it possible for us to live in the present.

Getting started

Once the interviewees had started to talk to me recollections came back to their consciousness in a stream they had not expected. One memory led to another. To get this process going, my strategy was always to start a first meeting by asking my interlocutor to give me the history of his career: his training, the ranks he achieved, the location of his various posts. Such an introduction could last anything between five minutes and two hours depending upon the propensity of the interviewee to add details to the backbone of the administrative details. Starting with career facts presented two major advantages: it provided me with a profile of the person in front of me and it established for him a frame from which other memories could emerge. A philosopher, whom I shall quote again below, has remarked: 'Any memory is recognised because it fits in with other memories, other knowledges …, i.e. it is part of a system of relations [and] it has a specific location' (Filloux 1952: 57). He continues: 'When a memory is voluntarily recollected, it is as if it was emerging from the surrounding frame' (ibid.). Interviewees could generally remember career facts without difficulty.[12] Having remembered and thought about their career, they were ready to fetch up in their memory more and more images of the Congo.

The transformative work of memory

Speaking of 'images' is appropriate in this context.[13] One should be wary, however, of mistaking memory for an exercise in the mere recall of images. Memory is a complex function which involves *working* on images. Claude Filloux, whom I have already quoted, makes this point in the 'Que sais-je?' he wrote on memory some fifty years ago. So does Ian Hunter in a Penguin book which appeared around the same time (1957, with a revised edition in 1964). I came across their books, written from a philosophical and a psychological perspective respectively, in second-hand bookshops. Although I find them extremely illuminating, I have never seen them being quoted,[14] which suggests they are not much read anymore. This is a pity, for they both beautifully demonstrate that memory organises the past in order to make life in the present possible.

The experiment of what I shall call 'the eating donkey', conducted in the 1920s by a certain Kluver and reported by Hunter (1957: 146–50), is a compelling illustration of the pervasive influence of the present on the way memory works. Kluver was interested in the phenomenon of eidetic imaging, i.e. the ability by some individuals, generally children under the age of twelve, to continue to see with almost photographic fidelity an image which has been removed from their sight after they have been staring at it for a short while. Allport, for example, had worked with English children who were able to read the German word *Gartenwirthschaft*, meaningless to them, in the background of an image at which they had been looking for thirty-five seconds. What is interesting is that the impressive recall of the details of the original image does not mean that eidetic images are literal reproductions of the model image. Kluver presented children with the image of a donkey standing some distance from a manger; on his suggestion that the donkey was hungry, the children began to see the animal racing over to the manger and eating. The point which Hunter makes when he reports this experiment is that memory never fixes images of the past somewhere in our mind, making them ready to be fetched intact. Memory involves using and transforming the past in a way that enables us to meet the requirements of the present (ibid.: 152).

Memory does not aim to conserve the past just as it was, but works by constantly transforming it. In this light, it could seem appropriate to say that memory distorts the past. However, one should be wary of the negative connotation of the word 'distortion', for the function of memory is not to conserve the past. This is why I leave the term in inverted commas when I use it below. Having said this, from the perspective of the objective reality of the past, distortions do occur. To demonstrate this, I shall discuss, and illustrate with my own material, four aspects of the transformative work operated by memory: the incorporation of new experience, the forgetting of unpleasant experiences, the pursuit of coherence and the drive towards synthesisation.

If we are very conscious of the fact that some elements of the past get eliminated through the process of forgetting, we are less aware that new experiences get incorporated. Childhood memories of events which took place when we were very small, perhaps not even born, provide an excellent example of this process. Such memories are necessarily based on what one has heard subsequently to the supposedly remembered event rather than on one's direct experience of it; yet we sometimes can see, or rather imagine, the scene so well that we have the feeling of directly remembering it (Hunter 1957: 125). This incorporation of new experience should not happen if memory was to achieve a faithful reproduction of the original event. But this is not the aim of memory, and original and subsequent experiences are probably amalgamated in most images we recall. I shall illustrate this through the answer of a respondent to the following question in my written questionnaire: 'If you thought that you were bringing progress, did you see any results? In which areas? What do you think of this today?' Vallaeys first spelled out the positive aspects which he saw in the colonial action. He then continued:

Negative results:
a) a secondary education which was insufficiently developed at the time of independence;
b) a university education which was still in its infancy and the almost complete absence of university graduates at the time of independence;
c) the paternalistic attitude adopted by Belgium in the Congo which failed to give the Blacks responsibilities and to train them in such a way that they could govern themselves. This was fatal and the excessively rapid granting of independence to the Congolese political authorities, who requested and demanded it, led to the unfortunate events which we lived in 1960 and the following years (Dembour 1991b: 82).

These words do not evoke the *personal* experience of Vallaeys in the Congo. Rather they express retrospective criticisms on Belgian colonial policy in the light of what happened after the Congolese independence, criticisms which have come to be widely accepted since then. Inviting my respondents to make the difference between what they believed then and what they thought today, which I did through the careful phrasing of my question, was asking too much of them. Experiences do not get pigeonholed in one's memory in a chronological order; rather they are amalgamated in what already exists, slightly changing the tone, adding a dimension, or completely 'distorting' the images of the past one keeps.[15]

The second aspect I wish to discuss is generally associated with Freud and with repression, which Hunter defines as the 'unconscious blocking of the recall of those experiences and actions which have either immediate or remote potentialities for causing pain' (1957: 110). Not having resorted to psychoanalytical tools, I shall not try to decipher repressive dynamics at work during the interviews. It is important to note, however, that the forgetting of unpleasant experiences does not occur only through repression. Hunter remarks: 'In our conversation and probably also in our private reveries, we tend to recall (and so rehearse) our pleasant experiences [...] The unpleasant is not actively inhibited but merely loses out in competition with the pleasant. And, of course, an experience which was originally disagreeable may, in being recounted to others, lose its unpleasant tone and even seem pleasant on recall [...] (ibid.: 130).

It is tempting to see such a forgetting process in 'Mignolet''s readiness to lend me a thin folder of personal archives after he had seen a call for documents I had inserted in a newsletter for former colonials. This folder contained the reports, called *bulletins de signalement annuels*, which his superiors had written about him each year. The report for 1950 described his attitude towards the natives as 'firm and sometimes too harsh'. Accompanying remarks included the following: 'Warned against the danger of being excessively repressive, he has failed to take much notice of this remark and continues to be intransigent towards both the Europeans and the natives.' Three years later, having accomplished his period of probation, 'Mignolet' became definitively accepted in the territorial ranks. The district commissary observed on that occasion: 'Will need to be supervised at the beginning, especially as far as moderation and political sense with the natives are concerned.' 'Firmness' is a word which comes back over and over again in these reports. Although 'Milnaert' tells me that a reputation of weakness attracted contempt and that his colleague may have received these criticisms as flattering, I find it difficult to believe that 'Mignolet' had not forgotten the existence of the negative appraisal of his person in the documents he lent me. Otherwise it is fair to suppose that he would either have taken some sheets out of the folder or at least provided comments, of the kind that 'd'Ave et d'Ove' spontaneously offered in respect to prestige, which attempted to make sure that I understood the words I would read in the 'right' way.

If I cannot be sure that 'Mignolet' had forgotten what the documents he had lent me contained, there can be no such doubt as far as 'Bertrand' is concerned. 'Bertrand' had also lent me his personal archives related to the Congo. As I was taking them back to him during a subsequent visit, I asked him for some explanations about an episode which had been the object of a lengthy correspondence between him and his superiors. After less than ten minutes, he closed the folder and said: 'Look, I do not like doing this. I did not remember that it was like that. I did not think we were so harsh in the way we communicated.' To me, the tone of the letters appeared administrative and innocuous, but it obviously did not correspond to the way 'Bertrand' had come to imagine the atmosphere in which he had worked. It is helpful to introduce Hunter's notion of 'rehearsing' here. Hunter uses it to refer to the fact that often we do not remember so much the original event as the image we have kept of it and 'rehearsed' in the interval. He illustrates this process through a personal experience. Introduced to a Scandinavian student at a party, he had invited the latter for tea along with other students. When the student turned up for tea the following month, Hunter failed to recognise him. At their first meeting, he had been struck by the fact that the student perfectly embodied the image of a Viking. As a result, what he had remembered was less the actual traits of the Scandinavian than his own stereotype of what a Viking looked like. The image he kept recalling drifted so far away from the student's real appearance that the latter had to introduce himself again when he arrived. Hunter comments on this kind of experience, which need not be restricted to people but can include buildings, objects and, I would add, images which are not visual: 'characteristics originally noticed as dominant [...] have become sharpened and accentuated in being recalled until the building, object, or person – as recalled – is but a caricature which is much larger, more gloomy, or more colourful than the original ever was. On being seen again, the original is now almost or completely unrecognisable' (1957: 76–7).

Interviewees must often have recalled 'images of images of images', which became increasingly 'distorted' in the thirty or more years which elapsed between their colonial experience and my asking them to recall it. This appears to be confirmed by the fact that each interviewee tended to have his favourite stories which he would tell me, almost in similar terms, over a period of time. 'Dehon' for instance came back over and over again to his walks with the chief Lukale Albert; 'Milneart' to the choice of the Malebranche book by Thourdelin; 'Parmentier' to the systematic search at 5 a.m. of his post in pursuit of infractions related to the fabrication of alcohol. Examples could be multiplied. Of course, these increasingly stereotyped and symbolic stories turn around an event which has taken place and may well appropriately convey the central point which the interviewer wishes to make. It nonetheless remains, to borrow the words of Elizabeth Tonkin, that: 'As reminiscences are repeated over the years they lose all the characteristics of immediate experience – they may almost become hearsay, since they happened "a world away" to a different person than the teller has become' (1982: 280). The question arises whether they describe the original reality at all.

Pondering the answer to this question requires taking into consideration the pursuit of coherence that characterises the memorising process. The most frequently cited experience in this respect is that of the story of 'the war of the ghosts' conducted by Frederic Bartlett some sixty years ago. It involved the telling of a story to a first person who had to repeat it to a second listener, himself telling it to a third listener, and so on. At the same time as the story increased in coherence, it got shortened (although less and less so) through the various versions. By the end of the chain of transmission the original phrasing had been replaced by commonplace *clichés* and the story bore little resemblance to the one which had originally been told. Bartlett found that similar transformations towards coherence and convention occurred when he asked one particular person to tell the story at different intervals over a period of time. In both cases, the story retained (or even acquired) the characteristics which could easily be assimilated by the persons who had heard it. Because the story of 'the war of the ghosts' originated from a North Indian culture and was presented to a British audience, it could be argued that it was particularly amenable to 'distortions' – for it could not be properly understood in the first place. All social realities are complex, however. And what is remembered depends upon what is orginally perceived and understood.

Moreover, to facilitate their storage, memories are always further interpreted and re-worked. They become more and more sketchy through time, as has just been illustrated by Bartlett's experience and by the fact that the interviewees quickly run out of examples to illustrate a concrete situation, as if the whole of their colonial experience had been synthetised in a few favourite stories.[16] Filloux's observations are pertinent here. He has remarked that images eventually disappear, leaving one only with the knowledge of what they represented. Speaking of the memories that 'one loves and respects the most' (faces of dear people, loved places of the old days …), he writes:

> Eventually these old recollections have no more than a schematic appearance. They have gradually shrivelled, stiffened and no longer offer our memory images but only *schemata*. Only the main outlines remain; the rest has gone. We do eventually come to the abstract *knowledge* of the recollection containing such and such elements, but some kind of apathy or helplessness prevents us from recapturing it with all its colours and images (1952: 26, emphasis in the original).

This is exactly the process 'Milnaert' recognised to be at work as we were discussing problems of memory. I had asked him in a letter to tell me what a typical day involved and, as we met, he gave me various models. One of these involved a council of chiefdom. He commented afterwards: 'I cannot recollect anything concrete. I know I spoke a lot at this council, but I am unable to say about what. I searched for it yesterday [as I knew you were coming], but to no avail. All the concrete aspects of my tour have gone, but perhaps structural aspects have not.' The other interviewees must similarly often have 'known' that such and such a thing had happened rather than 'remembered' the scene they were recounting to me. To say, for example, that the day began at six o'clock with the ceremony of the raising of the flag, they did not need to have vivid images of that occurrence in their mind (not even one). They just had to remember, in an abstract way, that the day began like that.

Filloux has noted: 'The mind relies on the frame, assesses what seems probable, and exercises logic to link events together and attempt to reconstitute what really happened' (1952: 47). For an illustration of this process, we can again turn to 'Milnaert', this time as he was attempting to describe the settler he liked most in his post (the dashes indicate the alternation between his and my taped interventions):

– With Cristou, I speak of the whole region, little of his exploitation. It is funny, but I do not think we speak much of his exploitation, but we speak of the region. He knows everything, absolutely everything. He has an ear as big as this and he knows everything. He also has a great influence.
– And how many people does he employ?
– I do not remember. I think very few. I shall say twenty for his lime-ovens. I do not know.
– And what, he sells …
– He sells limes, there is a big demand for limes and this is one of the few places where you can find some.
– And he sells it far?
– In the territory, in the missions
– In the territory itself, or further away?
– In the territory, at least in the district, but not further I think.

Although 'Milnaert' was able to answer my circumstantial questions, it is clear that he had to rely on his intellect to do so. His words also make it clear that he has kept general impressions, for example of Cristou's character at the beginning. This again is not surprising, for it is how memory works most of the time. In everyday life, as Filloux observes, general schemes are more useful than a concrete vision of experience. He gives the example of University degrees: 'It can be useful for me to let my interlocutor know which University degrees I have. To do this, I need only to call upon what I "know"; and abstract memory is both necessary (for I need to be brief) and sufficient' (1952: 26). In a very different way than the experience of the eating donkey, this brings us back to Hunter's contention that the primary function of memory is not the mere conservation of the past, but the use of the past to meet the requirements of the present.

Memory and history

So far I have suggested that we cannot rely on memory to discover the past. This is in line with Hunter's contention that '[m]emory seems to have been evolved to deal only incidentally with those rare situations where we are required to give a flawlessly accurate account of the past' (1957: 152). When we act as witnesses or receive the testimonies of other people, however, we are generally convinced that memories represent a reliable account of the past. The problem is that external evidence to the contrary is most often needed before our faith in our memories gets eroded. Thus, in the absence of contradictory oral testimonies or written documents, we tend not to question our sincere belief that our memories accurately represent the past.[17] Hunter warns against the dangers of this all too human attitude in the legal system (1957: 101). The warning can also be addressed to historical projects. Claire Tancré-Van Leeuw's confidence in the accounts she solicited from former territorials, for example, appears disarmingly naive. She writes:

> The value [of the] testimonies cannot be doubted. The competence of the witnesses is certain. They experienced the events which they report; theirs is a direct testimony. One could nevertheless fear that they let some mistakes unconsciously or unwillingly slip through. For example, the testimony of those who are very old could appear dubious. I can refute without any hesitation such a suggestion, for I met almost all of them personally. The possibility of mistakes due to the long time which has elapsed since the reported facts took place seems to me to be minimal too. A lot of former colonials wrote or told me that they consulted their personal archives before recording their recollections. Out of interest in the research project, they went through their study, cellar or attic, in search of photographs and other documents which could help them reliably to reconstruct their past (1992: 402).

Had Tancré-Van Leeuw read either Hunter or Filloux, her unabated assurance would presumably have crumbled, for she would have been forced to take seriously the problem inherent in looking for an unmitigated past in the products of memory.[18]

Adopting an extreme view, one could say that the memories of witnesses of long-past events have very little to do with the reality supposedly recalled. This is what the historian Benoît Verhaegen, a strong advocate of the use of oral sources, found to his dismay as he was working on the living conditions which had prevailed in Stanleyville during the Second World War. He knew from the contemporary official documentation emanating from the colonial institutions that life in the extra-customary centre had been extremely difficult. Contrary to his expectations, however, this was not the memory of those who had lived in the centre forty years before; they had built a romanticised view of the period of their youth, partly in reaction to the harsh conditions prevalent in Zaire when Verhaegen was conducting his research. While the intention of the historian had been to go beyond the unilateral character of the official documents, it was in these and not in the oral sources that he found the material for a critical appraisal of colonial power (1983: 489).

Turning to my own research, we have encountered the firm evidence of a clash between the written word and its memory when I reported that 'Bertrand' had closed the folder which contained the correspondence about which I was asking him for further explanations. He obviously did not like to be confronted with his own archives which documented the existence of a Congo, and perhaps of a self, other than those he remembered, even though he happily talked about the Congo for hours-on-end. A similar process must have been at work when Grévisse chose to refer to his reproachful essay of 1949 in his defence of the territorial elite in 1984. I also suspect, without having read them, that the archives 'Adam' offered me could have fuelled the construction of a damning image of the Belgian Congo. I doubt that 'Adam' remembered what his papers contained any better than 'Mignolet' when he lent me documents which referred to his harshness.

Does this mean that memories never reveal the past? Karen Fields beautifully argues the opposite in a paper pointedly entitled 'What one cannot remember mistakenly' (1989: 44). There she discusses the problems she encountered in using the memories of her grandmother, born black in 1888 in South Carolina. She introduces the paper by acknowledging 'the certainty that memory fails'. She points out, however, that there are times when it does not. One day, her grandmother, who had been a teacher, was having tea with a friend, a former pupil of hers, and was recalling how the brother of the visiting woman had been a bright pupil and was expected to have a grand future. Karen Fields' attention awakened when her grandmother added that his being sent to jail had been a tragedy. Fields asked what had happened. The sister of the boy said: 'Well, he didn't do it. The other boy did it, but he never would admit, *never would admit*, so all those years my brother was in jail for what he did. He walked all around us big as day, year in, year out, may he rot ... '(ibid.: 51, emphasis in the original). It turned out the incident was a request for a drink of water from a white girl. Fields comments:

> I piped up that neither one of them should have gone to jail for twenty years over asking for a drink of water, not [her] brother and not the other boy either. If I hadn't seen the mountain yet, the awful way she looked up at me, and then ignored me, let me see it. I let further comment die in my mouth. I then saw what she saw, a black teenager who let his friend be convicted in his place. She did not see what I suddenly saw, a Southern tableau: the impressionable white girl and her oppressive male kin (or perhaps the oppressive girl and her impressionable kin) enforcing an unjust etiquette of domination. A black young man did not ask a white young woman to address any sort of personal or bodily need. Her outrage at the wrong injustice revealed the Jim Crow order with an immediacy that intentional testimony never could. For this kind of unintended memory, I submit that cross-checking is redundant (ibid.).

It is difficult to disagree with Fields. But one can ask how many such 'unintended' memories a researcher comes across in the course of research – 'unintended' presumably because the informant provides the researcher with a precious piece of information in the eyes of the latter, but not his own. If not impossible, oral history is a difficult art in which I prefer not to venture. I feel more secure in considering that, if memory signals the past, it does so in a way which cannot be exactly ascertained.

This book accordingly focuses on the way colonialism is remembered in Belgium today without attempting to reconstruct how things were in the Belgian Congo. But such a presentation is arguably a cop-out: the two projects, one would-be strictly historical, the other would-be purely descriptive of memory, cannot be thoroughly separated. When I quote the interviewees, I take it that their words express their present vision of colonialism; but I also accept that they reveal something of the '*grandes lignes*' (main outlines) (Filloux 1952: 26) of their life in the Belgian colony. In other words, the presentation of my study as related to memory in present-day Belgium does not allow me to evade the problem of the relationship of the memories of my informants to the past, for my analysis inescapably contains and makes statements about the past. To make matters worse – worse in the light of the above discussion on the transformative work of memory – it calls on memories in a way that suggests they describe the past as it was. And indeed, the trick, or major difficulty, is that it is important for memory to get the past right. What 'right' means in this context is a question to which I shall now briefly turn my attention.

Remembering well

When colonials suddenly found themselves in Belgium at independence, all they kept from the Congo where many had planned to remain after retirement was – almost literally – their memories. This is not to be belittled, for memories are extremely important: ultimately they constitute us.

Memory is normally what remains when everything else has disappeared; we could say it functions against loss both at an individual level (for example when one loses a loved one) and at a collective one (which is why Claude Lévi-Strauss recommended we study primitive societies before it was too late). Memory is also, whatever our circumstances, what makes us. Whether our lives are reasonably peaceful or full of incidents, we carry it with us. As Tonkin says, 'we are our memories' (1990: 25). If we did not forget, however, we would equally be unable to function; we would be – ironically – at a complete loss. But to be able to forget well, we first need to remember well.

This seems to be crucial if traumatic events are to be overcome. Psychologists, for example, repeatedly warn against the danger for families not to acknowledge important events, which become the more negatively powerful for remaining taboo (such as the unspoken death of a young child). What is true of families also applies to the individual – think of victims of sexual abuse – and to collectivities – the avoidance by post-War Europe to confront its collaborative past with the Nazi regime springs to mind (Rousso 1991, but compare with Rousso and Conan 1994). This is to say that trying to forget the past, to put it behind one's back before having integrated it through memory, is no solution. The repressed events are bound to resurge in unexpected ways, possibly causing more damage than recognition, however painful, would have entailed.

The way we remember, or fail to remember the past, is crucial. Too great a distortion between the past and what is allowed to be remembered can be unbearable. This is why it can appear worthwhile to instigate lawsuits in defence of the truth decades after the contested events took place – think again of victims of sexual abuse who sue their perpetrator well into adulthood and of the trials regarding the revisionist accounts of the Second World War. Memory requires us to be faithful to the past, even as it constantly transforms it.

It is beyond my ability (and my aim) to assess the quality of the individual memory of the persons I met in the course of my research. By quality, I mean the ability to integrate the past experience in the present self – not the accuracy of the minute details of the past experience. What

I can say is that former territorials' memories must be at least in part painful. In 1960, they suddenly found that they were colonialists, and then could not fail to be aware that the populations they used to care for were falling in ever deeper and more abject poverty through the years. Interviewees often told me how sad they were at hearing the news about Zaire. I have no reason to doubt the depth and sincerity of this feeling.

Their memory shapes their identity as former territorials, an identity they are proud of (cf chapter 7). It (either their memory or their identity, for each constitutes the other) gives them the ability to fight, even if only privately, i.e. for themselves, the negative image of colonialism which comes from the outside world and which itself constitutes a simplified, sclerosised, and distorting memory. Even though their recollections must become rosier and rosier through time, they also catch something fundamental about their past. Thus, we should receive their words as being neither absolutely located in the present, nor strictly referring to the past.

Unavoidable misunderstandings

The intention of this chapter is to point to the complexity of the underlying processes which determine the dialogue between interviewer and interviewees. In seeking to do this, I have already highlighted a number of ways the interviewees' statements cannot be taken to reflect their experience of the Congo in a straightforward and neutral way. For example, I have pointed out in the second section that the interviewees had their own idea of how my research should develop and that what they decided to tell me was the subject of a constant, if often implicit, negotiation between us. Also, as indicated in the previous section, the way memory works means that their recollections could not but distort the past. This is so even though they aimed, as I stressed in chapter 4, at objectively recalling their experience of the Congo so as to make it possible for me to understand its reality. However, this aim was never going to be easily fulfilled. In this section, I want to concentrate on the difficulty for us to be on the same wavelength. Irrespective of my leftist political orientation when I approached my research project as explained in chapter 3, the fact that the world I grew up in was very different from the world in which they had worked was bound to make it difficult for me to receive what they were trying to convey in the way they intended. I will now review some misunderstandings which crept in, and suggest that there are many others of which I am not and cannot be aware.

The interviewees, or at least some of them, were perfectly conscious that what had been accepted as natural thirty years ago would appear shocking today. Over and over again I was told that I could not judge attitudes of the past by present criteria. I was accordingly urged to replace testimonies in their historical context. For example, 'Melonnier' attached the following warning to the Annual Report of Territory he sent me for consultation: 'In interpreting this report, you must keep in mind that thirty-two years[19] of evolution have happened in our European countries since it was written.' 'Melonnier' (with whom I exchanged correspondence but did not meet) did not elaborate on how present-day European mentality was at odds with that which prevailed more than three decades ago nor on how this could constitute an obstacle to the production of a sound interpretation. However, he was obviously concerned that my analytical ability could be impeded by spontaneous reactions learned in a very different society than that in which the report had been issued.

To be sure, the first annual report of the kind I read (which had been lent to me by 'Bertrand' at the very beginning of my research) had given me the impression of a police state.[20] These one-hundred-and-fifty-odd pages, with their notes on the whereabouts of the African population and their assessments of the African chiefs, which were not to be read by those directly concerned, appalled me; they also seemed to me to encompass every possible piece of political information related to the territory. Going over them months afterwards, however, I wondered why I had forged the feeling of a police state. It is possible that I revised my earlier perception because I was becoming increasingly acquainted with the world of the territorials and better able to share their vision. Now the elements which the report contained appeared matter-of-fact, pieces of information that the administration indeed needed to be able to function properly.

This perspective was confirmed by 'Dehon', who exclaimed when I told him how I had originally conceived of the annual reports as a means to ensure that everybody and everything was kept under control:

> Oh, but this is not a control. The A.T. [territorial administrator] feels responsible for his territory, and of course, he is, be it for tax collection – the money which comes in is necessary to start anything – or for agriculture – he must feed the populations. He also feels responsible because he is the central figure of the public order and he must give a detailed description of all that exists. The same goes for the roads. He must say whether he has enough money – he never does – and why the roads are not as one would wish them to be. The same applies in respect of the native authorities: he must say what is going OK and what is not, why this and why that. Whatever the area, he

must present a detailed report. All the more so because he must answer all the questions of the questionnaire he is sent. In fact, he fills in forms, and he does so in whatever way he likes.

The last words of 'Dehon' (which end an oral discussion which I taped) counteract what he had been saying so far. They also point to an alternative explanation for my new way of looking at the reports: instead of an accurate reflection of a carefully examined situation, could they be nothing but words written to please a superior? Reading, for example, that 'the atmosphere continues to be excellent' in the report of the Kivu district for the year which preceded the Masisi-Lubutu revolt (quoted in Lovens 1974: 12), I could not but reassess the significance of their content.[21]

My concern is not, however, to decide once and for all whether the reports point to a police state, whether they were intrusive for the local populations, or whether they were justified. I am more interested in the way one was given to me and the fact that I was specifically warned against the danger of producing an anachronistic study. Over and over again, the interviewees reminded me of this danger, and almost invariably when the interview came to touch upon the colour-bar which existed in the Congo. On such occasions, more often than not, my interlocutor would stress that nobody at the time gave a second thought to the segregationist rules and practices which pervaded everyday-life. I was repeatedly told that segregation was deemed absolutely normal, a part of the natural course of life, and thus neither discussed nor reflected upon.[22] Ironically, the result may be that I tended to imagine the colour-bar at work everywhere, including where it possibly had no place. Let me give three examples where I was tempted, at least at one stage, to read the situation as being modelled by the colour-bar that characterized the Congo.

The first was signalled by the expression '*style Louis-caisse*' (which I shall translate as 'Louis-box style'), which was used to describe the furniture which found its way into the houses of the members of the administration. This furniture, with which the government furnished the houses it built for the members of its administration, was constructed in the Congo, by African carpenters, apparently in a similar fashion throughout the colony. Its designation as 'Louis-box style' was meant as a joking comment on its rough appearance, not comparable to the real various Louis styles which are represented in Belgian bourgeois houses. Having used many wooden boxes as tables, chairs, or bookshelves myself as a student, I took the words of the interviewees quite literally and assumed the furniture they were given was indeed angular, tough and unplaned. This image fitted with that of the uncomfortable life they led, which emerged for example from their accounts of the tours they used to take in the bush. When I saw pictures of interiors, however, I had to revise my idea about the furniture: if not highly decorated, it nevertheless contained curves and appeared reasonably comfortable; the houses (and lives) of the territorials were obviously less in the nature of a camping site than I had imagined.[23]

As it became clear that I had misunderstood the exact compass of the expression 'Louis-box', I began to wonder whether the significance of this nickname could lie elsewhere. In particular, I was tempted to associate it with racist and possibly unconscious prejudices against the work of African carpenters, doing in fact as good a job as many Belgian ones. Retrospectively, I cannot help thinking that this interpretation was perhaps far-fetched; certainly it was not necessary. Another which springs to mind is that the nickname helped colonials to celebrate and rally around home by expressing a slight contempt for what was being produced in a foreign land (a contempt which need not repose on a colour distinction). It is also likely that the territorials who enjoyed a middle-class background missed the 'beautiful' pieces of furniture which they would have been able to display in their house, had they stayed in Belgium.

The first example concerned a piece of information that led me to mis-imagine the material conditions in which the territorials lived. The second relates to the territorial functions and the qualities required to accomplish them. Many interviewees recalled how they had been sent to the bush days if not hours after they had met the chief of territory in the very first post to which they had been assigned. They usually had a specific task to accomplish, for example, the building of a bridge. If one is to believe them, the only instruction they received was contained in the words '*débrouillez-vous*', which can be translated in this context as 'get on with it'.[24] Such accounts of their first jump into the deep end (which forced new recruits to learn at least the rudiments of the lingua franca) never failed to impress me. They reinforced in me the often projected image of female inadequacy in DIY as opposed to that of the male gift for engineering, and left me feeling that I would never have known where to begin, had I ever been put in a similar situation, while the men before me had somehow managed. I looked up at them with admiration, at least until 'Parmentier' added: 'You know, of course *I* did not know how to build a bridge. But the Blacks did. They had been remarkably trained; one only needed to leave it to them for things to take their course smoothly.'

This remark acted as a trigger: suddenly I saw territorials less as supermen than as trainee-supervisors, and their deeds as rather mundane achievements. But why had this piece of information been silenced for so long? Various interpretations seemed possible, which need not have applied to all interviewees in the same way. Perhaps some indeed enjoyed impressing the young female in front of them (as well as themselves) and, consciously or unconsciously, projected the self-image of a man able to confront difficult situations. It is also possible to bring again a racist explanation and to suggest that the most prejudiced among them refused to recognise the value of the work of the Africans. More innocuously, however, it is probable that most interviewees never thought that there was any piece of information to give. To them the reality was so obvious that it did not require further explanation – and indeed it took a comment on my part for 'Parmentier' to volunteer his illuminating remark. What the accounts may have conveyed is the sense of complete loss the new recruits actually felt, for although the task, thanks to African know-how, was not insurmountable, they might not have realised this when they received their first instructions (cf Samarin 1989: 52–3).

I finally want to turn to a story 'Milnaert' and his wife told me more than once. It involved a couple of white South Africans who were travelling during their honeymoon in the Congo. The road they were taking happened to be blocked as it went across the post of which 'Milneart' was in charge: the bridge over the river was being repaired just as the newly-weds arrived. Their trip was bound to suffer a serious delay whether they chose to head for another bridge (a five hundred kilometre detour) or whether they waited for the bridge to be reconstructed. On the spur of the moment 'Milnaert' decided to call a number of men who put planks over the pillars of the bridge and carried the car to the other side. This unusual crossing proceeded smoothly – except for some anxiety on the part of 'Milnaert' in case a man fell, which was unlikely but not impossible. As I was told the story for the first time, I had taken it to illustrate the will of a territorial to help, in all circumstances, the two South Africans who happened to be in difficulty, and thus to express the solidarity which linked Whites in Africa. It was clear in my mind that the colour of the persons involved had played a major role in 'Milnaert"s decision to improvise the crossing; I could not imagine the same degree of risk taken for Blacks. After I had suggested this interpretation in a letter, however, 'Milnaert' vigorously opposed it during our next interview. He assured me that he would have done the same thing for the driver, whatever his colour, as long as the car was not too heavy. On his wife's suggesting that it was '*de la conscience professionnelle*' (a sense of professional duty), he added: 'I do not like the word, but, whatever, the road always has to remain open.' What puzzled him the most was my own interpretation. He continued: 'But where did you get this idea that Whites always helped each other? The Whites did not constitute a mafia, you know.' If 'Milnaert' is right, this episode illustrates how my own prejudices led me to hear something other than what I was told – and which could not be inferred from the material.

I have just given three examples of misinterpretations on my part, and thus of misunderstandings between me and my informants. There are a few more of which I am aware but probably many whose existence I do not even suspect. They point to the weight of my presuppositions – 'Parmentier' and 'Milnaert' would say prejudices – in the interpretation of the material I offer. They also suggest that it may be problematic to determine exactly how to interpret uncontested facts, as becomes clear in the next two chapters.

At first sight, this chapter could seem to have addressed rather disparate themes. Let us remember that it started with a section which discussed the guarantee of anonymity and other apparently mundane modalities such as the time and place of the interviews and the methods through which they were recorded. The next section of the chapter explored either subtle or not so subtle processes of negotiations between interviewer and interviewee as to the subjects to be tackled during a particular interview. The third section proceeded with discussing how memory always works in a way which transforms the past so as to adjust it to the requirements of the present. Finally, the fourth section considered misunderstandings which arose between the researcher and her interviewees. What unites these four sections is their attempt to problematise the dialogues by revealing what goes on beyond apparently straightforward statements. As one often hears, things are not as they seem. This chapter showed that the dialogues developed along lines and according to processes which are less obvious than may appear. For example, the so-called guarantee of anonymity is often presumed to make the interviewees freer to talk; but it was found ultimately to work for the benefit of the publishing researcher, whose writing it freed. To give another example, memory is generally thought to give access to the past; but it was stressed that memory is as much about the present as it is about the past, making ambiguous the significance of statements uttered out of memory. To give one more example, it was noted that a statement can appear straightforward both to the interviewer and the interviewee, without the former therefore seeking nor the latter offering further explanation as to its meaning; the fact that interviewee and interviewer belong to different worlds and have different reference points, however, can easily result in misunderstandings creeping in between them, of which they are not even necessarily aware. This chapter thus occupies a vital place in this book which is ultimately concerned with the question of how one can communicate with an 'other' and achieve some understanding of the world he represents. What the chapter suggests is that one can only try to achieve this by being aware of the complexity of the processes involved and by recognising that 'understanding' is never final. Understanding has to be continually sought, in a way which remains receptive to the exploration of new avenues. This view also informs the next two chapters, which leave behind the question of how the interviews developed to ask what can be made out of them.

Notes

1. Anthropological discussions of the guarantee of anonymity in British mainstream literature seem to be confined to Jenkins (1979) and Davis (in Ellen 1984: 317–8). Mayer (1989: 206) has remarked on the lack of transparency of anthropologists' methods of recording their material.
2. Of course, no interviewees declined the offer I made to preserve their anonymity in my work: the role of the interviewee they agreed to play entailed that they provided me with information, not that they decided what to do with it. They were not in a position to ask me specifically to use the interview I had had with them, still less to cite and acknowledge them by name.
3. A historian who considered the publication of the manuscript indeed asked me to persuade the seven anonymous authors to drop anonymity. It should be noted that social pressure can also work in the other direction and incite participants to a 'combined' effort not to 'stand out'.
4. But two came to my office at the University of Brussels.
5. Many of my interviewees had recently retired from professional life when I started to conduct the interviews. This had a double advantage: on one hand, they could find time to receive me for reasonably long hours with relative ease; on the other, their memory was still very good. Being in their their mid- to late- sixties in the late 1980s, they had joined the territorial service in the late 1940s, i.e. they had been part of the relève. The period which followed the Second World War saw a peak in the history of territorial recruitment. There were never as many recruits as in 1946 (at least 295) (Dembour 1992a). Out of the twenty-five interviewees I cite in this book, nine entered the territorial service between 1945 and 1947. See Appendix 1: 'Basic career information on territorials cited in the text'.

6. The 'Milnaerts', the 'Michels' and another couple to whom I had come in the morning nonetheless invited me on the spur of the moment to stay over lunch.
7. The one notable exception is the interview with 'Delporte' which lasted some five hours during which we sat at a table without interruption.
8. Looking through the private archives of my interviewees, I discovered later that the broken arm had been 'Praet''s.
9. Another disadvantage of the note-taking was that, in order to carry on with the conversation, I generally could not afford to write down my own interventions which in turn prevented me later from exactly analysing how, why and by whom particular subjects were introduced. Moreover, some statements by the interviewees obviously could not be written down – one example is the remark 'de Glaise' made about the 'slap in the face' of the Portuguese ('But you're not interested in this kind of thing for your study, are you?') (above: 84). Had the tape-recorder been on, the same words most probably would have been uttered and found their way onto the tape, thus providing me with the exact record of what had been said.
10. Although Bucher, Fritz and Quarantelli mention six hours for transcribing one hour of tape (quoted in Ellen 1984: 191), Gravois and Andresen reckon that every hour requires eight to ten hours of transcription time (1988: 231), while Samarin speaks of eleven hours (quoted in Ellen 1984: 191).
11. My aim, in sociological jargon, was to conduct interviews of the semi-directed type. Sociologists have said of such interviews: 'The whole technique [for the interviewer] consists in never interrupting a "development" by the narrator while starting him again when necessary, or even refocusing what he says so as to cover the field of research as much as possible' (Poirier et al. 1983: 62). I find this statement much too simplistic. On one hand, it suggests that the success of the interview depends on the interviewer possessing adequate skills; whatever these are, I would say that different interviewees will react in their own personal way to them. On the other, my experience is that the aims expressed in the statement are often contradictory, making it impossible simultaneously to fulfil them.
12. 'Peters' nevertheless originally told me he had left for the Congo in 1950 and realised this could not have been the case after he mentioned his wedding (the date of which he was sure) during his first leave in Belgium. He had in fact first embarked for the colony in January 1948.
13. One of the French definitions of the term 'image' reads: 'mental reproduction of a previous perception or impression, in the absence of the object which gave rise to it' (Petit Robert 1982).
14. I have nonetheless occasionally come across citations of Hunter's work (in Lowenthal 1985; Borofsky 1987; Thompson 1988).
15. Luisa Passerini (1988) accordingly warns against the danger of imposing a chronological sequence onto the life-stories of our informants. Although I began the interview with a chronological theme, I let my interviewees associate events as they wished after we had reviewed the development of their career.
16. Cf Lequin and Métral who speak of interviews 'which are built on flashes recalling a series of intense experiences while entire life spans seem to have been swallowed up in oblivion' (1980: 153–4).
17. Cf Pat Caplan's discussions with her informant 'Mohammed'. He provided her with reminiscences which seemed plausible until she checked their accuracy by consulting the note-books she had kept over the years (forthcoming).

18. Oral historians do not seem to have been inclined to address this problem. The leading British oral historian Paul Thompson talks about a 'curve of forgetfulness' (1988: 111) and about the way in which the interests of the remembering person shape testimonies in his book *The Voice of the Past* (chapter 5), but he never really questions the value of the remembering process for reconstructing the past. Similarly, David Henige, a specialist in the African field, devotes only a few pages to memory in his book on *Oral Historiography*. In these he repeatedly hints at problems caused by memory, as illustrated, among others, by the following statements: 'In reconstructing the past from innumerable tiny fragments, which might be likened to the dots of paint that characterise the pointillist style of art, the historian will never be sure that he has all the pieces he needs or even whether the pieces he has belong to a single whole' (1982: 67); or later: 'No matter how careful we may try to be, remembering is just too casual and too unconscious to be adequately controlled' (ibid.: 111). Although these passages indicate that Henige is aware of memory's possible shortcomings, he does not seem to have digested either their range or depth. For a more sophisticated discussion of the use of memory in oral history, see Perks and Thomson (1998: Part IV).
19. By giving the exact number of years, 'Melonnier' probably wanted to reinforce the impression that he was an objective and reliable informant.
20. On colonial knowledge as colonial power, and its investigative modalities, see Cohn (1996).
21. 'Milnaert' strongly disagrees with my interpretation. He writes: 'You say: "It could just be words". This is not true. These were words which were attempting to say to one's superior: "Here is the situation in my territory." I cannot conceive that one would have tried to please a superior by fabricating annual reports. At the same time, there were some questions which touched upon such ultra-administrative aspects that it was impossible to give appropriate answers; so that we said almost anything which came through our mind. But this does not mean that we did it to please our superiors, absolutely not'.
22. For a forceful anecdote involving the prohibition for Africans to enter restaurants, see Turnbull (1984: 229). For a different presentation of exactly the same practice, see Brausch (1961: 23–5). For a dissident colonial voice, see [Rubbens] (1945).
23. Although it remains true that the level of comfort varied within the Territoriale according to ranks, the sophistication of interior decoration must have partly depended upon what the boxes sent from Belgium contained, i.e., upon the Belgian social background of the colonials.
24. For an analysis of the French verb '*se débrouiller*', albeit in a completely different context, see Reed-Danahay (1996: 62–5). This analysis rightly insists on the idea of resourcefulness.

6: My Story

The preceding chapters have underlined how my general approach to colonialism differs from that of my interviewees. Our different memories of colonialism are evident in our consistently contrary interpretations of events. Let us take as an example the obligation under which the Africans were to cultivate. I associate it with coercion, but former colonials stress its central role in the avoidance of famine. I see its primary object as a means for the coloniser to draw economic benefits, an interpretation in my opinion warranted by the emphasis the coloniser put on the cultivation of cotton; former colonials retort on the other hand that cotton was part of a cycle of cultivation which included other crops such as cassava, peanuts and paddy, and that the Africans were glad, even anxious, to buy cloth, bicycles and sewing machines with the money they made from the cultivation of cash crop. Asking who is right and who is wrong is not helpful in this kind of discussion. It is more illuminating to observe how our respective perspectives come to be articulated and why they do not converge. This is what I shall do in the next two chapters. In this chapter, I spell out what I heard during the interviews by offering my own interpretation of the territorial experience. It is not surprising, considering my starting point, that my analysis points to domination. In the next chapter, I present the criticisms 'Milneart' levied against my text, and thus highlight the coherence and pertinence of a perspective at odds with mine.

Being immersed: The pretence of closeness

'There, as a fresher, one lives exclusively amongst the natives'
(interview with 'Vastenakel').

The Belgian colonial administration placed strong emphasis on touring. The agent was supposed to spend twenty-one nights a month away from home and the administrator fifteen. As for the fresher, he was commonly sent to the bush for a relatively long period, for example two months, during which he was unlikely to meet many Europeans. There is a sense, then, in which one can say that the territorials lived amongst the natives. But which sense? Tancré-Van Leeuw, who finds it important not to distort her informants' testimony, suggests intimacy. She writes: '[During their tour, the territorial administrators] sometimes found themselves the sole Europeans among the Africans. Trustworthy discussions around the fire ensued, with legends being retold and other moments of grace which made it possible for them to know, understand, and value their African auxiliaries and the administered populations' (1992: 401). In this section, I wish to question the merits of such a description by stressing the limits within which the contacts between the Europeans and the Africans could develop.

A sense of immersion

Former territorials often give the impression that they knew the Africans well. I was thus very surprised when 'Bertrand' recounted that he had asked the policemen to identify the leaders of a riot. The riot – the only one he personally came across – had taken place between two tribes during the year which preceded independence. It lasted three days during which he told his policemen: 'Watch carefully who is at the forefront so that you can tell me afterwards.' The story, which he told me on the third day of my initial visit to him, surprised me because it did not fit with the picture I had built during the preceding two days. I had been under the impression that he knew all the people he had been administering; in my mind, he would not have needed to rely on others to be able to identify individuals living in his territory. This was naive, considering the number of people who lived in the administrative unit of which a territorial was in charge. The 'constant contacts', as the law called them, were mainly restricted to the 'intermediaries'. 'Milnaert' observed that the tribunal of territory was about the only place where the territorial met ordinary men and women. Tancré-Van Leeuw was thus absolutely right to mention the African auxiliaries in the passage I quoted above.

She suggests immediately afterwards that the privileged atmosphere she had described was not maintained through time. Her text continues:

> Unfortunately, the paperwork was going to grow and grow (correspondance, various reports, statistics to be provided, enquiries to undertake …); the time spent in the Territory office would never cease to increase. Add to this the constant shortage of manpower and the consistent improvement of the means of transport, which made it possible for the territorial administrators to come back home in the middle of a tour. In these circumstances, it would appear that the ties with the Africans were bound, little by little, to lose some of their tightness (ibid.: 402).

The Second World War assuredly represented a pivotal point in the history of the colony: as if, comparatively speaking, things were done at their own pace and with an in-depth quality beforehand, with haste and superficiality afterwards.

One former territorial, who had arrived in the Congo after the War, commented to me: 'The old ones knew a lot of things.' Another of his contemporaries recalled having read with eagerness the papers which his predecessor had left in the archives of the territory where he was posted. In the 1930s territorials had been involved in the application of the 1933 decree on the native circumscriptions. One of their tasks had been to prepare the redrawing of the limits of chiefdoms and the creation of sectors by collecting relevant information on the political organisation of the societies in which they worked. As a result, they had spent a lot of time enquiring about the groupings of the Africans, the history of their migrations, and the way authority was transmitted in particular groups. Even though their ideological position and the concepts they used are heavily criticised today, the articles and books which ensued testify that they sometimes gained an insightful understanding of the political principles on which local societies were based.[1] One can therefore understand why some of their successors talked almost with envy about these elders who had had the good fortune of working in a way which led them to get to know the African populations in more depth than they themselves were allowed.

This does not mean, however, that the territorials who worked in the 1930s were closer to the Africans than those of the next generation. If anything, distance was more strongly enforced before the War than after it: the colour-bar was stricter and the emphasis on the maintenance of prestige (a notion I analyse below) greater. Also, a few decades later when only memories remain, the 'broad lines' conveyed by the interviewees of the post-War period appear hardly distinguishable from those of the pre-War period. The impression one gets from what the former say and write is that they wanted to know the Africans, enjoyed being with them, and would have liked to be even closer to them than they already were. For example, 'Peters' remarked that, given the choice of reliving his life, he would remain single longer than he had done in order to have the opportunity of spending more time with the Africans. Whether he would actually have decided not to marry during his first leave in Belgium, had he been put back in the 1950s, is beside the point; what is significant is the interest he expressed in getting to know the Africans.

In what follows, I shall pay attention to some recollections 'Bertrand' shared with me, all of which suggest that his contacts with the Africans were good – something he repeatedly told me. In my view, however, each story lends itself to a more nuanced interpretation, which puts the territorial sense of immersion in an unfavourable light. The first recollection is related to the passing of a judgment. To quote from my notes: 'The judgment made a strong impression on him, for it was done in a truly customary manner. Proverbs followed one another. The judge started one, and the people ended it together, like in a chorus. Although he did not understand the language, ['Bertrand'] could see that it was really just. He spent the whole afternoon listening.' These words express a fascination for a different way of administering justice than the one to which 'Bertrand' was accustomed. The feeling of enchantment that arises from them is admittedly naive: it rests on a flawed vision which assumes a consensual exercise of justice – while power relationships must have been at work. It also fails to acknowledge that customary law was not a given but a problematic colonial practice. For 'Bertrand', however, this afternoon may have appeared, to return to the expression used by Tancré-Van Leeuw, as a 'moment of grace'. If so, it was not one in which he was directly involved, for he would have been sitting at the back rather than taking a consciously active part in the proceedings. In other words, whatever enchantment he felt, the afternoon did not represent a moment of shared communion.

Later 'Bertrand' explained that he could be said to have been racist in so far as he thought that there were different races and that it was therefore normal for different kinds of people to be treated differently. He gave three examples of such differentiated treatment in the Congo: the natives were not allowed to go into hotels and restaurants; they could not make chits and receive credit through this means; they did not live in the same place as the Europeans but in their villages or *belges*. (The term '*belge*' commonly designated the place of residence of the Africans in extra-customary centres). This led him to make a remark which I reconstituted in my notes as follows: '[Bertrand]'s house was situated at two or three hundred metres away from the village. At six o'clock in the evening, he sent people back to their homes. They left him alone and he did not bother them either – they were at home amongst themselves.' A sense of peaceful cohabitation emerges from these lines, but also a complete blindness to the effect of power. 'Bertrand' does not seem to realise that if he and the Africans retreated into their respective quarters at night, it was because they were expected to do so.

The third story is related to an initiation dance. 'Bertrand' told me he had allowed it to take place even though it was in principle prohibited because of the casualties it could involve. He had just warned the Africans to keep it 'on a moderate level'. My notes then read: '['Bertrand'] attended such a dance once, but the locals certainly preferred to be amongst themselves. He did not want to disturb them either. Moreover, he did not really have the time.' The first two sentences again suggest that a sense of good neighbourliness characterised his relationship with the people he was administering, as if each was in his home and neither encroached on the other. They could even seek to indicate that 'Bertrand' assumed a self-effacing role, one in which he was careful not to intrude upon the privacy of the people he was administering. The final remark on time may have been dropped in as an aside. It implicitly points, however, to the main concerns of the administration. These included doing the census and collecting the taxes, controlling and assuring the development of economic activity, maintaining public order – but not observing the 'ritual' life of the natives. Ethnographic interests were needed and encouraged, but within limits: they could not impede activities considered essential. The territorial was not there to share the lives of the natives.

By his own account, 'Bertrand' was the one who either prohibited or tolerated the dance. The fact that he chose to tolerate it may indicate magnanimity on his part, a readiness to understand the natives, and a certain closeness to them. I would, however, object to such an interpretation. To me, his decision to let the dance proceed – within some limits – demonstrates that the Africans were not the masters of their own actions in their own land. They may have been at home, but they were under the control of a foreign power. They were under some kind of occupation.

Speaking of occupation

Some interviewees used the term 'occupation' themselves. The first to do so in front of me was Mrs. 'Van Gansbeke' who went to the Congo in 1946 to marry her husband. On her arrival, she was quite astounded at how beautiful and developed the Congo was. She expressed her admiration and surprise to her husband-to-be, a settler, who replied : 'Maybe, but we shall always be the occupier here.' She commented to me: 'And we knew what we were talking about – we were barely coming out of the occupation [in Belgium] ourselves.' 'Milnaert' is another interviewee who came up with an explicit reference to the German occupation when he told me at the end of our first interview how shocked he had been the first time he had seen an African being whipped. After having heard the term spontaneously used twice by the interviewees,[2] I tried to drop it in myself during the interviews to observe the reactions it arose. There were few objections, and my interlocutor would even take up the topic sometimes. This happened, for example, with 'Dauw' during a discussion on the differences between the territorials of the pre-War and those of the post-War periods. His reply follows my intervention. To quote them in turn:

> – The impression I got is that they [the young territorials from the relève] perhaps arrived with very different ideas – as you say, it was the end of the war – ideas about freedom, about fighting the occupation
> – Yes, exactly, ideas about the occupation – I was going to say that. Perhaps we were the occupying force for them [the Africans], in a certain way; some certainly thought so.

The 'I was going to say that' indicates that 'Dauw' was not just following a leading comment on my part; the comparison had crossed his mind too. Further examples of occurrences of the term could be provided from other interviews.

In the last quotation, the words 'in a certain way' are crucial. As 'Milnaert' used the term 'occupation' during a subsequent interview, his wife intervened from the kitchen where she could overhear us. She came to him and interrupted, saying: 'What an awful word.' 'Milnaert' maintained the expression was appropriate. For him, it conveyed two crucial characteristics of the coloniser: his foreignness and his commanding role. His wife retorted that the diabolical aspect of the German occupation was not to be found in the Congo. 'Milnaert' agreed. So, I suppose, would his colleagues.

This important proviso notwithstanding, the fact that domination governed colonial society does not appear to have been a moral problem for the interviewees. We have already heard 'Milnaert' saying that he was no more shocked by what he saw on his arrival in the Congo (i.e. segregationist practices) than an officer who takes charge of a platoon. This explains the absence of second thoughts with which, to my original surprise, former territorials often integrate clear signs of domination in their account. Consider for example the following sentence: 'I returned to my war effort, to the fields, marshes and hills of the Bashi, a land and a people who represented what I knew best in the world '(Willaert 1990: 43). The author of these words is Maurice Willaert, a former territorial who ended his career in the Congo as the governor of a province and who has recently published his memoirs. The quoted passage refers to the end of a short holiday he took in 1942, when he had been in the Congo for ten years. Leave aside the expression 'war effort', and the sentence can have a romantic appeal, conveying a sense of in-depth knowledge and understanding; bring it in, and the picture changes dramatically. The 'war effort', as it was called, designates the contribution made by the Congo to the Allies during the Second World War.[3] It consisted mainly in the production of raw materials. By all accounts it involved heavy demands on the African population (as well as on the European one). Africans might not have welcomed the 'knowledge' Willaert had of them. One may also wonder what the term meant in this particular context. The book offers some clues, in that Willaert hardly speaks in it about his relationship with the African 'land and people', concentrating instead on his links with, and opinions of, various colonials he met in the Belgian Congo. Almost the only thing one learns about the Bashi from the pages which precede the quoted passage is that they lived in the territory of Kabare where Willaert had spent most of his then ten territorial years and that they were still refusing to pay taxes when he had arrived in the region. As a result a military occupation and a police operation were decreed in 1933 and 1934 respectively. Put in this context, the words I have quoted above express domination rather than peaceful intimacy.

The figure of the ménagère

Occupation implied segregation in the Congo; in other words, distance was a correlary of force. In turn, the insistence on distance prevented relationships between Europeans and Africans from developing beyond a certain point, not only by setting up material obstacles, but also by raising conceptual ones. The colonial figure of the *ménagère* poignantly illustrates this point. Strictly speaking, the ménagère is a housewife, i.e. a woman who keeps the house, who does the housework and takes care of the domestic chores. In the Congo, however, the term (which I shall keep in French in the text) was used to designate an African woman who was living in the house of a European man – including but not necessarily a territorial. The primary object of her presence on his side was not housekeeping as the etymology of the term would suggest. Although that element could play a part, it was well-understood that she was there to meet the sexual needs of the unmarried man. However, she did not do this as the unattached woman living in the centre and officially categorised as a 'free woman' ('*femme libre*') may have done, for the relationship between the European and the ménagère was understood to be of a more or less longstanding character.

During the interviews I was often told that she was the concubine of the European, but this was because my interlocutor wanted to make sure I understood the role of the ménagère. Nobody would have used the term 'concubine' to designate a 'ménagère' in the Congo. The idea of illicitness implied in the former term was absent from the latter. It was considered normal for a single European man to have a ménagère and not to marry her, except perhaps according to custom. No disgrace or moral condemnation was attached to him (or to her) by the European community.[4] The practice was widespread throughout the colonial period, although less so after the Second World War when European wives appeared in greater numbers. Some considered the ménagère as a political asset, a means of accessing African society, understanding it, and generally knowing what was going on (cf Stoler 1989b: 636–9).

The term was exclusively applied to the African woman who lived with an European man. According to 'Milnaert', the term derived from the decision by the couple to '*se mettre en ménage*' (create a household together). How this decision came about (and who took it), what kind of relationship ensued, how the latter came to an end, must have varied according to experiences. 'Ransquin', who joined the territorial service after the War, told me that a chief had 'given' him during his first term a 14-year-old virgin whom he had kept as a ménagère until his leave and marriage in Belgium. This account fits with my prejudices and expectations of how things were done in the colony. But, to give an example which sheds a different light on the institution, 'Parmentier' mentioned a judge who had an enduring relationship with a ménagère and who refused any social invitation if the latter was not extended to her. Although she never accompanied him, he insisted that she be given consideration. He finally married her.

The ménagère generally did not appear in the house when the European[5] was receiving other Europeans. The interviewees would say that 'she made herself invisible' ('*elle ne se montrait pas*'); I would be more inclined to say that she was not introduced. According to the interviewees, she would have felt uncomfortable in European company because she would not have known how to behave. Hearing them, it was almost as if they were doing her a favour by sparing her the obligation of entering a cultural milieu into which she did not fit. This may well have been the case, but the practice resulted in an exclusion which was not always respectful. For example, Roger Depoorter, a former territorial who has written a collection of short stories concisely and beautifully rendering the colonial atmosphere, does not mention her in his account of the lazy Sunday afternoons, which bachelors spent after having eaten a *moambe* (a rich dish where chicken is cooked in palm oil), 'often exchanging spicy remarks'. He only hints at her presence towards the end of the story: 'In the garden outside, two half-cast children were playing, indifferent to the burning sun' (1983: 68). The author of the story had presented the host of the party as a 'bachelor – of course' (ibid: 67), as if the mother of the children with whom his host obviously lived did not exist.

'Dehon' explained to me: 'Officially, she did not exist.' This is not to deny that a sentimental attachment between the European and his ménagère could develop in the privacy of the home. 'Milnaert' for instance recalled how the assistant in post when he first arrived was surreptitiously waving behind the van or making other little affectionate gestures to his ménagère just before he left his house. To me, however, the point is that these gestures were, in the words of 'Milnaert', surreptitious. Of course, it is impossible for me to know whether the assistant would have behaved differently, had he been married to a European woman.[6] Even so, I cannot believe that the absence of public recognition of the ménagère was nothing but the reflection of a wider pattern of gender relations.

The vocabulary which some former territorials use to describe the African populations warrants my seeing in the lack of recognition of the ménagère an attitude which goes beyond gender. Let us again listen to Depoorter. He explains in a story which comes just after the one on 'The bachelors' that he sometimes found himself in a depressed mood of which he then reasoned himself out. This represents for him the opportunity to make the following judgment:

> The native populations did not always understand that the effort requested of them was in their interest, so as to make them progress. Yes, progress.

Thinking about it more closely, it appears that even the most futile and seemingly tiresome task was part of a vaster programme, which aimed at assisting these simple and ignorant beings, victims of superstition, prone to illness, tribal wars and famines (1983: 70).

Without being typical of all former territorials, such language is relatively common. It points to relationships which are characterised by a lack of consideration and recognition of the dignity of the other. It also demonstrates, if I am allowed to make up a word, mis-knowledge, i.e. the fact that the Europeans thought they knew the Africans but did not.[7] I can already hear some of my interviewees objecting, as they often have, that the Africans liked them and see them producing letters where Zairians ask them to come back because, as I once read, 'We need you.' Invariably such letters come from former servants or *plantons*.[8] To me, what they show is that *some* Africans indeed liked the Europeans in a way which conformed to the paternalistic mode expected of them.

I would therefore conclude that it is less a sense of immersion which emerges from the interviews than one of distance. Of course, my account has not done justice to the variety of territorial experiences and personalities. Some were more respectful towards the Africans than others, and the quotations inserted in this section were selected for my own purposes. Nevertheless, the territorials kept apart from the African society. Either they did not wish to penetrate it or could not achieve closeness, because the colonial situation made this impossible. 'Peters' implicitly formulated that the territorials were not that close to the Africans when he told me of Jan Vansina who had been working in his territory: 'He really lived at their level. He even spent a night in a tree.' I did not check whether Vansina's fieldwork involved spending nights in trees, nor do I know what Peters means by saying that Vansina 'lived at their level'. It may be, but is not necessarily, derogatory. Neither do I wish to suggest that the anthropological encounter escaped the colonial logic (cf Asad 1973; Copans 1974; Said 1978; Fabian 1983; Pels and Salemink 1994a). It nonetheless remains that those who constitute the focus of this book, i.e. the territorials, could not develop relationships with Africans beyond a certain point. Of course, all human relationships are limited, but the colonial context limited relationships across 'races' to a degree which I feel is morally unacceptable.

Preferring the authentic African: An expression of imperialistic nostalgia

> 'So [X] goes to Leo[poldville]. I really would not like to be there; I much prefer to be inland'
> (Private correspondence of 'Bertrand', undated).

In the fourth year of his career, 'Bertrand' was transferred from an outpost in the bush to a more important centre. He wrote in a letter to a friend in Belgium, dated 24 November 1955, that his new post which counted about fifty Europeans was second only to the chief-post of territory in terms of European concentration in the region, i.e. for two hundred miles around. After describing the nature of his tasks in this new environment, he added: 'Of course, as far as the natives go, it is not as nice as at Kipeku [his former post]. They are evolving!!!' Considering that the proclaimed aim of colonialism was to help the Africans develop and 'evolve', such a statement can appear paradoxical in the mouth of a territorial. I shall explain the nature of this contradiction by drawing on Renato Rosaldo's discussion of 'imperialistic nostalgia' and shall argue that a feeling of power underlay the territorials' commonly declared preference for the bush.

Downplaying change

The interviewees constantly down-played the changes which their presence brought about. They talked as if they really did not wish to interfere with the ways of the natives. For example, 'Fontor' told me: '[The natives] settled their problems between themselves, but they came to us if they wanted us to know something.' Whether 'Fontor' was referring to judicial settlements or not, his phrasing suggests that it was possible for the Africans to keep on settling their problems as they always had: they had the option to go to the European but were not forced to do so. In a superficial analysis, this view may hold with regard to minor criminal offences and the so-called 'disputes between natives', as both resorted to the jurisdiction of the chiefs. However, it overlooks a number of crucial facts, including that European judges were ultimately competent to rule on any case, that the coloniser introduced a written procedure which affected the judicial system, and that substantial changes were brought to customary law (cf Chanock 1985; Moore 1986).

'Fontor''s perspective negated the profound influence of colonial action. It puzzled me so much that I asked him whether the life of the natives had changed in any way under colonialism. His first reaction was to answer negatively. He then immediately added that something had changed, which was that migrations and never-ending wars had come to an end. Thus, apart from the benefits of stability and peace, 'Fontor' did not think any other transformations were worth reporting. And yet it was clear that even his post, which he referred to as being '*au bout du monde*' (in the middle of nowhere), was the seat of major transformations. Later during the interview, he mentioned that a large development project, including a fishing enterprise and pastoral farming, was taking place there.

I asked the same question about change to 'Peletier', who gave me a much longer answer than 'Fontor'. For 'Peletier', whether the life of the native had changed depended upon the situation of the individual. He first took the example of a man who left his village to go and work in Aketi or Stanleyville. For that man, he said, life had changed. Whatever his occupation, he was not a farmer any more – but a mason, a brick-worker, a carpenter, a driver, a mechanic, an unskilled worker. Even more important was the fact that 'he was now living in a community which was not bound by the tribal hierarchy'. 'Now', 'Peletier' concluded, 'he was in all respects a man of the White rather than a man of custom; he was confronted with completely different customs'. I proceeded to ask whether this was also true for the native who lived in Mahagi, a rural territory where 'Peletier' had also been posted. His answer was:

> Much less so, for Mahagi was not a big economic centre. [… Whether the man was] a roadman, a flock-keeper, a worker in a plantation …, he was not […] removed from his customary environment. Perhaps he even went back to his village at night […]. Even if he worked at one day's walk from his village, if he had a problem which was really customary […], he was not far from his chief and could go to his tribunal. Therefore he was not at a loss. [For him, the change was not an upheaval].

'Peletier' added the last sentence after he read a transcript of our interviews – which is why I put it in square brackets in the quotation. It seems that rereading himself, he realised that he had implied (or could have been taken to imply) that change was occurring only in urban areas. What he probably wished to convey, however, was the idea that the change happening in urban areas, where the so-called customary setting was lost, was of a radically different nature to that which affected the Africans who remained under customary influence. He thus corrected himself by drawing a distinction between (simple) change and (confusing) upheaval. He could see that change was occurring everywhere, but he associated it first and foremost with a break-up of the 'customary', or 'tribal' milieu.[9] Presumably he thought that custom in rural areas had basically remained custom,[10] hence the little significance he attributes to the drastic transformation of occupational activity.

Like the other interviewees, 'Peletier' readily admitted that custom evolved – everywhere. Like them too, he presented this evolution as being slow and following the aspirations of the Africans. In his view, the Europeans were not directly pushing for the evolution; they just observed it. Thus he vehemently protested when I asked him whether he had ever '*rédigé des coutumes*' (literally: drawn up customs): the touch of personal creation connoted by the verb '*rédiger*' (which I had frequently encountered to describe the activity to which I was referring)[11] upset him. He told me to use the verb '*transcrire*' (to transcribe) instead. Similarly, when I asked Salmon, who had written an article in the *Bulletin des Juridictions Indigènes* in 1953, whether he had encouraged the evolution of custom which he was describing there, he replied negatively and said: 'we recorded, that's all'. Hearing the interviewees, the evolution came about internally to the Africans: if they wanted to take advantage of the new possibilities offered by colonialism, they could, but the evolution was not forced upon them.

At one stage, 'Peletier' even told me that polygamy had never been prohibited. This happened in the course of a discussion about the attitude of the coloniser towards African customs and traditions. He was telling me that territorials intervened very little, even in response to practices which they were not naturally inclined to approve. I remarked that this contradicted the literature of the time which always emphasised the fact that 'they were bringing …'. He interrupted me in the middle of my sentence and exclaimed:

> Of course, we were all very conscious of bringing something, but from there to say: "we're going to change everything". […] But the fact that we were there, the way we looked at things, the way we treated them, emphasised this or that. […] It's true, we were conscious that we had an influence and that we had to play on this influence to bring about, little by little, a modification in the way they thought. But we did not confront them directly, of course not – which is why polygamy was not prohibited.

I was very surprised by the mention of polygamy in this context as I knew that a decree had specifically been taken to prohibit it in 1950.[12] I pointed this out to 'Peletier', who replied that the territorials never cared about this decree which they did not apply. Other interviewees confirmed that the decree, adopted on 4 April 1950, had received no implementation in practice. Common sense supports this contention: it would have been time-consuming and devoid of much practical effect to annul customary marriages which did not meet the condition of monogamy. Using polygamy to illustrate the absence of European intervention nevertheless remains incongruous: measures were taken, and applied, to discourage it, including the payment of a tax for each so-called 'supplementary wife'. All the interviewees knew this, as they were responsible for tax-collection. 'Peletier' spontaneously mentioned it. But for him the continuation of the practice of polygamy must have been the significant fact, which proved his point that Europeans did not challenge African ways of living. One can argue otherwise: marriage is one area where the impact of colonial presence was arguably highly disruptive.

Regretting change

The fact that the interviewees were not inclined to stress change can be seen as paradoxical. Possibly even more surprising is the fact that when they talk about change, they seem to regret it. For instance 'Bertrand' related to me the following anecdote about a *capita* (African overseer) who converted to Christianity and subsequently abandoned his 'African' ways:

> There was a village capita whom I liked very much. His name was Tambwe, which means lion. He had a loin-cloth, was covered with tucula [red colour], and twisted his hair. I really liked him. I always greeted him when I was going through his village. I think he had three wives. One day, I see a man who is wearing a capitula [shorts]. He says 'hi'. I did not know who he was. He tells me: 'It is me, Tambwe.' I say: 'What?!' And then I say: 'What about your wives?' – 'I repudiated them. […] I am baptised, I could only keep one wife, so I repudiated the other three [sic].' Then I said: 'And what about your tucula?' – 'It is over too.' He was now wearing a capitula and a shirt. He had cut all his hair, and he was unrecognisable. […]. I thought to myself: 'What a pity.'

'Bertrand' says that he liked the man. Perhaps as proof of his attachment, he mentions that he greeted him when he went through his village. If he indeed felt a particular affection for the capita, he seems to have expressed it in a rather paternalistic way – which points to the limits to which the relationship between the coloniser and the colonised were allowed to develop. However, 'Bertrand' may also have been emphasising how much he liked the man so as to underline his own sense of nostalgia when he had to face a new figure who had left behind the 'authentic' African ways.

If so, 'Bertrand' is not alone in pitying the transformations he witnessed. Other interviewees expressed similar feelings. In doing so, they followed a general pattern which has been widely reported. As Renato Rosaldo writes: '[…] agents of colonialism – officials, constabulary officers, missionaries […] – often display nostalgia for the colonised culture as it was "traditionally" (that is, when they first encountered it)' (1989: 69). Rosaldo calls this phenomenon 'imperialist nostalgia'.

Rosaldo remarks that the peculiarity of this phenomenon lies in the fact that the 'agents of colonialism long for the very forms of life they intentionally altered or destroyed' (ibid.: 69). He explains it as an 'attempt to use a mask of innocence to cover […] involvement with processes of domination' (ibid.: 86). The nostalgia would 'transform the responsible colonial agent into an innocent bystander' (ibid.: 70). Rosaldo's explanation seems to apply perfectly to the story of the converted capita. 'Bertrand' told me it just after having remarked that he did not agree with the action of the missionaries. He could have meant: 'See, I had nothing to do with cultural destruction, those responsible were the missionaries.' It can also explain the way the interviewees presented the 'problem' of polygamy. As far as the administration was concerned, the Africans were free to marry as they wished. Any disruption was due to the missionaries who insisted on monogamous and religious marriages. In this perspective, territorials are not to be blamed for unnecessary transformations, which is why the interviewees could not see, or did not mention, that they partook of a system which was bound to disrupt the social fabric.

Despite its explanatory appeal, Rosaldo's observation nevertheless falls short on three points. First it does not allow for ambivalence towards change, including when it is self-induced. Change often comes as a package-deal which involves both advantages and disadvantages. While one can welcome the former, one can still regret the latter, even if the benefits presumably outweigh the losses. Secondly, it explicitly attributes a feeling of guilt to the colonial agents. As far as I can see, such a feeling was not part of the territorial psyche.[13] The explanation Rosaldo provides may tell us more about him than the psychology of the colonial agents; in the same way as my reluctance to use the word 'domination' did. Thirdly it confers on the 'imperialist' nostalgia a peculiarity which it does not have. Rather, the paradox highlighted by Rosaldo must be seen as a general phenomenon which derives from the ubiquity of power and is therefore not specific to the 'agents of colonialism'.

Let us listen to an Irish student reflecting on the 'small rough island' where he spent his summers:

... It was always summer there because I never went during the winter. There were no roads and no electricity. It was heavenly. In the ten years since I have been there the natives have tarmacadamed the place, installing toilets and telephones, widening the harbour, adding a hostel, a restaurant and countless new villas. [...] Of course, I genuinely begrudge the natives their comforts, never having to live there all year myself. Dammit, you could escape there. Now ignominy has been heaped on insult. The ancestral cottage, the oldest on the island, has been converted to a Take-Away [...] (McCabe 1990, 81–2).

One can long, to use Rosaldo's words, 'for the very form of life [one] intentionally alters or destroys' without being entrenched in a guilt feeling. Of course, in this case, the author was not actively engaged in the transformation of the island. Nevertheless, he only reluctantly admits that the natives deserve comforts, even though he recognises that his nostalgia is directed towards a way of life which he does not have to adopt all year long. It was his 'escape', not that of those who were living permanently on the island and who benefited from the changes (which came in a package-deal including toilets, telephone, take-aways, and the disappearance of the ancestral cottage). What holds for a 'small rough island' off the Irish coast applies to 'backward' areas in general. The example of the arid but sunny regions of the Mediterranean springs to mind. The tourist recognises that modern facilities should be brought in to alleviate the hardships of the 'traditional' peasant, but is attracted by the 'bucolic' atmosphere of the place and hopes it will be maintained as 'in the old times' (cf Waldren 1996). Backwardness appears to hold a true value and genuine quality of life behind it. The same fascination applies to poverty (Schaffer 1985), or for that matter, to the 'noble savage'. The feelings described by McCabe could have been those of the 'agents of colonialism'.

This leads me to the merit of Rosaldo's denomination, which is that it emphasised the relations of power involved in the process of '*imperialist* nostalgia'.[14] Those who share these paradoxical feelings come from a powerful centre and look at a marginal periphery. They do not dream of becoming permanently 'backward', 'poor' or 'savage'. The attraction is limited to a convenient personal 'escape' which can be mixed with contempt. Moreover, the imperialist may have a vested interest in keeping the other backward, poor or savage, namely the preservation of his domination. In this light, regrets about change can be interpreted as regrets about loss of domination. This is exactly what some interviewees suggested when they explained to me their preference for the bush.

Enhancing one's authority

In the remark I have placed as an epigraph to this section, 'Bertrand' pities a friend who was posted to the capital of the colony, Leopoldville. The feeling he expresses epitomises the territorial attraction for the bush, which most interviews echo. Let us for example listen to 'Vastenakel': 'I personally preferred the native of the chiefdom to the native of the extra-customary centre. [...] He was more straightforward, more natural, he was at home. [...] In the bush, I am closer to the native.' The myth of the noble savage resonates in the two reasons given in this passage to explain a supposedly personal preference for the natives who have not left their customary milieu, i.e. the better character of this type of native and the closeness of the relationship one could develop with them. Later during the interview, however, 'Vastenakel' implicitly spoke of a third reason, which had to do with the authority the territorial enjoyed in the bush. In his words: 'For the Blacks, we were God. We were the masters. Especially in the bush. We could have requested anything and they would have done it. Because we were white, that's all there is to it. We were the Whites, you see.' This remark about authority, which came at a completely different moment during the interview, could be viewed as independent from the explanation about the beauty of working with 'good natives'. By putting the two remarks together, I am admittedly establishing a link which 'Vastenakel' probably did not intend. My argument is, however, that the two realms of explanations are very much related to each other.

Interestingly, 'Peletier' explicitly made the link I am suggesting in the course of a long conversation. This conversation began with my saying that many interviewees seemed to think that the true territorials were those of the pre-War period who were single, spent nights talking with the Africans, and were generally closer to them. 'Peletier' retorted that there were two ways of looking at this proposition, which he agreed represented a common opinion. One way was situated, as it were, at a 'mythical' level. This was 'Peletier''s word. I take it to refer to the myth of the noble savage and to the pure life which 'simple' people supposedly lead. The second way was to adopt a political perspective sensitively attuned to the future of the colony. 'At that level', 'Peletier' continued, 'the clever one was perhaps not so much the one who sat around the fire as the one who had a drink at the club of the évolués.' I expressed surprise at this remark, observing that I had heard many former territorials saying that they were positively looking for the company of the authentic Africans, but few expressing an interest for the évolués.[15] 'Peletier' replied:

Someone who follows this line of argument may have the unconscious feeling that he cannot cultivate in his dealings with évolués the good-natured condescension he shows to the black man in the bush. Now there is something ambiguous about this, because the black man in the bush, who is supposedly a primitive, may in fact be very subtle. His thoughts are not unworthy of interest, far from it. But because the black man in the bush adopts a deferential attitude and is, you could say, more or less admiring of the European, you feel in a more flattering position with him than you do when you face évolués who are starting to use your own dialectic, your own language, and who take a closer, critical look at the European, living as they do in permanent contact with them and being able to observe the pettiness of white life. (reworked tape-transcript)

His explanation was simple enough: the African in the bush did not question the authority of the European; on the contrary, he continually enhanced it by his deference. The position was comfortable for the European, satisfying for his ego. Even the person who would not have been able to attract respect in a European (Belgian) milieu could feel he was important in the bush. 'Peletier' expressed more or less this idea when he declared:

> It is undeniable that [...] finding yourself the little chief in some bush district [...] brings you moral comfort. Consider by contrast the position of the territorial administrator who is in town. He must respect a hierarchy, rules about deference, and a rather strict protocol [among Whites]. [Moreover] he is dealing with Blacks for whom he is a white man among many others. He is a *mondele [white man]*, but not a *mondele moke* (great white man). He is a White in between.

In other words the 'bush' was comfortable not only because of the presence of deferential Africans, but also because of the absence of Europeans in a competitive situation.

The quasi-automatic authority the territorial enjoyed in the bush illuminates some life-stories, including that of 'Ransquin' which I shall briefly reconstitute from what he told me. 'Ransquin' wanted to escape the narrow-minded milieu in which he grew up. His father had been a clerk who worked from 8:00 to 5:00, he had never read a book, and would not let his son go to University. 'Ransquin' decided to enter the Colonial University (which had the status of a college of secondary education rather than that of a University).[16] He left for the Congo in 1946 as a territorial. During his leave in Belgium between terms, he studied law at University 'for fun' and took the exams. He qualified as a lawyer in 1957. After independence, he entered the Belgian judiciary, where he still had a post when I met him. In his own words, seldom shared by other former territorials, he wasted his time in the Congo: 'I arrived there and realised I did not like living in a hot country. [...] I felt there was malaria, dysenteria, it was too hot, I was in the bush, people had nothing interesting to say, all they could discuss were servants, buildings, roads. I was bored. Here I had a richer life. [...] I have never been very keen on Africa. [...] I regret having gone there. It was a waste of time.' I asked him why he did not consider becoming a judge in Belgium as soon as he took his law degree. He answered: 'I was not going to leave my career just like that.'

Although career considerations may well have played an important role in this decision, it is also clear from his account that 'Ransquin' found some attraction in his job as it stood. He may have complained that the bush had nothing to offer him culturally, but this was nonetheless the place where he wanted to be. During the interview, he mentioned that a friend of superior rank had offered him the possibility of joining him (the friend) in town. 'Ransquin' refused. I asked him why he was so determined to stay in the bush. His answer was straightforward: 'There I was chief of territory.' He reiterated the same idea on different occasions during the interview. While he was telling me that he went to the Colonial University because of his father, he added: 'Having said this, deep down, I liked the imperium. I must admit this. This is why I liked territories in the bush.'[17] Amidst an account of the influence of his family background on his entrance to the Colonial University, 'Ransquin''s remark seemed to fall out of nowhere. However, the introductory words (in French, '*C'est pas ça*') indicate where the thread of the conversation lay. The Colonial University and territorial career were not such secondary options for 'Ransquin'; he was looking forward to the power the territorials enjoyed. The interlocution '*je l'admets*' reinforces this message. The perspective of the imperium also informed 'Ransquin''s following remark: 'I wanted to have a territory in the old style. A territory in the bush, a life in the Congo a little bit old-fashioned. I thought it would be fun.' The Congo 'a little bit old-fashioned' is probably nothing else than the Congo where 'Ransquin' felt he could successfully use 'paternal' authority: raise his eyebrows in front of the children who did not go to school and their parents, make fun of the headman whose village had added only one supplementary concrete house since the last annual visit, or ask the man who had not cultivated his field if he was going to do it, in an appropriately intimidating tone. (I have picked all these examples from our taped conversation).[18]

It would nevertheless oversimplify the nexus of possible motivations to relate the preference for the bush expressed by the former territorials exclusively to a feeling of unchallenged authority. 'Peletier' mentioned other factors worth reviewing. One was the greater initiative the territorial enjoyed in the bush and the opportunity for him to devote his energy to what he felt was most useful. Another was the satisfaction of seeing the result of his work. To quote him: 'In town, [the only thing one did was] pile after pile of paperwork. [...] In the bush, if one builds a road, the road appears. Same with a house. And this is rather flattering. What's more, one has done it with Blacks – Blacks who appear to be nice Blacks.' The last remark brings us back to 'Peletier''s mythical perspective and to the image of the noble savage. The myth, however, was only a myth; it did not stand up in reality. 'Peletier' immediately continued with an observation to the effect that there were as many murders in the bush as in town, but that in the bush they escaped territorial notice. Notwithstanding this, the feeling of working with nice Blacks was gratifying.[19]

The preference for the bush was mythical in another and completely different sense. Living there involved major drawbacks, especially as far as family life was concerned. Spouse and toddlers could follow the territorial on his tours and often did so – happily I was told.[20] But comfort was not at its height and health problems could become dramatic in places where no doctors were available within easy reach. The spouses of the interviewees have often told me stories of birth-deliveries which would appeal to no women of my generation (for instance in a pirogue before arrival at the hospital or involving a six-week stay in hospital before the expected date). Furthermore, children of school age were almost inevitably sent to boarding-school (not a common practice among Belgians), except in the first years if the mother was prepared to take care of their education. Territorials were thus hoping to be posted in town sooner rather than later, for there they would enjoy greater comfort and better medical services, more stability (tours were reduced as a result of the greater load of administrative tasks), possibly educational opportunities for the children, and more frequent and diverse social events. The posts in town were scarce and territorials who went there at the outset of their career were considered lucky – except by a few people such as 'Bertrand' who, noticeably, married after 1960.

The trend in the territorial career seems to have been from bush to centre, if not a town. However, the interviewees hardly talk about their urban experiences, concentrating instead on the bush, as if it represented the locus of their true territorial years. The bush acquired a mythical significance and became 'the bush': an authentic place where Blacks remain in a pristinely pure state, untouched by civilisation. This image, akin to that of the noble savage, has a different resonance when seen against the backdrop of the power relationships which provided the context in which the myth developed. From this perspective the bush becomes the place where the territorials enjoyed uncontested authority. Admittedly this is not the whole story – I have noted that working in the bush was also gratifying for the territorial who saw the results of his work. Nevertheless, the territorials' declared attraction for the authentic African cannot be divorced from the political context in which it was founded.

Acting through persuasion: Prestige as violence

> 'You know perfectly well where prestige comes from.
> It comes from the whip – and nothing else'
> ('Dehon', imaginary answer by an officer to a territorial administrator).

In his answers to a questionnaire devised by Claire Van Leeuw, 'Amory' recalls how he dealt with a strike by not dealing with it, as it were. This is what he writes, using a telegraphic style: 'Total strike in a mining camp. The A.T. arrives in the evening, escorted by a few G.T.V. [soldiers]. Sleeps at the camp chief's. The next morning, all the workers responded to the call. But what would the A.T. have done if the strike had continued? Question raised after the event. No answer.' The territorial administrator (A.T.) whose experience 'Amory' recalls is none other than himself.[21] He seems to look back at the strike and especially the ease with which it was broken with slight astonishment, as if suddenly realising that he might not have managed to bring things back to their normal course just by sleeping for one night on the spot. This is nonetheless what happened. In this section, I wish to explore how this virtually magical effect could come about and why it may not have appeared surprising until years later, when 'Amory' came to reflect back on the event.

The reference to the voluntary territorial guards (G.T.V.) situates the episode during the Second World War: the G.T.V. were retired African soldiers of the colonial army who were recruited within the territories to replace the regular soldiers called to fill the central units of the army. This implicit inscription in time makes sense: a number of strikes racked the Congo during the War.[22] 'Amory' tells the researcher very little about the strike. He does not say what the claims of the workers were, for how long it went on, how many workers it involved. Instead, he concentrates on what he sees as the significant event, namely his presence, which broke the strike. He writes as if he genuinely wondered what would have happened if his presence had not had the effect of bringing the miners back to work. While he states that he is unable to formulate any answer to this question, a scenario involving the use of force irresistibly comes to mind.

Force had resulted in the deaths of workmen on some occasions, for instance whilst crushing the strikes which erupted in Lubumbashi in 1941 and in Matadi in 1945 (Markowitz 1973: 125; see also Perrings 1979: 224). Could his 'no answer' implicitly encompass such a scenario? If one follows this line of argument, one would argue that 'Amory' was aware that force was a real alternative, even though he does not say it in so many words. The mention of soldiers by his side could be seen to support this interpretation. By stating that he does not know and cannot imagine what would have happened, 'Amory' could mean that he has no clear idea of the exact course events could have taken and how coercion would have been implemented. Another interpretation is nonetheless possible: his 'no answer' would point to the fact that 'Amory' did not think, or did not want to think, that force was a real possibility – and that he cannot see that force was very much present when he was 'just' sleeping. Force would in this case be excluded from his mental representation of the Congo, which he saw as having been run smoothly, peacefully, without arms and without violence. From this perspective, the point of the question left unanswered would be precisely to emphasise that force was in reality superfluous in the Congo. Thus his account would make it implicitly clear that force was not needed and not part of the scene. Such an absence would, in retrospect, be astounding not only to his audience but also to 'Amory' himself, who looks back at his colonial experience with the knowledge of the 'events' which followed independence and the troubled post-independence history of the country. The common view of the interviewees is indeed that force played a very minor role in their actions. By contrast, my view is that it played a crucial role.

The idiom of prestige

The paradox between the low number of personnel in the various colonial administrations and the little difficulty the colonisers encountered in controlling the countries under their domination has tantalised scholars (see e.g. Kirk-Greene 1980; Berman 1990). The interviewees generally explain the overall success of colonial administration by reference to prestige. This idiom implicitly underlies 'Amory''s text. For an explicit reference to the term, we can turn to 'Peletier'. The slightly defensive tone of the passage is due to my question which specifically mentioned violence. To quote 'Peletier':

> Why are you trying to make me say that the Territoriale could realise its aims only through violence or force?
> During the fourteen years of my service, I experienced one military occupation — if you can call it that: the army only arrived after my assistants and myself had managed to calm down the situation and had stopped, through peaceful means, the violence (involving human casualties) which had erupted between two clans in the wake of a murder.
> We exercised domination through persuasion. And our persuasion was successful simply because we, the men of 'Bula Matari', had a lot of prestige.

The last sentence is particularly relevant for the present discussion, but I have quoted the whole passage for it shows how 'Peletier' pushes violence to the background and persuasion to the foreground. I have no reason to doubt he experienced only one military occupation from 1947 to 1960. L. F. Vanderstraeten notes that between the repression of the Bas-Congo strike in November 1945 and the Leopoldville incidents of 4 January 1959, the army did not fire a single shot to maintain order in the Congo (1992: 520). But suggesting like 'Peletier' does that persuasion was the principal tool of the administration is to forget the high number of criminal convictions, the often routine flogging of prisoners, and the passive but real role played by the army in maintaining the 'Pax Belgica'.[23]

'Peletier' asserts that persuasion was successful because the territorials, otherwise referred to as the men of *Bula Matari*, enjoyed a lot of prestige among the Africans. In this statement, persuasion, prestige and Bula Matari are three key-words which reinforce each other. 'Bula Matari' is a Kicongo expression which came to designate the colonial state and/or its representatives, the territorials. F. Bontinck (1969) argues that, being a verb in the imperative form, it should be translated as 'break the rocks'. He thinks it became the African name of Henry Morton Stanley in 1879 during the building at Vivi of a station for the Comité d'Etudes du Haut-Congo, probably as a result of Stanley constantly telling the workers to 'break the rocks'. The expression is nevertheless generally translated as 'breaker of rocks'. It is generally assumed, apparently wrongly, to have emerged to designate Stanley in 1880 when he had explosives used in Ngoma to make a way for his dismantled steamers which could not be carried by the side of the rapids of the lower Congo river because of the rocky and mountinous landscape. Some interviewees gave me yet another origin of the expression, attributing it to the construction of the railway between Matadi and Leopoldville in the years 1889 to 1898, which had involved the use of explosives. This was seen, they told me, as a real feat by the impressed Africans of the region. What is beyond contention is that the expression spread throughout the colony and became a metaphor commonly used to designate the colonial state.[24]

According to Young and Turner, the image the expression conveyed was of 'a force which crushes all resistance'. They quote the Zaïrian scholar N'kanza to support their contention: 'For all Bakongo, the name of Bula Matadi signified terror' (1985: 31). However, when 'Peletier' uses the metaphor, he certainly does not have terror in mind. He may agree that it suggests 'crushing all resistance', but for different reasons than those implied by Young and Turner. The latter must have in mind the forced character of African labour and the numerous deaths it involved. Such reality, however, is not part of the perspective of 'Peletier' or the other interviewees. For them, 'Bula Matari' conveys the idea of success in the accomplishment of a task deemed impossible to realise. In other words, far from denying that force played a role, they situate it at the centre of their interpretation. But they see it in a positive rather than a negative light.[25] We can now understand how Bula Matari connects with prestige and persuasion in 'Peletier''s view. His argument runs as follows: the territorials were the men of the crushing force Bula Matari; this made them prestigious, and thus persuasive. To put it differently, the territorials did not need to resort to blatant force, for the Africans were convinced that the action proposed to them was right and appropriate. The prestige of the territorials was such that it ensured the obedience and even cooperation of the Africans.

The territorial administration admittedly sought the cooperation, and when possible even the assent, of the Africans. This especially happened through the council of chiefdom. Negotiation was allowed, and even encouraged. It occurred regarding matters of detail and even sometimes principles. However, not everything could be questioned. If a disagreement persisted, territorials had to resort to coercion, or to the threat of coercion. When the native authorities did not voluntarily accept the measures which had been decided in higher instances, the decisions were forced upon them. This barely comes out of 'Peletier''s account, which gives the impression that the Africans were easily persuaded, presumably because they admired and looked up to the territorials. In the passage I quoted above, 'Peletier' appeals to a notion of prestige which is devoid of a forceful, overtly coercive, element.²⁶ As we shall see later, however, another picture also emerges from his testimony. Before discussing it, let us first examine the possible causes of the admiration he and his colleagues claim they enjoyed.

Many interviewees recall that the Africans often told them, when impressed by their deeds, that the Europeans had '*mayele*'. Mayele is a quality attributed by someone to another who displays intelligence in matters beyond the understanding of the former (Davis 1991). Davis, an American anthropologist who was in Zaire in 1969, remembers her informants telling her that Americans had mayele when the first man stepped on the moon. During the interviews I conducted, the word generally came up in relation to technological performances. For instance I was told of a driver who was praying in front of his broken car in the hope that it would make it work again. The mechanics involved were beyond his comprehension. For him, the fact that the Europeans managed to construct and maintain cars was a clear sign that they had mayele. Of course Africans also had mayele, which is applicable to diverse types of knowledge. But presumably, in the technological domain, Europeans were recognised as the champions.

European knowledge was not thought to be restricted to mere technological abilities. According to 'Milnaert', the Africans believed that the Europeans were repositories of a secret which enabled them to command even the forces of nature (cf the anecdote of Thourdelin above). Considering the wonders which explosives, railways, planes or cars could represent, it appears thoroughly plausible. The admiration could of course be made up as much of fear as joyful excitement. Many interviewees commented: 'For them, we were [like] gods.' Once this overstated image was created, all kinds of things added to reinforce it. To return to 'Milnaert' sociological insights once more, he mentions in his notes-for-himself: 'the great prestige of the White who, by contrast to the Black, hunted head-on (conscious that he could rely on an excellent weapon, while the Black's first reaction was atavistically to run).' 'Milnaert' also mentioned that the speed at which he was riding his bicycle and the distance he cycled in one day provoked the admiration of the Africans. He prosaically explained the sources of the 'amazing' deeds: a gun and gears. In doing so, he reduced the aura of the imagined hero by showing that supposedly extraordinary capacities were the fact of very common men. Not all colonials were as modest. For a different type of account, we can turn to J.-M. Domont's tale of his successful fight against a cobra. By the same token, we shall see how mundane occasions could reinforce the image of the 'amazing' European.

Domont, a former territorial, has recently published an account of his administrative dealings with the Kibanguist 'sects' during the Second World War (Domont 1988).[27] In the text which concentrates on strictly administrative matters, Domont inserts an anecdote which takes up a page and a half about an 'herpetological incident' (ibid.: 58–9), i.e. an incident connected to 'that part of zoology which treats of reptiles' (SOED). The text begins by noting that deskwork was monotonous. Such monotony, however, was interrupted one morning by noisy shouting. 'Was it a demonstration? The beginning of a riot?' No, comes the answer, it was a snake. There follows a description of the author's bravery: how he rushed to cut off the snake's path with a ridiculous stone picked up from the ground as his only weapon; how the snake attacked him as soon as he found himself in front of it, amidst what had become a complete silence. And then: 'Not another sound. The Blacks, assembled at a safe distance, were wondering with some anxiety what their white man was going to do.' There follows a dramatic account of the snake uncoiling, the swelling of its neck, and the venom spat towards Domont's eyes. But, the story goes on, Domont quickly turned his head away and threw the stone. The serpent fell flat and: 'It was the end [*hallali*]. The shouting increased, but now out of happiness. "The White was not afraid", "the White killed the snake", "the White is the most clever and the strongest", "the cobra is dead" …' Unfortunately, the whole passage is too long to be reproduced in full. Its vocabulary, construction and tone perfectly encapsulate the psychology of colonialism, as viewed by the European. On the one hand, it provides an image of the White as courageous, determined and always in control, even when he is rash. On the other, it presents the Africans as if they were at a complete loss, waiting for *their* White to do something. When the latter successfully does so, they celebrate him and recognise that he is '*malin*' (clever), a word connoting both intelligence and cunning (and perfectly rendering, at least in relation to some contexts, the idea of mayele). Although the term 'prestige' does not appear as such in the text, it is at its very centre.

Vellut notes that prestige was a general and constant concern among the colonisers (1982: 97; see also Kennedy 1987: 153). Whether one reads a paper of the time, opens a book, or listens to a former colonial today, the word is bound to come up. Although relevant to the whole group of the colonisers, it took on a particular significance when applied to the State representatives. Let me quote a few statements in which the term appeared in an administrative context:

> The Right to punish considerably increases the prestige of the territorial officers before the natives (*Bulletin des tribunaux de police congolais* 1953: 1);

> [...] the chief of territory was most upset because the prestige of the administration was at stake as much as, or rather even more than his prestige as a white man (Tinel 1956: 114);

> Each time I see a group that appears to be hostile, I go right towards it. This could spark aggression, but the prestige of the State – and perhaps also the fact that I am tall – keeps them respectful (Augustin n.d. [circa 1985]: 30).

The first statement is understandable as it is and can, for now, stand by itself. The context of the second quotation is a judicial investigation of the murder of a chief which was conducted by a territorial and greeted with stubborn silence by the Africans. The third quotation is part of an account by a territorial of his visit to a leper colony. The lepers, who had been cultivating and smoking hemp, and generally living outside European control, were fiercely unwelcoming at his arrival (above: 102).[28] The three passages are extracted respectively from a law journal, a novel and the memoirs of Augustin I have already quoted. I chose them from different types of sources to emphasise how pervasive the vocabulary of prestige was, and still is, in the language of (former) colonials.

Prestige was a group matter rather than an individual one. This emerges from all that I have said so far about the Bula Matari, mayele, hunting attitudes, and so on. It also appears clearly from the last quotations. Let us take the second one as an example. What the novel presents to be at stake when the chief of territory does not manage to get ahead in the investigation is not the prestige of the territorial as an individual person, but the prestige of the white man and particularly of the administration. This ties in with the fact that the colonial was regarded in the colony as the representative of the colonial group to which he/she belonged before being considered as a single individual. This will become clear as we proceed.

As prestige was a group matter, it was attached to the performance of the group rather than to the achievements of the individual, and it benefited any newcomer. Personal qualities were largely irrelevant, though they could reinforce the perception of the European as different and superior. This can be seen when Domont successfully fights the snake and gives the reader (most probably a Belgian historian considering the type of publication) the picture of a daring personal character. Even then, Domont presents himself as representing a group (cf. 'what their

White was going to do') rather than as standing as a mere individual. The relative neglect of personal qualities is also well exemplified by the first quotation in the above group of three, which declares the exercise of judicial functions to be a source of prestige. Prestige presumably resulted from being imparted with judiciary functions, regardless of more specific and personal qualities such as impartiality, patience when listening to the parties, or soundness of judgment.

I have never heard a lawyer in Belgium making a link between judicial function and prestige. But such a link is repeatedly made in colonial legal literature. The difference between the two countries cannot be explained by the fact that prestige did not depend on strictly personal qualities in the colony. This happens everywhere. When one speaks of the *'prestige de l'uniforme'* ('prestige of the uniform'), a phrase commonly used in French, one similarly fails to refer to personal qualities. There also, it is the mere fact of wearing a uniform that is supposed to bring prestige regardless of the person who puts it on. I shall argue that the distinctiveness of the colonial situation lies in the fact that a stronger link was made between prestige and coercion in the colony than in Belgium.

No prestige without the whip

The 'uniform' bestowing prestige to the territorials in the Congo was presumably not so much the loose khaki shorts and shirt they were required to wear on a day-to-day basis, but rather the official authority with which they were endowed. This gave the territorial prestige a specificity compared to that of the white man in general. The prestige of authority encompassed, and was perhaps best expressed, by the use of coercion. It is worth recording the exact wording of the statement on judicial activities, which explicitly referred to the 'right to punish' (above: 159). In the early 1920s, Fernand Dellicour, then Procureur Général at Elisabethville, established a similar link between prestige and criminal sanction. To quote him: 'How much … the prestige of the administrator increases when the natives see him as the fearsome figure who not only gives them orders in the name of Bula Matari, but can also resort to punishments to sanction disobedience to his orders' (n.d. [1956]: 233). Interviewees recurrently linked prestige with the ordering of the whip. For example 'd'Ave et d'Ove' thought that: 'He had less prestige […] than those of the previous generation […] who had enjoyed more coercive power (whip), which gave them prestige.' (Dembour 1991b: 104)[29] In the original and much longer sentence 'd'Ave et d'Ove' wrote in answer to a question of mine, the tautological construction of the statement is less obvious. Presented in this reduced form, it appears more clearly that 'd'Ave et d'Ove' considers that the whip was a source of prestige, even though he did not approve of it, for he immediately adds that he does not feel that what he is reporting was a good thing.

A link between the whip and prestige is also found in the novel *Kufa* (Cornélus 1954). The hero of this novel, published in the early 1950s, is a young man who arrives in the Congo from Belgium and does not manage to adapt to his new circumstances. In particular, he refuses to act according to expectations in the outpost where he exercises territorial functions. At one stage, his superior rebukes him for deliberately avoiding to order any strokes of the whip during his absence. The chief of territory tries to impress him with the following argument : 'When a policeman accuses a prisoner, you must use the chicote. […] It is a question of prestige and discipline' (1954: 158).[30] This argument, which leaves the hero indifferent, makes an explicit connection between prestige and the whip. What is suggested is that the failure to order strokes of the whip damages the prestige of the territorial.

Perhaps it is not so much that ordering strokes of the whip was positively seen as enhancing prestige, but rather that failing to so so was regarded as diminishing it. 'Peletier' would probably find it difficult to disagree. Among the various reasons which justified the practice of the whip in the colony, he included the following: 'If I fail to resort to the whip, will the black population not label me a white nobody, which will prejudice a certain form of authority? Perhaps we [territorials] thought: OK, I must do it otherwise I'll have no prestige – even though the concept of prestige is not exclusively linked to this, but perhaps it is part of it.'[31] Although 'Peletier' hesitates to associate prestige with the whip, he does formulate the possibility that the latter may have been part of the former. We are suddenly very far from his use of the word prestige in the sense we encountered above of the guarantee, through persuasion, of the success of the Territoriale's action. Here force undoubtedly arrives on the scene, even though 'Peletier' implicitly indicates that ideally the source of prestige should have reposed on more positive qualities than the capacity to order physical violence.

'Dehon' would agree with him. He sets up the following (imaginary) dialogue between a chief of territory and a chief of post:

> – 'But, my dear fellow, you must have prestige, you really must. Make your prestige felt by the chief, by the blacks.'

– 'Do you think I am stupid?' (the subordinate retorts). 'You know as well as I do what prestige is, it is this.' And by this he means the whip, you understand.[32]

(– *Mais mon vieux, tu dois avoir du prestige, hein. Fais intervenir ton prestige auprès du chef, auprès des noirs.*
– *Mais tu me prends pour un imbécile (parce que ça répond hein). Tu sais très bien que le prestige, c'est ça – et ça, c'est la chicote, hein.*)

The answer of the chief of post suggests that territorials fooled themselves if they insisted in talking in terms of 'prestige' while the key to their action was the use or threat of force – taking for instance the form of the whip. For him, the whip is not prestige, or at least not real prestige, but it nonetheless passes as prestige. Having started with the vocabulary of prestige and persuasion, we end up with a notion of prestige where force plays a central role. Although fear and deferential esteem can be close to one another, it must have been that the former rather than the latter underlay the mechanism through which prestige allowed respect to be gained – or imposed.

A concern for distinction

We are now in a position to answer the question of why the coloniser was so concerned with the notion of prestige. To put it in one sentence, they needed prestige to keep themselves differentiated from the colonised in order to survive as a group.[33] Phrasing it differently again, the concern for prestige amounted to a concern for distinction, so that 'prestige' and 'distinction' stood as equivalent terms in the colony. Anything which helped to distinguish the group of the coloniser (or one of its sub-groups such as the Territoriale) from the group of the colonised was presented as reinforcing the prestige of the former. This is why a link was made between prestige and judicial functions while such an association never surfaces in Belgium. In the Congo the most trivial of things came to be conceived in terms of prestige as long as it served as a marker of difference.

We are used to 'distinction' covering different semantic fields. The term can indicate both a factual and a qualitative difference. When qualitative, the difference is regarded positively. Saying that someone has distinction is necessarily to imply that s/he is outstanding in a way that commands admiration. In common parlance, prestige is generally associated with distinction in the latter understanding of the term. In the colony, however, it embraced the material sense as well as the character-related one. In fact, the two senses were not divorced from each other.

Material separation, expressed for instance through rules of residence, went along with moral, cultural or social separation (and vice-versa).[34] By the same token, the infringement of one kind of separation involved the infringement of the other.[35]

The figure of the European 'gone-native' illustrates this mechanism. In the novel *Kufa* (which I have already cited), the chief of territory Van Leeuwen flings the following remarks to the hero, Pottier, whom he sees as taking the side of the Africans: 'But if you like them so much, why don't you go and live with them? You would not be the first! There is already Borman [...] an old lice-devoured dotard, repulsive to see ... [...] One day he'll disappear [...]. He may take care of the negroes and all the trash they catch, he has lost in their eyes the prestige of the white' (1954: 160). The portrait of the doctor, as depicted by Van Leeuwen, epitomises physical and moral decrepitude.[36] Whatever his qualities, including medical skills and concern for the Africans, he has lost the prestige of the white man. This is because he has not kept the required distance. By abolishing the material distinction, the other distinction has also gone. The consequence is that he has no chance of survival: 'he'll disappear'. For the chief of territory, Borman's life is lost in the literal sense of the term.

Van Leeuwen regards all relaxing of distant contacts as a real threat. He makes this remark to Pottier: 'You arrive here with completely made-up ideas! [...] If you had your way, we would lose the Congo in five years!' (ibid.: 160). These lines, found in a novel written at a time when nobody thought about independence, convey the sense of absolute necessity the Van Leeuwens felt in keeping a strict demarcation between the group of the coloniser and that of the colonised.[37] The 'you' of the quoted sentences implicitly encompasses all the Pottiers of the post-War period. The conflict between the two protagonists of the novel obviously reflects the divide between the generations of the pre- and post-War periods. Remarks I heard during the interviews echo it. For instance Mrs 'Milnaert' recalled how the superior of her husband, who had been trained before the War, disapproved of 'Milnaert' giving various talks to the évolués of the post. The couple found it difficult to explain to me the reasons for the reproof beyond the statement that the contact the lectures implied was felt to be 'too close'.

The lectures 'Milnaert' gave in his real post of Eastern Zaire were probably much less conducive to intimacy than the conversations the novelist imagined Pottier having. One is left to wonder how different the attitude of the younger generation was compared to that of the previous one and how different a contact they were seeking to establish with the

Africans. My guess is that the divide between generations, if very much felt when the relève first arrived after the War, came to fade away as time went by. On the one hand, I suspect that the 'old' generation came to adapt to the revised code of conduct called for by the new social, economic and political circumstances. The fact that segregationist legal provisions came to be removed in the decade preceding independence or that Africans would have brought complaints quicker than in the past, testify that changes were happening to which the 'old guard' could only but adapt. On the other hand, the young so-called idealists probably increasingly integrated into the group of the colonials and came to share its code of conduct.[38]

Significantly, the novel ends with Pottier seeking death in a storm. Though his kind of suicide must partly be attributed to disappointment in love, it also indicates that Pottier cannot adapt to colonial life. Van Leeuwen had warned him that, without a change in his attitude, he would have no choice but to report him to superior authorities – presumably (although the text leaves this slightly ambiguous) for 'incitement to revolt' (ibid: 177–8). Even after having been informed of this, Pottier persists in refusing to behave in the way which is expected of him. His inflexible determination can be analysed as a lack of adaptation to the colonial situation, and this is what distinguishes him from his contemporaries, also newcomers of the post-War period. The example of the whip is particularly striking. In the novel Pottier is shocked by it and refuses to order it. Although the interviewees also recalled the shock they experienced the first time they saw it applied, they then integrated the practice into their routine. As we have seen above, they were thus displaying the prestige of the White.

The consensus is that the prestige of the European diminished after the Second World War. We can recall here the story of 'd'Ave et d'Ove' about the chief who complained to him that the White was losing the prestige he used to have. The chief substantiated his claim by recalling how a White had thrashed the carriers who had failed to prevent a branch from hitting his eye. He deplored the fact that the White would no longer have acted like this in the time of 'd'Ave et d'Ove'. Illustrations of this kind could be multiplied, all pointing to a decrease in the prestige the Europeans enjoyed or fostered. But prestige did not disappear and could not have disappeared, for the end of distinction would have meant the end of colonialism and the lost of prestige would have signalled the disappearance of the coloniser group. The relationships remained colonial throughout the colonial period, i.e. founded on distinction and articulated around a concept of prestige ultimately based on force, however unwilling some former territorials may be to recognise this fact.

This chapter has highlighted three contradictions or paradoxes in the discourse of the former territorials. They talked as if they were 'immersed' in the African society while they actually lived in a segregated way. They agreed they were there to bring development and change but expressed a preference for the 'authentic' African. They spoke of a 'persuasive' action which in fact rested on violence. In these three cases, power is central to my analysis. This is ironic, considering I had specifically decided to leave aside legitimation as a focus of analysis so as not to make my informants appear as the powerful 'baddies'. Revising my topic did not have the radical effect I had anticipated. The resilience of my original approach is much to the regret of my best informant. As we shall see in the next chapter, his feeling is that I have failed to understand the position of the former territorials.

Notes

1. Jewsiewicki expresses 'double comments' in regard to the study by the former territorial Tonnoir (1970). Although highly critical of Tonnoir's 'ideological position and approach', Jewsiewicki recognises that one merit of the publication is to highlight how valuable it would be to organise the 'systematic collection of the memories, notes, traditions and observations kept by former administrators, missionaries, and commercial agents who spent their life in Zaire' (1974: 591). See Alexandre (1971) and Cochrane (1971) for an appraisal of the knowledge administrators, as opposed to anthropologists, gained of the African societies in which they worked. See also the excellent essay by Pels and Salemink (1994a) on ethnography as colonial practice.
2. It also occasionally appears in the literature. See for example Kestergat (1985: 77 and 85), who quotes André Ryckmans.
3. On the way the Belgian Congo came to side with the Allies, see Lovens (1975) and Vanderlinden (1988).
4. As revealed by the way the ménagère comes out in the fictional literature. See for instance the short story '*La maison écroulée*' by de Valkeneer-Briard (1950). Vellut nevertheless observes that the practice of having a ménagère, once unanimously accepted, progressively came to be considered as a stain on colonial decorum (1982: 103).
5. The European is never referred to by a term qualifying him in relation to the ménagère. This usage is not especially surprising as it reflects the different ways in which man and woman are commonly defined. In this respect, it can be noted that the masculine of 'concubine' does not exist in English – although the term 'fancyman' exists, which implies subordination to a rich woman. In French '*concubin*' exists

but is less frequently used than '*concubine*'. Both have pejorative tones and non-married couples who live together nowadays generally avoid those terms altogether.
6. After having read the draft of my work, 'Milnaert' expanded on this relationship in the following way:

> In the very first months of my arrival in the Congo, I shared a house with a young man (who was killed soon afterwards). He was living with a ménagère. In a way, she lived with us. She had traditional reactions. For example, she refused to eat with us because a wife does not eat with her husband according to tradition; she had her little house at the side, where her White man came and visited her. In contrast to this traditional attitude, she displayed such tenderness and enjoyed playing such games with him that it is impossible to qualify this relationship as a service. There was on both parts a loving relationship in our sense of the term. I should add that they also had their arguments as a couple – and it was not always the White man who won.

7. The latter was reciprocal. It is for example well-known that stories of Whites eating Africans circulated in African societies (Ceyssens 1975; see also Vellut 1982: 112; Vellut 1983: 515, note 46; Verhaegen 1983: 485–7; Kestergat 1985: 170–71; de Lannoy et al. 1986: 209–10 and 214–5; Jewsiewicki 1986). Although eating is part of the witchcraft metaphor, the legends must also partly be attributed to the fact that limits were imposed to the development of personal relationships and therefore mutual understanding (cf White 1997).
8. The planton was a key-figure among the 'intermediaries'. Formally a messenger belonging to the administration of the territory, he was in practice the *factotum* of the territory, and more than that. In the words of 'Vastenakel': 'The planton was an extremely precious man. When he trusted you, he came and told you things you would not have heard anywhere else.' Examples of help which cropped up in the course of the interviews are related to various matters, including the cultivation of hemp, activities of a sorcerer, understanding of judicial decisions. 'Milnaert' with his usual sociological insight classified the planton along with the boy among the Africans who had a domestic relation with the European – in the sense that they belonged to the household (*domus*, home). 'Dauw' also told me: 'The relationship was extremely personal; there was something like a symbiosis.' As an illustration of this, 'Milnaert' referred to the planton of his first chief of territory, who used to fill the pipe of the latter.
9. A link, similar to that which 'Peletier' makes between 'custom' and 'tribe' occurred when one spoke of the 'detribalised' ('*détribalisés*') of the 'extra-customary centres' (*centres extra-coutumiers*'). In both cases, the tribe is conceived as the lieu where custom appears and receives its unity.
10. Contemporary anthropological work, which cannot be accused of lacking sensitivity to historical developments, indeed suggests that the African 'essence' remained. For instance MacGaffey argues in his book *Religion and Society in Central Africa* (1986) that the Kicongo mental equipment did not collapse under colonialism. Of course 'change' and 'continuity' are neither juxtaposed nor measurable. They make up reality and whether one or the other is emphasised depends on the perspective adopted.
11. On the use of the term '*rédaction*' in this context, see Vanderlinden (1962: esp. 233–6).
12. For an interesting exploration of the significance of this measure, see Hunt (1991).
13. For a discussion of the absence of guilt of an anthropologist towards domination, see Clifford on Griaule (1988: 75–80).

My Story

14. Without relating it to this heading, Rosaldo points to another manifestation of 'imperialist nostalgia' when he remarks : 'So-called Third World social critics (such as Fanon, Gayatri, Spivak and Edward Said) often are dismissed … [as if] only the poor and illiterate [were] truly people of color' (1989: 243). On the one-hand universal access to higher education is conceived as a desirable goal; on the other hand Western influence is conceived as entailing the loss of an essential quality.
15. It is generally agreed that the Europeans treated the évolués with great disdain, mocking their attempts to conform to European behaviour and their efforts at being integrated (Balandier 1951: 65; see also Anstey 1970; Bhabha 1984).
16. The limited survey I made among former students suggests that the Colonial University mainly attracted lower middle-class students, and a minority of upper middle-class students.
17. The original reads: '*C'est pas ça, au fond, ce que j'aimais bien, c'était l'imperium. Et ça, je l'admets. C'est pour ça que j'aimais bien les territoires de brousse.*'
18. Compare with the description provided in respect to another part of Africa by Berman and Lonsdale (1992: 239).
19. The missionaries similarly tended to hold a view which romanticised the countryside and demonised township (Markowitz 1973: 13–14). It should be noted that the cliché between country and town worked in the reverse way for the educated Africans who looked at the former (the 'traditional' world) as the world of the dupes and at the latter (the 'modern' world) as secreting civilisation (Jewsiewicki 1983: 56).
20. One exception includes the family of a friend of mine who told me his mother was so unhappy in the Congo that she entered a deep depression and stopped caring for her five children. The family came back to Belgium after one term to the regret of his now late father, who very much enjoyed his job in the Territoriale.
21. By avoiding to say 'I', 'Amory' may be seeking to objectify his personal experience (cf Tonkin 1982: 281). As for the telegraphic style, it characterises all the answers 'Amory' sent Claire Van Leeuw – and subsequently transmitted to me. It is probably best explained by the fact that he did not deem it necessary to write full sentences in a text which he did not think would go beyond the researcher(s)' eyes.
22. For a detailed study of the colonial labour policies of the French and the British in Africa, whose insights can be extended to the Belgian Congo, see Cooper (1996).
23. Thus Bertrand 'explained' the end of the riot in which he had been personally involved in the following way: 'I was in contact with Kikwit which was four hundred kilometres away and also with Leopoldville which was one thousand kilometres away and where the army was based. They sent the army and then everything stopped. People went back to their houses as soon as they saw the soldiers and the guns.' It is difficult to say that no force was involved even though it was not used in a way which resulted in casualties. Let us note that this riot admittedly took place after 4 January 1959, i.e. during the disrupted year which preceded independence.
24. For an example of such a use in the colonial period, see Quinet (1955). The metaphor was so pervasive that Young (1994) entitles the first chapter of his book on the African state 'Bula Matari and the contemporary African crisis'.
25. The same holds when 'Peletier' refers in the above quotation to 'domination', a word he uses because of the phrasing of my question. Thus he recognises the fact that the coloniser exercised domination. But in doing so, he does not attach a negative value-judgment to it.

26. Compare with Bourdieu who speaks of paternalism as enchanting and consistently denying calculation (1981: 70).
27. Kimbanguism is a religious movement of the Lower Congo, which developed out of the teachings of Simon Kimbangu in 1921. Repression by the colonial authorities, including the arrest and deportation of Kimbangu to Katanga, failed to mark the end of the movement. It finally became a recognised Church in 1957 (the Church of Jesus Christ on the Earth by the Prophet Simon Kimbangu). On the changing attitudes of the administration towards the 'sects' associated to Kimbanguism, see Raymaekers and Desroche (1983); see also MacGaffey (1992).
28. Augustin, the author of the mémoires, is *not* the interviewee to whom I gave the name of 'Vastenakel' (and who also mentioned hemp in relation to lepers) (above: 107).
29. The number of strokes of the whip legally allowed decreased through time.
30. Kirk-Green has noted the pervasiveness, in African colonial novels, of this type of clash of personalities within a hierarchical relationship (1991: 66).
31. Note the similarity of language between this passage and one quoted earlier. Here 'Peletier' talks of a '*Blanc de rien*' ('white nobody'); earlier he was talking, in reference to the territorial posted in town, of a '*Blanc entre les deux*' ('in-between White') who was not considered as a '*grand Blanc*' ('great White') (above: 150).
32. 'Milnaert' commented that the familiar tone of the dialogue was impossible to imagine in his territory where relationships between superior and subordinate, though excellent, remained formal.
33. This analysis can be applied, although in slightly different terms, to the native authorities whose prestige was also a key concern for the colonial administration.
34. Interestingly, Kennedy analyses prestige in the colonial context as an 'attempt at emotional disengagement' (1987: 154).
35. See Kennedy (1987: chapter 8) for a useful analysis of the need for segregation in the colonial situation. The analysis emphasises that fear by the Europeans of the Africans, coupled with economic reliance by the former on the latter, demanded that contact between the two groups be closely regulated, which was achieved through segregationist rules.
36. On 'degeneration', see Kennedy (1987: 173).
37. The judge Dellicour expressed the same idea: 'Prestige is absolutely necessary. It constitutes the most important force and a guarantee of security for the European isolated among the countless mass of natives.' (n.d. [1956]: 237)
38. This would be congruent with the fact that I find it impossible to classify the language the interviewees used in relation to the generation they belonged to. Of course the interviews took place thirty years after their departure from the Congo and this lapse of time could account for the homogenisation which took place in their discourse. But the fact is that their discourse is not homogeneous (as the various figures of interviewees which appear in this book indicate).

7: Their Response

*T*he underlying argument of the previous chapter is that former territorials are mistaken in not seeing, or at least not stressing, the role played by force in colonial relationships. This argument arises from my reading of the material; but what would the interviewees' own analysis of colonialism be? The present chapter indirectly addresses this question.

I had originally conceived of this chapter as a counterpoint to the previous one. My idea was to discuss former territorials' interpretations of the colonial experience after having presented mine. I quickly realised, however, that this was not feasible. How could I completely remove myself from the analysis I was about to provide? I could not. It was not possible for me to think and write like my informants, or even the majority of them, or just one of them. One solution, I thought, was to ask 'Milnaert' to write the chapter that I had in mind, but could not write. Not surprisingly, he did not take up the barely disguised invitation I made to this effect. He had always indicated that he was not interested in engaging in a public debate and preferred to think for himself, privately. Although he did not comment on this, the deal I was offering him was inequitable anyway: to counterbalance the six chapters I had written, I was granting him the space of one chapter. Had he been ready to accept this imbalance, it probably would not have been possible for him to fit into the structure *I* had given to the text anyway.

He nonetheless carefully read the first chapters I had written, and sent me three hours of taped comments. Some passages concerned matters of detail which helped me to correct the draft of my thesis; others consisted of general criticisms. He said the lens I had adopted was inappropriate, the focus wrong. In his opinion, the forest was indiscernable even if the trees were recognisable. As I listened to the tapes and returned to his comments on other texts I had written, I started to see that he had been expressing the same ideas over and over again, in various forms which I had failed to relate to one another. His remarks derived from a coherent system of thought. It is this system of thought that I try to put across in this chapter, for although I cannot write for 'Milneart', I can listen to him and articulate his point of view to the reader.

Put in a nutshell, his argument is that entrenched prejudices and naive ethics have led me to make a simplistic discourse from complex actions. Most if not all of his territorial colleagues would agree. This is why I feel entitled to refer to their response to my work, rather than that of 'Milnaert' specifically, in the title of the chapter.

Resorting to inadequate concepts: A rather common peculiarity

> '[In England], you probably could not feel at ease in such and such a bar, amongst such and such a group. And it is like that everywhere'
> ('Milnaert').

This sentence means in effect that no-one can ever be completely immersed in a group. It encapsulates one aspect of a two-fold objection which 'Milneart' levies against my use of the term 'immersion' in the last chapter. The second aspect of his objection is that moments of true communication happen everywhere; they happened in the colonial situation too. These two points deserve to be discussed, and I shall do this below. For the moment, I shall note that they are part of a general criticism 'Milnaert' levels at my work, namely, that I have failed to grasp what I would be tempted to call the banality of the colonial situation if it was not inappropriately reminiscent of Hannah Arendt's study of Eichmann's trial (1964). Subtitled *A Report on the Banality of Evil,* Arendt's study suggests that Eichmann, representing for many the very incarnation of evil, was in fact a very banal human being. 'Milnaert''s point, however, is not about the banality of evil, but about the banality of colonialism. In his tapes, he repeatedly points out that I have presented rather common events and attitudes as if they were peculiar to the colonial situation, which they were not. This is an important point, and my conclusion to this section demonstrates that I believe it deserves to be taken on board.

Let me first clarify the general feature I think 'Milnaert' is trying to capture by reviewing a series of comments he has made about my text. I have spoken of loopholes in the Territoriale's system of internal checks and balances, but I have not observed that no administrative system ever manages to fill all possible loopholes. I seem to have been surprised to hear about the existence of caisses noires, but 'adjusting' balance-sheets is a widespread practice among private companies and possibly public bodies. I have spoken of the pressures under which the territorial worked in the Congo, but have failed to compare them with those to which, say, a burgermaster is subjected in Belgium. I have interpreted the toleration of a dance by 'Bertrand' as the expression of blatant domination, but have not taken into consideration that any public social event in Belgium also requires administrative authorisation. Examples could be multiplied. I shall not provide more, however, for I am less interested in discussing the validity of each analogy 'Milnaert' is proposing than in highlighting how this particular train of thought gets articulated.

My impression[1] is that 'Milnaert' has misinterpreted the reason which has led me not to draw the attention of the reader to the similarities which exist between colonial and metropolitan practices.[2] This appears clearly when he castigates me for having noted the absence of women in the Territoriale. He exclaims: 'There were no women in the Territoriale, that's true. But was there any woman in the army or in the administration at the same period in Belgium? Not only do the poor territorials have to be blamed for the sins of Leopold II, but they should also have been in the vanguard of a social movement which only started to develop in the 1970s!' In this instance, my aim was certainly not to pillory colonialism for female exclusion within the territorial service, although the outburst transpiring from the quoted passage indicates that 'Milnaert' imputed to me such an intention. Difficulties in communication occur both ways: I may have misunderstood the former territorials, but they also misunderstood me; we both read the other in accordance with our own framework of reference.

It may not be going too far to say that 'Milnaert' tends to read the book as an unabated attack on the territorials in particular and colonialism in general. This, of course, was not exactly my aim. But one can appreciate why 'Milnaert' should reach such a conclusion. Once he began detecting in my text critical comments about colonialism which he found unjustified, he integrated in his reading the fact that my stance was an anti-colonial one, thus expecting more of these unwarranted comments and interpreting all my words in this light.

My failure to note the banality of the colonial situation became but one factor which reinforced his suspicion that I was singling out colonialism for negative appraisal. For him, my use of the concept of 'immersion' illustrates this process particularly well. In the last chapter, I have criticised the territorials for not being immersed among the Africans. 'Milnaert' notes that I have done so without analysing the concept I was using. He questions the meaning of the term through a series of examples. Thus he mentions De Gaulle who liked to 'mix' in French crowds and Giscard d'Estaing who invited himself into middle-class homes, and asks: 'Were these Presidents immersed among the French population?', a question with an obvious answer.[3] He raises a similar question in regard to the feudal lord of the Middle Ages: 'Was he immersed among his subjects – or was he not?' Leaving political figures aside, he turns to the position of the anthropologist, such as Vansina who I had heard he had slept in a tree. 'Milnaert' asks: 'Was Vansina immersed in the village because he lived and ate with the Africans?' He answers: 'Not any more than anyone else', and continues:

> A thick veil of strategies and mental structures separated Vansina from the Black who hosted him and with whom he lived. He was there to get to know something about the native society. But the Black had similar claims towards him, for he was a strange White who did not fit the usual model of 'the White'. The fact that he lived there probably made it possible for Vansina to get information on local life, but the fact that he slept in the middle of the village, that he was not separated from it, does not add anything to what you name immersion.

If 'Milnaert' is right, perhaps I can be accused of having been influenced too much by classical writings in anthropology. Powdermaker opens the preface of her book *Stranger and Friend* as follows: 'To understand a strange society, the anthropologist has traditionally *immersed* himself in it, learning, as far as possible, to think, see, feel, and sometimes act as a member of its culture and at the same time as a trained anthropologist from another culture' (1966: 9, emphasis added; but for a critique see Crick 1982: 21). The process of immersion which is referred to concerns the move from a familiar to a foreign environment, where one abandons the former and 'completely' lives in the latter.[4] But 'Milnaert' senses that I have something else in mind when I refer to the concept. My aim is to stress the circumscribed nature of the relationships which existed between the territorials and the Africans.

'Milnaert' contends that, as far as depth of relationship is concerned, my position is no different from that of the territorials. He remarks:

Let us take you as an example. You reside in England. Can one say that you are immersed amongst the English? No, you select a restricted number of people with whom you are more 'intimate' (I do not like the word) than with others. These are persons who touch you in one way or the other, for example professionally. You probably could not feel at ease in such and such a bar, amongst such and such a group. And it is like that everywhere. When you come to my house for an interview, are you immersed? There remains between us a distance [an enormous distance].

(I have put the last three words in square brackets because 'Milnaert' underlined the qualification 'enormous' and put a question mark underneath it when he read the first draft of this chapter).

My tendency to speak of immersion as a process which allows two or more individuals to fuse in their feelings and thoughts irritates 'Milnaert'. In the concluding remarks of the relevant section (above: 142), I noted that human relationships are by nature limited. But I did not *emphasise* that I was referring to a general phenomenon.

More importantly, I used a model of relationships which 'Milnaert' finds naive: neither empirically valid nor desirable as an ideal. This is consonant with his observation that I do not escape from the phenomenon I am criticising: I fail to be immersed both in my daily contacts and when I endorse the role of the anthropologist and meet even the informant with whom I have become the closest. 'Milnaert' does not blame me for this, for a situation of perfect immersion is unattainable, whether by me, Vansina, or anyone else. What he objects to is that I give the impression that my description is peculiar to the colonial situation, when it applies to the full spectrum of human relationships. He has a second objection to my analysis, which is that I deny that territorials entered into contact, and indeed established contacts of quality, with the Africans. I shall come to this aspect after a detour through a comment involving the use of the term immersion by a political scientist.

Dominique Darbon, whose work focuses on French Africa, also uses the term 'immersion' in reference to colonial administrators, but he arrives at a conclusion contrary to mine. He writes: '[…] for these European officers, in practice the State […] meant […] the *immersion* of isolated and foreign individuals in the middle of vast and socialised territories of which they had to learn, accept and respect the governing management rules if they were not to be thoroughly marginalised' (1990a: 40, my emphasis). In his article, Darbon hammers home the idea that colonial officers had to negotiate with the Africans for their activity to be successful. His concept of immersion is thus related to practical knowledge and efficiency (and not very far removed from that used by Powdermaker in the passage quoted above). He places a similar emphasis in his review of a colonial officer's memoirs (Clauzel 1989). There he speaks of a colonial administration 'able to adapt to the societies it encountered', and of commanders (the French colonial officers were called '*commandants*') and district officers who could not conceive of an 'administration which would have existed outside the sociological local reality' (1990b: 149). No doubt he would extend his remark to the Belgian territorials, for he is concerned with the main characteristics of administration throughout colonial Africa.

It is all the more remarkable that Darbon chooses to use the term 'immersion' and to speak of 'links' between the colonial administrators and the African population (1990a: 41) in that he is a regular contributor to *Politique Africaine*, a journal which prides itself on adopting a bottom-up approach and could probably be broadly characterised as holding leftist views. He could have been expected to emphasise distance and power. To understand Darbon's unlikely praise of the colonial administrations, one needs to take into account the aim which he pursues in the article I have quoted. His aim is to denounce the inadequacies of the present African administrations by contrasting them with their predecessors.[5] Thus he forcibly argues that members of present African administrations are cut off from the societies which they are supposed to serve in a way that was not imaginable in the colonial era. The personnel which has taken over the 'colonial carcass', as he calls it, remains aloof from the civil societies: it does not negotiate, let alone live with them. Representing the 'divine surprise' of the state, the administration nevertheless claims and receives legitimacy, including international recognition (ibid.: 44), for it is perceived as a vehicle of civilisation, modernity and development (ibid: 37). It is nothing more, however, than the embodiment of a 'predatory state', an expression which gives its title to Darbon's article.

In comparison to the present state of affairs, one can no doubt say that the French commanders and their Belgian counterparts were immersed. Darbon's argument thus highlights that 'immersion' is a relative concept. If I disputed its relevance in relation to the territorial experience, it is because I was implicitly *comparing* the latter experience with one which could have taken place in a world founded on different premisses. In doing so, I did not wish to imply that the territorials had no contact with the Africans. Nevertheless, I doubted the quality of these contacts.

It annoyed 'Milnaert' that I should blame the territorials for not having achieved an immersion which he felt I conceptualised in an utopic way. It annoyed him even more that I refused to grant them the experience of having met African fellow-men. He explained:

> Of course, our contacts with the Blacks were professional ones. Whether with those you call auxiliaries or with ordinary Blacks in villages, these contacts were not intimate ones. We were neither 'immersed' nor 'drowned'. We were ourselves, and they were themselves. But there was a true contact; and to suggest the contrary is to go beyond what your material says. At least it is to go beyond what *we* felt.

In this passage, 'Milnaert' denies that a concept of immersion implicitly referring to an ideal of fusion between human beings would be analytically helpful: the territorials were themselves, and so were the Africans.[6] He also states that true contacts existed between the territorials and the Africans. I am ready to accept that 'Milnaert''s statement reflects his experience, and that it might have been wiser to give a bigger place to this aspect of experience in the book. I find problematic, however, his phrasing in the plural form ('we' instead of 'I'), which suggests that all territorials, or at least the great majority, shared in this experience.[7] I doubt that a respectful attitude towards the Africans was the rule.[8] The diversity of experiences must be acknowledged. It is, however, easily left aside – both by 'Milnaert' who speaks of 'we' and by me who concentrates on the attitudes which I expect and have learned to make sense of.

'Milnaert' returned to the phrase 'moments of grace' which Tancré-Van Leeuw had used to describe the time a territorial spent with Africans around a fire at night (above: 134) to explain:

> There were moments – it happened often at night – when all strategies and obstacles were lifted. Then the only thing which remained was men talking to each other. Vansina enjoyed such moments, but so did your informants, although perhaps less frequently. In these moments, there were no more Blacks and no more Whites, no ethnologist and no ethnologised,[9] no administrator and no administered. There were men in contact with each other. I mean, there was a pure contact between them. This is what Tancré-Van Leeuw calls a state of 'grace': functions and obligations do not matter; we are there as two men on earth. Such a state is not false, it is true.

What can the anthropologist of the memory of colonialism add to this? She could persist in saying that the colonial situation did not favour the meeting of men or that power relationships nevertheless underlay such meeting. This interpretation is arguably suggested by the terms of 'Milnaert', who speaks of 'moments of grace', taking place in the obscurity of the night, allowing the 'lifting' of strategy, obstacles and roles, conducive of 'true purity' in the meeting of 'simple' men who talk to each other. The depicted atmosphere is one which is specific and privileged, one could almost say spiritual. But my guess is that 'Milnaert' wishes to hint at a more general phenomenon. Let us recall his assertion that 'race' was forgotten on both sides when territorials and Africans were involved in the discussion of problems of construction, agriculture, or customs (above: 90). When he read the draft of this chapter, he remarked that the moments he had in mind in the passage just quoted occurred also during the day. Because of this, rather than pursuing an analysis of domination, I find it more appropriate to *listen* to 'Milnaert' and to accept that moments of grace did exist, which had nothing to do with an ill-defined notion of immersion.

Leaving out the texture of life: A rigid picture

> 'He made men out of them, men like we see living everyday'
> ('Milnaert').

More than once in his comments, 'Milnaert' implicitly criticises me for leaving out the empirical context of the facts I am reporting. The result, in his view, is that my descriptions suffer from a rigidity. For example, he regrets the absence in my work of the other Europeans (settlers and traders, missionaries, other members of the administration …), for this prevents me from conveying how life evolved in a small, white, community. He similarly feels that my presentation of the Territoriale, admittedly more technical in the originial thesis than in chapter 2 of the present book, is unduly rigid. To quote him:

> You give the impression that the territorial activity was wholly turned towards administrative and judicial matters, that our work was thoroughly organised by law – cf your discussion on the councils of chiefdom, the control of native tribunals, the activity of the judge of police. In fact, the territorial spent very little time on these things, even though he had to do them. He mainly went to check the road work, asked where the pit-sawyers were and went to visit them, took care of hygiene matters in the villages, and whatever else … – in other words, a lot of very concrete, as opposed to legalistic, tasks.

'Milnaert' seems to be saying two things in this passage. On one hand, he points out that the territorials were involved in a range of activities which were not necessarily legally oriented. On the other, he may wish to direct attention to the fact that the territorial activity took place in a social context and required social interaction; the territorial could not fulfil his functions simply by following the letter of the law.

When he complains about rigidity in my work, I take him to refer to a lack of sensitivity on my part towards the way relationships were established in the colony. This comes out clearly in his criticism of the way I talk about the Africans. He contends that I give them a purely passive role: 'For you, the African seems to be the passive subject of all the actions by the European. In the colonial situation, however, there is a symbiosis. Each actor exists on the horizon of the every-day presence of the other, influencing him, simultaneously organising and dismantling him. Behaviours are always correlative; you do not stress this point enough.'[10] His comments on my discussion of prestige illustrate further what he means. He takes exception to the idea that the image of the all-powerful/knowledgeable European benefited newcomers. He corrects my assertion by saying that the Africans did not grant authority to anyone straight away. They always tested a newcomer, especially if he was young, and they even had a word for this testing – '*ku-pima*'; the Africans first *pimaient* ('peemed') the young European. Only after having observed and evaluated his reactions in various situations, did they grant him authority – if they thought he deserved it. In 'Milnaert''s opinion, my analysis wrongly suggests an automatic attribution of prestige by the Africans to the Europeans.

In his eyes, no one has better captured the idea of the prestige of the white man than Pierre Ryckmans when he recalled a conversation with two Africans who belonged to a pastoral group. Ryckmans had told these men that, for them, his horn-less horse probably was nothing but a contemptible animal. Although the horse was indeed without horns, his interlocutors replied, had it had some they would have been formidable, for the horse was the animal of the white man.[11] I suppose it is because prestige appears to have nothing to do with force, coercion and violence in this story (but is that really so?) that 'Milnaert' takes the dialogue to embody its very essence. Of course, in his opinion, I am wrong to persist in inserting question marks. Although he accepts that my text touches on certain attitudes and practices which he encountered, he denounces 'an abusive touch' on my part. In accordance with what is a leitmotiv in his comments, he denounces the fact that 'one does not see the African in [my] discussion of the notion of prestige'. He identifies the same defect when I attribute the institutionalisation of monogamous marriage exclusively to the action of the missionaries. He urges me to see that the African woman played an active part in this process: she envied the model of the European household and sought to realise it for herself, even to impose it on her husband. In other words, the evolution of monogamous marriage was not unilateral. The same is true of all the other transformations which took place in the colony: the Africans were tempted by the apparent facilities which the European civilisation brought, and 'they threw themselves at them'.

'Milnaert' posits that my obsession with the idea of a 'dominating strategy' prevents me from seeing the relational aspect of the colonial situation.[12] His analysis echoes the conclusion by Beidelman to the monograph *Colonial Evangelism*. To quote it:

> It is easy to criticize colonial rule in terms of exploitation, injustice, and ethnocentrism, such accounts are common and have led to cheap and easy judgments. Rather than this, what is required is analyzis and review that allow us to perceive the colonial world as a system, both in terms of its thoughts and values and in terms of the ways it was organized. We must see colonial rulers as acted upon by those they attempted to rule, quite as much as the reverse and more conventional approach (1982: 214–15).[13]

'Milnaert' of course does not say that I never talk about the Africans, but that I talk about them as passive actors. In a sense, it is also what he tells me I am doing with the territorials. At least, his opinion is that I present them as 'mechanical beings'. What he means by this is best understood by his referring me to a book about the early period of Islam entitled *La grande discorde* (Djait 1989). The subject of this book is the third khalifat, which marked the beginning of the rebellions and the development of various orthodox and heretical movements within Islam. Until Hichem Djait's book, this extremely important period in the development of Islam had been studied by Arab theologians who viewed it, so 'Milnaert' tells me, through the lens of the particular doctrine they were following. As a result, they described the actors involved in terms of stereotyped roles and produced a rigid image. By contrast, Braudel's student Djait manages to go beyond this traditional vision constructed around ideologies and allows for a new understanding of the period to emerge. In 'Milnaert''s words:

> Djait has got rid of the chains which constrained all these rigid figures. He made men out of them, men like those we meet everyday. They are cruel and

compassionate, brave and cowardly, intelligent and stupid. All of a sudden, the scene becomes animated, and convincing. I am not saying that Djait has reached the historical truth, but he allows these figures to become men again. And through him it is as if one could have a discussion with them.

This is the last comment I found on 'Milnaert''s tapes. The message is implicit, but clear: the figures in my text are not men in flesh, with feelings and contradictions. I have taken out their 'commonality' and turned them into mere stereotypes. Judgments of course permeate stereotypes, and judgment is what 'Milnaert' discerns underlying my whole work.

Inventing screens: A prejudiced approach

'The corpse is within you like a preconception that you cannot cast out' ('Milnaert').

According to 'Milnaert', a major problem with my work revolves around my entrenched prejudices towards colonialism. In his comments on my article about the whip, he puts this idea across by comparing me to a policeman who is vainly searching for a corpse in a closet. To quote the letter in which the comparison appears: 'Your expressions sadden me [...] You expect screen-like answers to your questions, but the answers are clear. You are like a policeman who acts upon his intuition, which he thinks infallible. He opens a cupboard sure that he will find a corpse. But there is no corpse. Or, rather, the corpse is within you like a preconception that you cannot cast out'. The message is plain: like the policeman who wrongly supposes a crime has been committed, I was determined to discover the deadly crimes of colonialism, even though none had been committed. The culprit is my biased perspective which prevents me from seeing this (to 'Milneart') evident fact.

Over and over again, 'Milnaert' complained that I could not get rid of 'preconceived ideas which made it impossible for [me] to see things as they were', to see that 'the answers are clear', to return to the expression he uses in the passage above. For example, he found the way I reported my natural reactions to the interviews astonishing. To him the jubilation I felt at hearing stories involving illegalities and/or arbitrariness demonstrated that I was blind to the reality I was attempting to discover. He commented: '[You write:] "I got it." It is a pity to see a sentence like this. And I recognise the feeling from other pieces of work you have written. Such a feeling stands in the way of any understanding, makes it impossible to understand.' 'Milnaert' was surprised that I could feel jubilation. How could this be? Or rather what did it say about my preconceptions?!

He saw these occurring through much of my writing, for example when I advanced the 'gratuitious' idea that imperialist interest may have demanded keeping the native backward (above: 148), when I suggested 'without any foundation' that a strike could have been broken by force (above: 154), or when I remarked that the expression 'Louis-box' could have had a racist overtone (above: 127). What he said about this last example is worth quoting, for his words again express the view that I have abandoned a clear reality for spurious interpretations:

> The expression 'Louis-box' covers something which is more or less objective. It is wrong to suggest that a racist prejudice underlay it. Excellent workers were in heavy demand, and we were happy to have someone who knew his job. This is *not* to say that they were doing the same job as Belgian cabinet-makers. In fact, the tools for this did not exist in the Congo. Congolese cabinet-makers had a hammer, some nails, a saw; they did not have electrical power tools, a lathe to turn the wood, etc. What I find shocking is that you have to say that a racist interpretation springs to mind. Why should it 'spring to mind' [as I wrote in the thesis]? This shows the idea is absolutely fixed in your head.

Further examples could be added, which all explain why 'Milnaert' finds that my work is replete with 'small indications that [I] see things from a particular position, that of a perch.'

He could understand why my vision should be so directed. At one stage, he even told me: 'If I was to [pursue] today a study similar to yours without the benefit of my Congolese experience, I think I would think like you because everyone more or less thinks like this in 1992' – which is the year Milnaert sent me his comments. This nevertheless did not absolve me from retaining my faulty perspective and he immediately continued: 'You do not insist enough on the fact that you are speaking in 1992 about events, opinions and mentalities which have nothing to do with the ideas you hold today.'

This theme is common to the other interviewees, who repeatedly warned me against the danger of failing to analyse and understand the material I collected in the context of its time. 'Milnaert' had specifically alluded to this danger on previous occasions. For instance, he had asked, having read my analysis of the answers to the written questionnaire:

'Have you considered the peculiar situation of the researcher?' To which he had answered:

> She lives in a world which has (partially) 'resolved' the colonial question. A world which on the whole qualifies colonialism as a sin (cf Lévi-Strauss). A world which enjoys security and therefore gets irritated with any military burden. A world which is incredibly rich, sufficiently affluent to elimininate below-subsistence levels (years of full employment); sufficiently scientifically developed to consider itself capable of resolving any problem in the future. A world whose coherence is not seen to derive from groups, but which encourages its dispersion in a multitude of dust-like individuals so autonomous that they come to resent any constraining factor. A world where 'power' and discipline are considered to be 'constraints'.

It is difficult not to consider the optimistic statements about security, economic wealth and scientific confidence, to be out-of-date today. However, to the extent that they apply to the 1960s, they are relevant to the way my generation learned to see the world. The handling and perception of disciplinary and coercive practices, especially in education, have also most certainly changed in the past few decades. 'Milnaert' has a point when he reminds me that the world which shaped me is not the one which moulded him.

However, he would not consider the generation gap to be the most important factor in explaining our different angles. He is perfectly aware that I am only following the view of others, many of whom belong to *his* generation. More importantly, he recognises that my tendency to analyse the material in terms of 'meta-logical' systems, and particularly of a relationship between dominator and dominated, has a long history. In his words: 'You have famous predecessors: Hegel (master and slave relationship); Heidegger (the annihilation of man); Marx (the proletariat); Saint Anselme (the "argument").' He continues: 'If I may say so, what you (and all of them) lack is to have had to act in the concrete world. Such an experience would have led you to realise that words are the meshes of a net we throw over things to "com-prehend" them. The meshes are too wide, and we only get the big fish.' I shall return in the next section to my presumed lack of experience which, in 'Milnaert''s view, is largely responsible for my inability to grasp the world. For the moment, I shall continue with his idea that words and concepts only allow us to capture 'big fish'.

Let me link it to a statement he had made in reply to my article on the whip, i.e. two years before he sent the letter from which I have extracted the above quotation (which was dated March 1993). Before I analyse the statement in question, I shall briefly explain what my article (Dembour 1992b) was about. Its starting point was a series of pictures entitled '*Colonie belge*' which all depict an African soldier or policeman giving strokes of the whip to an African prisoner under the supervision of a territorial. They have mainly been painted by Tshibumba Kanda-Matula, but occasionally by other Zairian painters belonging to the same school.[14] It is not uncommon to find them reproduced in the academic literature on the Congo, often without any accompanying comments, as if the reproduced picture spoke for itself. Presumably it is meant to represent the brutality and oppression of the colonial system. My article sought to make the point that it is too easy to reduce the reality to one image, even if this image cannot simply be said to be false. My contention was that the reproductions implicitly make a distinction between the (past) colonial officer and the (contemporary) scholar, but that links must be established between past and present practices. Moreover, I argued that the form and implications of the violence suggested by the picture could not be taken for granted. 'Milnaert' obviously did not think I had achieved my goal. He wrote on receipt of the draft of the article: 'It is rather disheartening to see our Congolese adventure summed up in this rather easy and demagogical image. Our agricultural project, for example, could not be illustrated in the same way.' When he uses the term 'image', he obviously refers to my article rather than just the picture by Tshibumba. As far as he is concerned, I have not managed to provide a balanced argument.

'Milnaert' ended his five-page letter with the following words: 'I see that I have written a lot. I have never spoken about flogging so much! I hope it is useful to you.' Perhaps this was a way of concluding on a light, humorous and engaging tone. But the second sentence may also contain an underlying message: the whip was not and should not be a central preoccupation. More important things deserve to be discussed, including the agricultural project mentioned earlier. If only I had adopted an appropriate focus for my research, 'Milnaert' may think, the data I would have come across would have taken care of my prejudices.[15]

But my prejudices were entrenched and I paid little attention to the economic achievements of the Belgian colonial administration. I suspect that most if not all former territorials find my near-silence in this regard most objectionable. After all, the Congo was a 'model colony' (cf Stengers 1989: 144; Vellut 1980: 265). The infrastructure which had been developed by the time of independence was an object of pride (cf the *Livre Blanc* 1962 and 1963, especially I: 2; Brausch 1961, chapter 1; Cornevin 1966: 313). As was repeatedly asserted, the Congo enjoyed in

1960 the best medical infrastructure in the whole of Africa, the highest percentage of children in primary education, and an extremely high degree of industrial development (Brausch 1961: 8, 11 and 1). In view of these uncontested figures, former territorials cannot understand why their accomplishments and/or colonialism (for the two go together) have subsequently been denigrated. As an informant remarked in a passage which I have already quoted: 'Twenty years ago, what we had achieved in the Congo was said to be astounding, whether with regard to education, health, transport, the elimination of famine ... Now [it is said that] we have done no good whatsoever; even health care is deemed to have been more detrimental than beneficial' (Dembour 1991b: 102).[16]

One question of my written questionnaire concerned the positive aspects of the territorial work. The most common answer alluded to the construction aspect of this work. Other elements were mentioned, for example the high level of autonomy the territorials enjoyed, the diversity of functions they fulfilled, the number of responsibilities they received even at a young age, the pleasure they derived from diverse and numerous human contacts. These items, however, ran a poor second compared to the sentiment of participating in a project of development, which was by far the most frequently mentioned (Dembour 1991b: 126). This feeling arose through the completion of the construction, kilometre by kilometre, of appropriate road networks; the careful supervision, from one season to the next, of the progress of agricultural work and experimenting with new techniques; the construction of one more school or dispensary to assist missionaries and doctors in their educational and health efforts, and so forth.[17] And now the former territorials see the core of their work, what really made it worthwhile, its very concrete achievements, completely denigrated. It hurts them.

Their bitterness is aggravated by having to watch the country in which they worked sinking ever deeper and deeper in more abject misery.[18] Hardly any trace remains of their achievements on the ground. Roads have been destroyed, transport is a problem, food cannot be obtained, corruption is rife, insecurity high. A former territorial stated in 1989: '[I] am proud [to have been a territorial], even if I fear that it did not help in any way: Zaire is returning to wilderness. The efforts of the territorials, as well as the doctors, agronomists, and others, seem to have come to nothing – unless there is another colonisation, which is unthinkable' (ibid: 95).

Another colonisation is indeed unthinkable; although some Zairians seem to have hoped for something like it to happen, which would recreate the dream-like feeling of security increasingly associated with the colonial period (cf De Boeck 1998: 33). For example, disappointment was expressed in February 1993 when the Belgian paracommandos left Zaire in the middle of a crisis between the then President Mobutu and Prime Minister Tshisekedi.[19] The Zairian population, a Belgian journalist observed, had expected wonders from the paracommandos' presence, not only as far as keeping order was concerned, but also in terms of economic reconstruction – a task which obviously fell outside the military remit (de Bellefroid, *La Libre Belgique*, 20–21 February 1993). A few days later, the same journalist quoted a Zairian politician, Albert M'Peti, who took the view that the catastrophic situation prevailing in Zaire created a moral duty of intervention on the part of Belgium towards its former colony:

> The population in Kinshasa [...] will soon begin to starve to death. As far as public health is concerned, Zairians are facing the return of serious endemic diseases: sleeping sickness, malaria, tuberculosis, cholera; without even mentioning AIDS. On the economic side, the whole system has collapsed; nothing remains of the industrial, transport and commercial infrastructures which existed at the time of independence and made most other African countries envious. Add to this the destruction of the education system: the universities have been closed for three years, primary and secondary schools are open only sporadically (*La Libre Belgique*, 24 February 1993).

M'Peti was asking: 'Confronted with such chaos, must our Belgian friends wait for images like Somalia to intervene?' (ibid.).[20] The nature and effect of foreign interventions in Somalia and other parts of the world raise questions beyond the scope of this study (but see Lewis 1993). My reason for quoting M'Peti's call is the implicit reference it contains to the model colony where 'things worked'.[21]

The contributor to *Politique Africaine* we encountered above echoes the nostalgia which transpires from M'Peti's words. As we have seen, Darbon praises the colonial administrators for having been immersed in the African societies in which they worked. He also commends their work for having been concrete and unassuming. In his review of Clauzel's memoirs, he writes that one interest of the book is that 'it presents a colonial administration which is unassuming (through acting in small projects of development)' (1990b: 149). He adds: 'University graduates, who are today's administrators, would have much to learn from the commanders and the district officers of the colonial period' (ibid). What are we to make of such a statement? Before answering this crucial question, I would like to examine Darbon's comments more fully.

The two characteristics of the colonial administration Darbon identifies presumably go hand in hand: it is because the administration carried out its action through small projects that it had no reason for vanity. In all likelihood Darbon would extend his comments to the former territorials. The territorials would certainly agree that their action proceeded through the completion of small projects which together added up to something bigger than their simple addition. But was the administration unassuming? Its former members can hardly be said to be modest. If anything, what they express is pride, so much so that when I devised my written questionnaire, I asked my respondents whether they were proud to have been a territorial as a warming-up device before turning to what I considered sensitive topics. I expected the answers to this question to be positive, which they were. Out of twenty respondents, sixteen said 'yes'. A seventeenth answered 'a little'; another noted that he mostly remembered his inadequacies. The last two (one of them 'Milnaert') answered that 'pride' was not a term which appropriately described their feelings.

The interviewees, however, do not necessarily all refer to the same thing when they say that they are proud. The pride of some may well be 'self-inflation', to return to the expression Ryckmans used and associated with the 'dangerous force' the territorials enjoyed (above: 35–6). 'Ransquin', who did not want to leave the bush because 'there, [he] was chief of territory', told me that indeed he was proud. He immediately added: 'A handful of territorials controlled the whole Congo' (Dembour 1991b: 66). This elaboration makes it clear that his pride rested on a feeling of competence and importance. For most territorials, however, pride could simply have represented the translation of the exhilaration they felt at having done a useful job, involving responsibilities and self-fulfilment. Still for others, it may have been nothing more than a psychological mechanism to defend themselves, today, against the relentless attack to which colonialism is regularly subjected. 'd'Ave et d'Ove' who tells me he is now opposed to the very idea of 'colonising' also said he was proud to have been a territorial. This statement may need to be understood in relation to the hostility he feels around him, which would explain why he wishes to emphasise the value of the work accomplished by the territorials.[22]

In conclusion, there is no necessary incompatibility between the lack of vanity of the colonial administration identified by Darbon and the pride repeatedly expressed by the territorials. The call for contemporary Africans to learn the lessons of their predecessors is disturbing for another reason, however. Darbon speaks in his review of the structure of domination pertaining to the colonial situation, but he does not seem to see that it is what actually made the work of the colonial administration possible. In other words, he misses the crucial point, discussed in the previous chapter, that prestige and distance were indispensable elements of the colonial machinery and that what colonial administrators, thanks to these 'tools', could achieve then, is out of reach today.[23] The question which must be asked is the following: did or does the end, namely 'development', justify the means, namely the colonial features including prestige? Darbon does not raise it. 'Milnaert', for his part, finds it neither pertinent at an individual level nor worth asking at a general one. On one hand, he argues that territorials who came like him into the service after the Second World War were involved in an on-going project. Wishing that colonisation had not begun was never an option for them (and became less and less so as they came to depend on colonialism for their livelihood). On the other hand, he notes that the question supposes the existence of a dichotomy between Good and Evil which, in his opinion, is contradicted by all practices and, hence, vain-glorious. My ethics, he would argue, catch only 'big fish'. As such, they are naive and simplistic. Why he should come to such a conclusion is the subject of the next section.

Lacking experience: An action reduced to a discourse

> 'Have you taken the measure of what an action […] requires?'
> ('Milneart) .

In the introduction to chapter 6, I spoke of a dialogue in which the interviewees and I would react to each other and discuss the pros and cons of the obligation placed on the Africans to cultivate. 'Milnaert' criticised my dichotomous presentation and observed: 'There is only one reality. It encompasses beneficial elements and others which are open to criticisms. One aspect is not possible without the other. We territorials did not have two options, one angelical, the other diabolical. We were confronted with a fact, a single fact, and when we decided to act, we knew we were acting in both a good and a bad way.' Throughout our long encounter 'Milnaert' had hammered home this idea that any action encompasses positive and negative moral elements. I had failed to understand, however, how central this idea was to his thought until I put together and logically organised his comments under a number of headings. Before probing its significance, I shall quote a number of passages which express related ideas.

Having read my presentation of the answers to the written questionnaire, 'Milnaert' had asked me: 'Have you taken the measure of what any action, any determination to modify the environment, to overturn the obstacles, requires? Speculating and thinking will not help you any longer; one needs to overcome the opposition, the unknown, the unexpected ... and of course, this gives you dirty hands! Your analysis does not bring out these ethics of action.' Later, in regard to my article on the whip, he explained how authority worked in practice. He did this by drawing on his personal experience after his return from the Congo to Belgium:

> I worked in Belgium for an American company. The Director never took a decision without having assembled us, having *pleaded* for his project, asked for our reactions, opinions and objections. The meetings were animated, often quarrelsome. Then he took his decision: bang! 'The discussion is over; it goes without saying that however opposed you are to my project, you do everything possible to realise it (otherwise ...).' I have never felt nor minded the 'domination' of this director whom, incidentally, I have always admired and supported. Why? Because chance had resulted in this man having been designated to lead the group and I admired his achievements, I trusted him [...].
>
> I have experienced numerous situations of command and I have always encountered the same scheme. Hegel would say that, for any master, there is a 'slave'. But this is because he speaks in terms of status. One could say: for each action carried through, there is (a) a group (b) which is led.

Finally I shall repeat a remark which he inserted in one of his last letters (and which I have quoted in a more extensive form above): 'If I may say so, what you [...] lack is to have had to act in the concrete world.'

To summarise the quotations in the reverse order to that in which I have cited them, 'Milnaert' argues that perhaps I do not realise what acting in the world entails; that a leader is necessary for an action to be successful or, to phrase it differently, have 'direction'; that taking a course of action requires stopping to think and taking risks; that an action simultaneously contains positive and negative aspects. The string of quotations thus express a series of related points. 'Milnaert' is saying that action, which requires the exercise of leadership and authority, never allows one to be completely 'clean'. He adds that this process is universal (thus returning to the theme, previously discussed, of the banality of the colonial situation). He further suggests that my lack of experience (my ivory-tower position) is responsible for my lack of understanding of the territorial world.

These ideas illuminate 'Milnaert''s following comment on my work: 'The territorials are reduced to their own discourse, while in fact discourse is not what they are made for, action is. They are men of action.' I had first understood this remark literally to mean that men trained to act should not be judged on their words; I thought it could refer to the absence of emphasis I reserved in my work for the material achievements of the territorials in the Congo. In the light of the quotations above, however, it is clear that the statement addresses the very foundations of the distinction between 'discourse' and 'action'.

'Milnaert' has urged me time and again to abandon my fascination for grand words and to study the ordinary character of colonial practice instead: 'If I could suggest something, it would be never to use spellbinding grand words. Without the writer even noticing it, they are a vector of deformation and ideology; they hide the reality which is much more "ordinary".' The term 'ordinary' does not merely designate the 'banality' of the colonial situation. Rather it refers to a vision of reality taking place at ground (as opposed to abstract) level, thereby echoing his idea that reality is not made up of big fish – the only things which grand words capture. 'Milnaert' insists that one must think in concrete terms. This, of course, involves an effort in precision, for it is the details of a particular situation which allow one to understand it – and 'Milnaert' indeed excels at paying attention to the significance of the minute details of a situation. But it also involves a particular cast of mind, as an example will show.

In the article on the whip, I noted that the young territorials who arrived from a country where corporal punishment was not practised were at first shocked at having to order, possibly on a daily basis, floggings for breaches of discipline by African prisoners. They nevertheless quickly came to integrate the sanction as a normal and routine practice. They learned to see it as a form of traditional punishment, which the colonial administration had humanised and which they perceived as relatively benign. 'Milnaert' objected to the significance I attributed to these 'meta-justifications' and contended: 'Of course, I needed a "justification", in the sense of a concrete reason in a concrete case, but not in the sense which you suggest.' These words imply that he needed a justification every time he ordered the punishment, in other words, that a singular justification which would have stood once and for all would have been of little help to him. Nonetheless, 'Milnaert' would probably not have been ready to order a flogging in Belgium. This demonstrates that a meta-justification underlined his practice, whether he is conscious of it or not. He and I are referring to different levels of analysis. These can be seen as complementary to, rather than exclusive of, each other. It is also possible, however, that our different emphases reveal a more serious disagreement, as a detour through another of our exchanges makes clear.

In the same article on the whip, I reported that 'Dehon' had told me that, placed in similar circumstances to those he experienced as a territorial, he would use the whip again. He said this just after remarking that he now thought, as he was talking to me, that the use of the whip was inhuman and unacceptable. 'Milnaert' detected in my interpretation of this last statement the attribution of an unconscious feeling of guilt which I would have had 'Dehon' share with the other territorials. In fact, by that time, I was in no doubt that the territorials felt no remorse or even guilt about the use of the whip. I thought, however, that perhaps *I* would feel so if *I* was in their situation, which of course is close to thinking that *they should* have felt guilty. By contrast, 'Milnaert' firmly asserted: 'There is no reason to feel guilty.'

Immediately after having written this statement, he went on to castigate me for judging the territorials according to universal and definite moral standards which, in his opinion, do not exist. I may have dropped my overt concern with legitimation which I felt discredited those in power in a way which was too simplistic. Nevertheless, even if I do not like to admit it, I implicitly pass moral judgment on the material I have collected, and through it, on the men I have met. For instance, I assume knowledge of right and wrong when I think that perhaps the territorials should have suffered from guilt (saying 'perhaps', although meaning it, does not suppress this fact). Similarly the doubts with which I have conducted this research attest to the persistance of my aloof morality. Thus, I wrote to 'Milnaert' that I was wondering how I could be 'fair' to all colonial actors in a letter where I was reflecting on the fact that I did not know 'what to think' of colonialism. Not surprisingly, 'Milnaert' did not like these questions which, in effect, amounted to saying that I did not know how to take what I was told, in other words, how to judge the men behind the material I was collecting. The same process was also of course at work when I was asking earlier in this chapter if the end ('development') justified the means ('colonialism').

'Milnaert' wrote in the margin of the draft of this passage, opposite this point: 'The question supposes an arrogant dichotomy between Good and Evil which the very nature of behaviour contradicts.' He repeatedly advised me to describe rather than to judge, and this can be seen as his answer to my 'doubts' and dilemmas'. To quote him once more: 'A historical process gets reported; it is not there to be judged. The only thing to do is to describe events which have existed.'[24]

The last two remarks, which are related to each other, tie in with the other criticisms which 'Milnaert' has levelled at my work and which I have presented in this chapter. To summarise, my picture is rigid because I am interested in 'big fish'; these, otherwise referred to by 'Milnaert' as 'spell-binding grand words', are judgmental, and in line with my prejudices; in turn, these prejudices blind me to the common character of the colonial situation; by trying to seize reality through grandiloquent concepts, I am missing its complexion and adopting a simplistic and arrogant ethical framework. All this points to the fact that I have adopted an aloof morality which is incompatible with the reality of the empirical world and its request for actions. The conclusion is that I have failed to research the 'ordinary' character of the territorial world and to describe the empirical complexity of a particular historical situation.

Most former territorials would probably accept the pertinence of the four sentences which I placed as an epigraph to each section of this chapter. My guess is that they would agree with 'Milnaert''s verdict that I have failed to place the material in the context of its time, to give 'life' to the territorials, and to pay due attention to the requirements of their actions, i.e., to look at the ordinary character of the colonial situation.

It is now time for me to say that I also think that 'Milnaert' has a point. Five years have elapsed since he sent me his comments on the draft of my thesis. The naivity with which I embarked on the doctoral thesis has further eroded. Through my job, I have gained some insight into the requirements of action. I have accepted and rejected applications to entry, taught students, marked their examinations, discussed their results; I have made friendships with some colleagues, fought others, and many times just kept quiet, which is still a way to get involved in the politics of a department. I do not like all that is going on in higher education in Britain, in my University, or in my Department. However, I neither wish to give up a job which I overall enjoy, nor can I put right all the things of which I do not approve. This is to say I understand much better that 'action' gives you dirty hands – even if I feel fortunate to be an academic and thus less actively involved than many.

With the hindsight of experience (a grand word for a banal and short career), it is even more clear to me than before that I am in no position to pass judgment on the moral standing of the territorials. But they tell me I have. It is true, I have submitted a thesis, written a book, and offered an analysis. As I explain in the next chapter, anthropology might seem to be by nature an arrogant enterprise. From this perspective, I might have no way out as an anthropologist but to live up to the arrogance of my discipline. At the same time, admiration must be felt when it is warranted. For all the 'de Glaises' present in the Congo, there must have been as many colonials whose integrity and humanity demand respect.[25] I salute them. Of course I invite the reader to do the same.

Notes

1. Let me repeat what I have already said in the introduction. The fact that I allow myself to come into 'Milnaert''s analysis and offer comments upon it, as I think I should do and would be in no position to refrain from doing even if I wanted to, makes it clear that this chapter remains *mine* (i.e. develops my analysis), however much it focuses on the ideas of my informant.
2. Samarin is fairly exceptional in doing exactly this in his book on colonisation and labour in Central Africa between 1880 and 1900. He writes: 'work in the colonies was only a variety, a racist variety, of patterns that characterised nineteenth-century Europe' (1989: 4). In support of this point, he includes a short description of labour conditions in France (ibid.: 26). See Keesing (1989) for a discussion of the tendency amongst anthropologists not to consider it worthy to write about that which is similar to their own practices.
3. The answer may be obvious but is easily forgotten. Verhaegen suggests in his review of Vanderlinden's biography of Pierre Ryckmans that the book is too soft on the personality of the Governor. Amongst other things, Verhaegen criticises Ryckmans for not having had significant relationships with the Africans, and Vanderlinden for not having made this clear (1995: 176). Vanderlinden pertinently replies by asking which official of comparable rank enjoys close relationships with the people he is in charge of administering (1996: 375).
4. Thus, in French, one talks of 'complete immersion' when one learns a foreign language in the country where it is spoken, without access to one's native language.
5. For an argument which links the present African crisis to the legacy of the colonial state, see Young 1994.
6. It is probably in the light of his remark that his statement on the 'enormous distance' which separated us must be explained. Informant and anthropologist stayed themselves, hence the distance between them : they did not fuse. 'Milnaert' must have wanted to emphasise our differences as he first put his point across, speaking in his microphone. Reading the transcript of his words in the first draft of the chapter, he must have thought that talking of an 'enormous' distance between the two of us was going too far. Such 'correction' points again at the fact that both 'immersion' and 'distance' are relative concepts.
7. Such phrasing, however, is not particularly surprising. Lequin and Métral remark that the past is most often talked about as a shared experience (1980: 157).
8. Vellut notes that the description of the two month transformation of a peasant into a worker in the brochure of a mining company dating from 1951 (i.e. very late in

the colonial period) uses a language more appropriate to the description of cattle. To quote one sentence: 'Our friend has put on weight and has become shiny. He's done to a turn.' ('*[N]otre ami a pris du poids et du luisant. Il est à point*') (Vellut 1981: 56). Although the words of a private company, the vocabulary reflects an attitude which must have been found among the various groups of colonials.

9. Instead of speaking of 'informant', 'Milnaert' speaks of '*ethnologué*', a word which does not exist in French, but perfectly renders what he has in mind. Compared to my translation, the French word has the extra savour that it rings very much like '*catalogué*' (classified).

10. This passage is strikingly reminiscent of that found in present scholarship. Mary Louise Pratt for example writes:

> By using the term 'contact', I aim to foreground the interactive, improvisional dimensions of colonial encounters so easily ignored or suppressed by diffusionist accounts of conquest and domination. A 'contact' perspective emphasises how subjects are constituted in and by their relations to each other. It treats the relations among colonizers and colonised, or travelers and 'travelees', not in terms of separateness and apartheid, but in terms of copresence, interaction, interlocking understandings and practices, often within radically asymmetrical relations of power (1992: 7).

Apart from the last words, Pratt's text echoes 'Milnaert''s critique.

11. The image of the horse is interesting. Kennedy reports an incident which involved the death of an African employee who had ridden a horse in colonial Kenya, thereby 'challeng[ing] a symbolic boundary that distinguished and separated the two races', for the right to mount a horse was an 'emblem of social rank and authority reserved for Europeans' (1987: 166).

12. No doubt some of my readers will agree with 'Milnaert' that I should have given more space to the Africans in my study, although probably for a different reason. My reply to this alleged flaw is that proper research could not have been improvised by landing in Kinshasa and staying somewhere in Zaire for a few weeks or even months collecting as many recollections from the colonial period as possible. This material would have needed to be analysed in the context of their structural position both in the colonial and the contemporary situations. Arguably, failure to provide such an analysis is the weakness of otherwise fascinating collections of Zairian life-stories which embrace the colonial period (De Lannoy et al. 1986; Jewsiewicki 1993).

13. These words would satisfy 'Milnaert', but I doubt that he would say that Beidelman achieves this in his monograph.

14. On Tshibumba's paintings, see the fascinating book by Fabian (1996).

15. This may not necessarily have been the case. Colonial policies have been subjected to sophisticated analysis which demonstrate their link to domination and pernicious effect. In the field of health, see for example Lyons (1992) and Hunt (1988; 1990) for Belgian Africa, and Vaughan (1991) for British East and Central Africa.

16. See previous footnote.

17. 'Fontor' is again exceptional in noting that, due to frequent transfers, no-one was ever in a position to complete what he had started. He said that this left him with a feeling of non-fulfillment rather than one of accomplishment.

18. What Laurent Kabila's regime reserves for the future remains to be seen. When I interviewed my informants, Zaire was still under the deplorable command of General Mobutu.

19. Etienne Tshisekedi was one of the thirteen '*ex-Parlementaires*' who founded the UDPS (Union pour la Démocratie et le Progrès Social) in 1982 (see Willame 1987). He was appointed Prime Minister by President Mobutu in September 1991, but removed from office the following month. The Conférence Nationale elected him Prime Minister in August 1992. Mobutu repudiated him in February 1993 and appointed in his place Faustin Birindwa (a co-founder of the UDPS) in March 1993. The result was that two governments coexisted. Because the Haut Conseil de la République (the transitional Parliament put in place by the Conférence Nationale) had never endorsed the appointment of Birindwa, Western governments solely recognised the government headed by Tshisekedi. But they never implemented their threat to take sanctions against Mobutu's government. The danger for Mobutu eventually came from inside Zaire. Laurent Kabila, after a military campaign which had started in the east in the spring of 1996, eventually arrived in Kinshasa and ousted Mobutu in May 1997.
20. UN intervention was formally requested by the government of Tshisekedi soon afterwards (*Le Soir*, 24 and 25 April 1993: 6). Although discussions took place in the summer of 1993 on its possible form, no intervention was ever decided on.
21. Such comparisons already surfaced in the 1980s. See for example Verhaegen 1983.
22. The same applies to another statement of his, which I had originally suspected of hiding guilt feelings: 'There is no need for us to feel ashamed of having been territorials.'
23. Moreover, 'Milnaert' pertinently remarks that the colonial and the present situations differ by a *range* of elements, including the fact that territorials were guaranteed a career in which they could foresee the various promotions and the fact that their emoluments, established at a Belgian level, made them incorruptible by African requests. While I find this remark convincing, the expectation that the European would receive presents such as eggs at his arrival in a village remains problematic. On present corruption as a legacy of the colonial period, see Gould (1980).
24. Many a historian would find this view of history untenable today (Jenkins 1997; McCullagh 1997)
25. The sub-title Vanderlinden (1994) chose for his biography of Pierre Ryckmans is most telling in this respect: *Coloniser dans l'honneur*.

8: Conclusion: The Anthropological Position

The argument so far

*I*n an important book which explores what the passage to anthropology entails, Kirsten Hastrup remarks that 'There is no way of seeing from "nowhere in particular"' (1995: 4). She founds her practical theory of anthropology (see below) on the premise that one always sees from somewhere. A feature of this premise is that one never remembers in the abstract, but by reference to the context in which one lives. These are the premisses upon which I have constructed my study.

Chapter 1 introduced the project of the book and chapter 2 provided a kind of glossary in the form of an introduction to the Territoriale. The ethnographic part of the book can thus be said to have started with chapter 3. This chapter was an attempt to elucidate the position from which I was approaching the world-view of my interviewees. It tried to recapture what I thought I knew about colonialism when I embarked on my research project and it explored the implications of this original position for the way the project developed. The question which guided its writing is: how did I approach my informants and what was I looking for through them? The chapter discussed the moral dilemmas in which I found myself entangled and the way these moral dilemmas transformed themselves into epistemological questions, forcing me to question my original image (memory) of colonialism.

Conclusion

Chapter 4 explored the position of the interviewees. All but two of the former colonials I contacted agreed to meet me for an interview which they knew was designed to discuss their colonial experience. Considering the general hostility the world in which they live today displays towards colonialism, this is perhaps surprising. Why did the interviewees talk to me, while many had consciously decided not to tackle colonial themes with non-colonials? The image I presented of a young, possibly naive and uncorrupted, female student may have helped. For those who were not moved by this image, the fact that I appeared ready to listen to them seems to have been sufficient to allay any reluctance on their part. They were willing, sometimes eager, to contribute to the historical project in which they mistakenly thought I was engaged. Many must have hoped that, through me, the 'objective' knowledge of the colonial experience they had no doubt they held might be passed on to society at large, including future generations. The final result, that is, the thesis followed by the present book, may be a disappointment to them, but one which they are ready to accept.

Chapters 3 and 4 positioned first the researcher and then the informants. Chapters 6 and 7 can be seen as their continuation in that they provided first the analysis by the researcher, then the objections by her best informant, on the material collected/produced. In between these two sets of chapters, chapter 5 acted as an intermediary. It was concerned with the interaction which took place between the anthropologist and the former territorials. Seemingly disparate aspects were treated: research modalities, the implicit but constant negotiation of issues to be taken up for discussion, the working of memory, the inescapable creeping-in of misunderstandings. What unites all these topics, however, is that they sought to problematise the very interaction which constitutes the interview and thus helped to understand the course taken by the conversations and the research.

Chapters 6 and 7 focused on the view of the researcher and of her informants respectively. Chapter 6 made it clear that I never completely abandoned my original perspective. Due to its particular angle, my vision led me to analyse the way my interviewees talked about immersion, authenticity and prestige, as revealing processes of domination in the colonial experience, which the interviewees themselves concealed or simply did not see. Chapter 7 articulated the criticisms my best informant levelled against my work. In the opinion of 'Milnaert', I have approached colonialism through the prism of grand concepts rather than examined its minute complexion. Because of this, I have attributed to colonialism a singularity which it does not have. His verdict is that I have failed to understand and convey the ordinary character of colonial practice.

This powerful critique raises the question of what constitutes understanding in anthropology. 'Milnaert' clearly thinks that I have not understood what he has been trying to tell me over the course of many years. If he is right, would this suggest that I have failed in my project as an anthropologist? Not if one accepts Hastrup's contention that the anthropological project entails a break from what she calls the native point of view (1995). This argument, which would not be put forward by all anthropologists, requires elaboration. In my view it offers a proper perspective on what the social science of anthropology is about.

The need to go beyond the native voice

The few interviewees to whom I sent a copy of my thesis in the summer of 1994 were disappointed with my work. None directly accused me of having exploited them,[1] but their congratulations, if any were forthcoming, were mitigated. Having followed (or been made to follow) the development of my research rather closely, 'Milnaert' was genuinely happy for me that the ordeal of the exercise was finally over. He was kind enough not to go back to his earlier criticisms. 'Parmentier' complemented me on having completed the doctorate, for he recognised the effort it required. He wrote he had read the text with attention and 'interest', a word which *he* put in inverted commas. As usual, he offered numerous, precise and valuable comments during a long session. 'Peletier''s were the most vocal of the objections I received. Presumably he could not wait to express his surprise and disappointment at my partiality (his main complaint), for he acknowledged that he had not yet finished reading the text in the letter he sent me in August 1994. His words, which I shall quote more than once in this conclusion, explicitly or implicitly raise the question of the aim and nature of the anthropological enterprise. This is a question undoubtedly worth tackling, and I shall address it in this chapter.

'Peletier' is appalled by the way I constantly cite other scholars to back up my argument. He remarks: 'But what I really object to is the way you call to your rescue a multitude of writers (whom we do not know, but perhaps this is our fault) without ever doubting what they say. They are, however, as likely to lie, to have preconceptions, and to make mistakes as the rest of us mortal beings.' In my reply to him, I observed that my motto was not to accept the words of other scholars and reject those of my interviewees, as a matter of course, as some passages in my work demonstrated. However, the important point – which 'Peletier' may have sensed or missed – lies elsewhere. As the practitioner of the scholarly discipline of anthropology, I was under the 'obligation to verse [myself] in earlier literature on and previous arguments about' my area of study (Hastrup 1995: 158). The primary aim of this exercise is not to display scholarly erudition, neither to show respect to one's elders, nor even to send a friendly (or not so friendly) nod to one's colleagues. Even though all these factors may play a role, the point of referring to the existing literature is that it makes it possible to engage in anthropology, that is, in a project which 'transcends local knowledge' (ibid.).

I expect Hastrup uses the verb 'to transcend' on purpose. She is clear about the fact that 'anthropology will always … encompass native understanding' (ibid.). To quote her again: 'the point of anthropology is to transcend self-description – not through a bypassing of it but by way of incorporating it into a language of a higher-order generality' (ibid.: 148). In these two quotations, the expressions 'native understanding' and 'self-description' are broadly equivalent. The term native is not meant to designate only those who have been the subject of anthropological enquiry. Every single one of us human beings is the native of a particular world, of which we have an intimate and largely intuitive knowledge (Hastrup 1996: 78). Thus, each of us has a native understanding and is able to provide a self-description of the world of which we are part. But anthropological understanding is different. It arises from anthropology 'being able to add another, deeper, higher, more general or more subtle understanding as the metaphors may go, and at least provide some statement about the world that is not already produced by that world itself' (ibid). This is why Hastrup views 'native anthropology' as a contradiction in terms. She convincingly argues that the native point of view cannot be conflated with the anthropological vision, because there is no way one can simultaneously speak from a native and an anthropological position (1995: 159).

Marilyn Strathern had already made this point in her contribution to the ASA volume on *Anthropology at Home* published in 1987. Speaking of her research in a village in Essex, she wrote:

> The Elmdon project might have begun in a milieu in which it could be assumed that the villagers broadly participated in the world view also held by

the anthropologist. Yet what started as continuity ended as disjunction. The ethnographic text was hardly continuous with indigenous narrative form; one was not rendering back to the residents of the village an account immediately contiguous with those they had given, as social history or as biography might be regarded. ... Commonsense descriptions are set aside. Indigenous reflection is incorporated as part of the data to be explained, and cannot itself be taken as the framing of it, so that there is always a discontinuity between indigenous understandings and the analytical concepts which frame the ethnography itself (1987: 18).

Both Strathern and Hastrup are in agreement that 'anthropologists have to distance themselves analytically from whatever local world they are studying' (Hastrup 1996: 78). Of course, one implication of the necessity for the anthropologist to step out of the native discourse (including her own), is that she could be said not 'to stay with' the native. This, in turn, could indicate that coevalness, the quality of existing at the same time, is being denied. The next section argues that such distancing is a necessary part of anthropological practice.

In limbo between distance and empathy

Johannes Fabian coined the expression 'denial of coevalness'. He did so in his seminal essay on *Time and the Other* (1983), which was intended to draw attention to the anthropological practice of denying we live in the same time as those we study. While 'we dogmatically insist that anthropology rests on ethnographic research involving personal, prolonged interaction with the Other, ... we pronounce upon the knowledge gained from such research a discourse which construes the Other in terms of distance, spatial and temporal' (ibid.: xi). Fabian's main thesis can be summed up as follows: during fieldwork, anthropologists share time with the other and accept to experience coevalness; during writing they leave the other behind and retreat into allochronism. This powerful critique obviously links up with those which point to the development of anthropology as a feature of imperialism and to the representation of the Other as the 'primitive' (of another, past, time). Fabian's point is that we cannot leave the Other behind, as if he/she were a primitive or a savage. They are in the same time as us. They are no different from us. They are us, and we are them (see also Fabian 1991: 198).

In my effort to analyse the interviews, I was all too aware of the allochronism Fabian denounces. While I felt a degree of closeness to the interviewees during the interviews, any such feeling disappeared as I was in my study trying to write-up. Or, rather, it would be more correct to say that the memory of the closeness and the sense of betraying it in the act of writing paralysed me. What was I to write? Whatever I wrote could not satifisfy the people who had trusted me and opened themselves up to me. We were too far apart. The distance was unbearable, and unbreachable. How was I to proceed, as an anthropologist?

More than four years have elapsed since I submitted my thesis. I remember how difficult it was to write it. At the time, the moral and epistemological conundrum in which I felt I was seemed insurmountable. I would never have thought it would vanish, but it has. I now feel satisfied that I have done (some kind of) justice to the words of the former territorials. I also realise that analytical distance was necessary. I nonetheless remember the fear of hurting my informants was difficult to bear, almost painful. In this section, I try to understand why my position was a difficult one.

Part of the problem arose because I was studying people to whom I did not naturally feel close. In a sense my informants were from home. One was an uncle, another two were fathers of friends of mine. Any of the others could have been my father. But home is a potentially infinitely receding notion, and thus not very useful analytically (Strathern 1987: 17). In fact, my informants were, or appeared to be far away from my own world and values.

Mine was not the most usual anthropological field. In a crucial footnote, John Van Maanen has remarked:

> [C]ollegial expectations hold that fieldworkers should come to appreciate, if not admire, the thoughts and actions of their informants. Displays of sympathetic understanding are quite common in fieldwork reports. The house norm seems to be one in which the fieldworker not only represents, but also takes the side of the studied and thus becomes something of an official voice for their aims, ambitions, and general perspective on the world ... (1988: 42).

This passage can hardly be said to apply to my study. The determination of my informants to achieve their aims and the wide range of their interests impressed me, but it took a long time before I started to admire the integrity and humanity displayed by some of them. I cannot fully share the enthusiasm former territorials express for their past actions and life, even though I understand it better. I remain opposed to the principle of going and colonising other people, be it for the seemingly most humanitarian reasons – as some men who joined the Territoriale must have believed. While I now conceive of colonialism as a historical process which was ineluctable, my position is still one step removed from taking the side of the people I have studied.

Van Maanen's note suggests that anthropologists are expected to share their informants' views. Not everyone would agree, but the fact that I was 'studying-up' (Nader 1974) put me in a particular predicament in this respect. The attention anthropologists rightly like to pay to what is happening 'on the ground' as opposed to 'high' spheres of discourse means that much fieldwork takes place amongst the poor, the oppressed, the underprivileged, those who generally do not have a voice. Indeed, much anthropology is based on the wish to denounce situations of injustice and to empower those without much power. Against this trend, I was studying 'the coloniser', often reduced to an undifferentiated class occupying the place of 'the dominant' in the colonial relationship. In other words, my task was to 'understand' the powerful. As Rebecca Klatch's account (1988) illuminates, this is a difficult position to be in today.

The paradox of my situation was never made clearer to me than when I attended the Amsterdam Conference on Critical Anthropology in December 1988 (Nencel and Pels 1991). I went to Amsterdam because I was attracted by the idea of a critical, emancipatory, postmodern anthropology. What I heard, however, did not help me to make sense of my research. It was as if people like the interviewees I had learnt to know over the previous year were completely by-passed, as if they were not worthy of attention. I felt too close to them to accept such implicit contempt. The neat division of the world between the haves and the have-nots on which most papers seemed implicitly to rest appeared to me ridiculously off-the-point.

The Conference was a turning-point in my ability to articulate what I had already sensed: a focus on legitimation would have in effect put my informants in the class of the 'baddies' subject to my contemptuous analysis. Such a focus would have to be abandoned. The certainty of this intuition was due to the relationship I had been building with a few interviewees. I was not able to consider them as elements of a – past or current – fieldwork whom I did not need to take into account in my analysis. They were far too present in my mind for this to happen. Perhaps paradoxically in view of the distance I always felt between them and me, I was applying the principle of coevalness identified by Fabian. To quote him again: 'To be carried out successfully, making and translating ethnographic texts in the absence of interlocutors still calls for (the substitute of) an inner dialogue in which the anthropologist who writes ethnography matches recorded sounds and graphic symbols with communicative competences, memories and imagination' (1990b: 100). In my writing, I could not help but pay attention to what I imagine the reactions of the interviewees to my text would be, were they to have access to my thesis written in English. Knowing I could not satisfy them had a paralysing effect on my writing.[2] Still, I carried on, with them in mind.

This does not mean that I managed to satisfy them. In his letter of August 1994 'Peletier' mentions in a long paragraph a number of (in his view) key-points about the colonial experience: transport, schools, justice, equality, agriculture, as well as a few other things. He bitterly concludes: 'Not a word of all this is to be found in your study.' This statement could suggest that I have fallen in the trap denounced by Fabian when he writes: 'When much or most of anthropology is ... perceived as tangential (beside the point, irrelevant) by those who have been its objects, ... it is yet another symptom of the denial of coevalness' (1983: 92). As his 1991 article makes clear, Fabian wishes to contribute to an emancipatory anthropology which helps to get rid of imperial structures and domination. His numerous monographs demonstrate that he does this by working closely with, and implicitly taking side for, the blatantly oppressed. In my case, however, the people I was studying did not fall in this category. As a result, there was not a side of the fence on which I could have unquestionably sat.

In my research, I recurrently experienced both empathy and distance, as well as the lack of either one or the other, as problems. Retrospectively, it is as if these problems, which appeared very real at the time, took care of themselves. Empathy is regularly presented as a must in anthropology (e.g. Lewis 1961: preface), but is not the point (Hastrup 1996: 79–80). As for distance, I have already argued that the anthropological project requires one to step out of the native point of view. In other words, working towards coevalness cannot be achieved by remaining on the same plane as the natives (Hastrup 1995: 21; see also Lemaire 1991: 38). It is worth noting, however, that the distance which troubled me as I was writing-up was not just of an analytical nature. The feeling of distance *also* emerged from the fact that I was not a native of the same world as the former territorials. Of course, it was impossible to disentangle the analytical distance from the native one. They were blurred, and this created its own problem. It made me feel terribly arrogant.

The seeming arrogance of anthropology

How did I dare to do what I was doing, namely, writing about and thus passing judgment on people I had to admit I did not even know that well?

Throughout the research and still at the time of writing the conclusion of the thesis, this question disturbingly remained at the back of my mind.

I have often heard anthropologists say that their informants would recognise themselves or at least their society in the analyses which they (the anthropologists) produce. Perhaps this belief, rarely put to the test by formally inviting comments by informants, only preserves the anthropologist from the unsettling realisation that anthropological analysis literally *subjects* the informants to the idiosyncratic examination of the reseacher. Perhaps anthropology would by nature be an arrogant exercise. Ducking this issue was not an option available to me. 'Milnaert' was there to remind me that, as far as he and probably also most of his colleagues were concerned, I had failed to understand the world of the territorials. The fact that I was working 'at home' (Jackson 1987) may have brought this issue more pressingly to the fore, but it is central to the whole of the anthropological enterprise. As Hastrup says, '[h]owever much the others are dealt with as equal historical subjects, anthropology still has to objectify them in writing' (1995:7).

I could only hope to justify my intrusion and my informants' subjection by believing that some form of knowledge and understanding would emerge from the process, which was of benefit to others. When I submitted my thesis, I sensed that the way my anti-colonialist feelings had shrunk in the course of the research because of my increased recognition of the complexity of colonialism and the variety of experiences within it was worth recording. Four years on, my conviction that the study was worth doing is much firmer. As a result, I do not believe anymore that anthropology is necessarily an arrogant enterprise, i.e. one which unduly assumes knowledge. On the contrary, I find anthropology often reaches out towards what is not well-known.

My findings

'Peletier' was surprised by the title of my thesis, 'The Memory of Colonialism', which he found misleading. In his words, 'I think it would be more appropriate to entitle your study: "What I, M.-B. Dembour, think about the memories that territorials I met have evoked in front of me".' The study indeed traces my itinerary from a disgust for colonialism, perhaps tainted by diffused guilt, to an awareness that the Congo was a place inhabited by people 'like those we meet everyday' – to borrow 'Milnaert''s expression. Being a personal itinerary, it may appear of little scientific value to 'Peletier' and his colleagues. By situating my position and that of my informants and addressing the question of why the interviews and the research developed the way they did, the significance of my study nonetheless goes beyond my personal itinerary. Speaking of anthropology, Strathern observes: 'We need to have some sense of the productive activity which lies behind what people say, and thus their own relationship to what has been said' (1987: 19). This is the sense I have tried to capture in this book, in an analysis where I consider myself as much the native of a world to be studied as I consider the informants to be.

Let me make clear in which perspective I have worked. Like all the scholars I have cited in this conclusion (and many others), I do not believe in the idea that there is one ultimate truth or that the aim of science is to produce a perfect representation of reality. Accordingly, my aim has never been to create an image which would act like a mirror of reality, because 'there is no mirroring but an attempt to understand how the world is disposed in the first place' (Hastrup 1996: 182). As Fabian points out, writing is part of anthropological praxis, a praxis is doing and doing does not mirror anything (1990c: 763). Moreover, 'there is no disengaged standpoint of knowing [so that] the former hero of science, who gained control through disengagement, has to be replaced by a scholar who achieves understanding by way of involvement' (Hastrup 1995: 173). This is why '[d]irect experience is not opposed to rational thinking' (ibid: 162). One feeds into the other and vice-versa. Of course, the 'recontextualization [which the anthropologist will thus produce] may easily involve a challenging of the native self-understanding, including [her] own' (ibid.: 157). This is what happened in my case.

My itinerary is one that I would wish others to follow. A friend of mine recently phoned me, all excited by a trip she had just taken to Paris. She had brought back an African statue she had bought in a flea-market. She had mixed feelings about it. The statue was beautiful, but she felt a little bit guilty about it. Was the price she had paid for it high enough? Did her purchase contribute to the exploitation of the Africans? Did her act partake of neocolonialism? I could not help recommending that she read Bruckner's *The Tears of the White Man* (1986). Although the book focuses on France, its relevance goes beyond this country. Its main thesis is that Third Worldism is Eurocentric in so far as it wrongly attributes responsibility for everything that goes wrong in the Third World to Europe, hence the subtitle *Compassion as Contempt*. My friend continued by saying something like: 'Well, I do not feel so guilty because there was not a strong tradition of colonialism in Italy [her native country] and no members of my family went to the colonies.' I could not help thinking: 'Why should I feel guilty because I have an uncle who has been a territorial in the Congo?' At this stage, I told her to read my book when it came out. She continued: 'But you must recognise the feeling. Even if you do not share my feelings, you know how I feel, don't you?' I said: 'Well, yes, this is exactly the point.'[3] We then changed topics. What this short, undirected, spontaneous encounter demonstrates is the pervasiveness of the frame of mind with which I entered the research project. By implication, it also points to the necessity of understanding its origin, articulation and limitations.

Ann Stoler has warned against the tendency to treat 'colonialism and its European agents as an abstract force, as a structure imposed on local practice' (1989a: 135, emphasis omitted; see also Comaroff and Comaroff 1991: 54). European agents were indeed *agents*. But their individual diversity is often buried under sweeping generalisations. Of course, ideologically, it is easier to make use of a memory of colonialism which remembers the latter just as blatantly oppressing (or just as enhancing development) than as a more complex phenomenon.

The colonial agents could be said to have been actors on the colonial scene.[4] They had not invented the scenario. The play had been produced elsewhere (by international forces as well as strong individuals) and it was directed from Belgium. Some territorials kept to their lines of the script better than others. Some proved excellent improvisors, others messed up the score. Good actors are not to be held wholly responsible for a scenario which was badly conceived to start with. But such a process of scapegoating seems to be common in regard to colonialism.

The academic literature offers many examples of what I would call gratuitous condemnations of colonial actors. Fabian provides one such, I think, when he reports the affirmation by a Zairian colleague that a white missionary of the colonial period was a 'true friend of the Africans', that he 'really understood them', and that he 'spoke the[ir] language very well' (1991: 198). In fact, the Zairian added, the missionary spoke the Lubumbashi Swahili as well as he, Fabian, did. Fabian writes: 'Something hit home. Not that I took being compared to a notorious missionary colonialist literally; it would have been an insult which, I am sure, my colleague did not intend' (ibid.). Why would the literal comparison *need* to be an insult? If the missionary was a truly despicable 'colonialist', which does not seem to be borne out by the comments of the Zairian, Fabian should have spelled this out.[5] If not, why is Fabian offended by the comparison? When a Ghanaian greeted James Lance one morning with the words 'Good morning, Captain Rattray', the reaction of the American researcher was to ask in a similar fashion to Fabian: 'Why could the old man and his fellow Mamprusi not see that I was … a "good foreigner" …' (1990: 337). Such remarks seem to posit an unbreakable divide between the old colonisers and at least some of the contemporary Westerners working in Africa. But who are we to assume that the colonisers were all so bad? Also, who are we to know that we can consider ourselves to be absolutely different from 'them'?

The territorials joined a process which had been under way well before they started to participate in it. When they took this decision, it was a decision which the prevalent ethos of the time regarded as a respectable one. More than this, the choice they made to serve in the Territoriale was often presented as a positively good thing to do. At least three interviewees mentioned their work as a continuation of the boy-scout movement of which they had been part in their childhood and youth. Whatever we may think of the paternalistic complexion of this movement, those who embraced it are not to be blamed for all its faults.

It is worth noting that territorials were not necessarily aware of the most horrific aspects of colonialism. One interviewee had the book *Cent ans de regards belges* (C.E.C. asbl n.d.) and a few other pieces of work equally critical of Belgian colonialism lying on his coffee-table when I visited him. He remarked, with some bitterness, that he had never heard of the atrocities committed under Leopold II's regime until he read about them in recent studies. He spoke as if he had been fooled into joining in an enterprise which was not as rosy as it had been presented to him when he was young. Still, the long memoirs he wrote, where he presented different styles and characters within the Territoriale, indicate that on the whole he felt his action had been a positive one.

All the men I met took part in colonialism. Some abused their position of power, as predicted by Pierre Ryckmans in his text on the 'dangerous force' (and elsewhere). Others handled it the best they could, with awareness and constant questioning of the ethical implications of their actions. There is no good reason why we should forget this. I would even say that it is important we remember it.

The value of anthropology

As the former territorials repeatedly told me, it is wrong to adopt a present lens to look at past events. But considering one cannot see from nowhere, what lens should one adopt? There is no easy or direct answer to this question. What I would say, however, is that it is important to be open to a dialogue and to the idea that there is no definite truth to be found so that one must remain in an attitude of quest and doubt. Through such an attitude, the value of anthropology is able to come through. It lies in the readiness not to accept the 'truths' which circulate about the unknown, i.e. the imagined. Instead of stopping at the apparent but falsely obvious, anthropology has the propensity to go against the grain by meeting those first concerned by these false truths and listening to what they have to say. This encounter with the unknown (or badly known) alters the original image by putting in a different light the situation which had been supposedly understood – once and for all.

Without realising it, I had met former territorials before I started my doctorate. I knew a few of them personally, one since my birth. However, I knew nothing about what they had done in the Congo and what they felt about it. Nonetheless I imagined, in a very vague way, that it was all rather gloomy and that they were full of guilt. The story they told me was different. Of course, the whole book indicates that we have not reached an agreement on what their colonial experience was about. To quote once more 'Peletier''s response to my thesis: 'We find ourselves in the non-enviable position of an accused who is charged before a tribunal … and who has the feeling that the tribunal … has already made up its mind. To say the same thing in other words, I think you are partial.' I need not say that I do not share 'Peletier''s verdict. Our views obviously remain very far apart. But I still think I have reached an understanding of colonialism which I did not even suspect could emerge when I embarked on my doctorate. Also I can live with the disagreement which persists between me and my informants, for I do not think that anthropology is about the creation of a 'happy agreement' (see also Fabian 1990b: 5).

This position is related to my belief that there is no Knowledge, with a capital K, to be discovered. There is, however, understanding to be sought. What this study has taught me is to try never to assume, to listen before passing judgment. This attitude is what posits anthropology at the opposite of arrogance. Most anthropologists attempt to reach out for other voices. This is crucial. It is true not only for the colonial discourse, but also for other discourses. Let me take as an example a field I have become increasingly interested in since I became a lecturer in law; that of human rights. Here is a discourse which is fraught with presuppositions about how people live their life and what they want of it. All this is done in the best of intentions, but often with very damaging consequences for the possibility of establishing a dialogue, and some understanding, between fellow human beings.[6] When I hear what I take to be undue comments, I am glad there are anthropologists around who are committed to listening and seeking a better understanding, rather than making sophisticated propositions in the abstract. For, of course, ultimately anthropology is, and reflects upon, practice.

While anthropology provides an analysis which goes beyond the native voice, it also has the potential of 'changing the world by infiltrating its self-descriptive modes' (Hastrup 1996: 80). By contrast to the atom which is just an object, the object of anthropology is also a subject. Thus, whereas any theorising on the atom will never affect it, theorising on people (especially if presented in an accessible way) has the potential of affecting their self-constitutions, -descriptions and -understandings (ibid.). The absence of a neat separation between analysis and practice may at times make anthropology paralysing, as I have experienced, but ultimately it makes it extremely exciting, for it may pave a way forward.

Notes

1. As Marilyn Strathern apparently was (1987: 32, note 5).
2. Fabian acknowledges a similar process when he attributes part of the difficulty of writing an ethnography on the material he had collected on working-sites to his ambiguous position in-between the employer and the employees. He suggests that the fact that he could not be just on the side of the latter contributed to a kind of writing-block (1991: 200, note 11).
3. This anodine conversation led me to wonder whether I had undertaken the study because I somehow needed to reconcile myself with colonialism. Hastrup recounts how a theatre group decided to make a play about her life. In preparation for this play, she was questioned at long length. This brought her to see her life in a new light, which she wanted to share with the group. But, she notes, 'They were not really interested in me; they had their own world to discover, not mine' (1995: 131). Similarly, it might always be more their own worlds than that of their informants that anthropologists are ultimately seeking to discover.
4. I am grateful to Bob Morton for having suggested the metaphor I use in this paragraph.
5. This is not to deny that some colonial agents were despicable in their attitudes towards the Africans. I have mentioned 'de Glaise' for the Belgian Congo. The Governor-General Ryckmans did not hide that he encountered many figures of dubious character. For an example outside the Belgian Congo, see Hayes (1996).
6. Female circumcision is a case in point. My own interest in this issue arose from my irritation with the way the human rights discourse portrays female

circumcision/genital mutilation either as a cultural right or, more commonly, as an abominable violation of physical integrity, without ever listening to what the women first concerned by the practice have or want to say about it (Dembour 1996). See Parker (1995) for an account, based on fieldwork, which leads the author to suggest that Western deep-felt indignation may have more to do with Western belief about sexuality than with what is happening in the societies which practise circumcision.

Appendix 1:
Basic career information on territorials cited in the text

Pseudonym	Degree	Period of Entry*
'Amory'	C.U.	1926–30
'Bertrand'	Law	1948–52
'Colman'	C.U.	1945–47
'Cornil'	C.U.	1945–47
'Dauw'	C.U.	1936–40
'd'Ave et d'Ove'	Law	1948–52
'de Glaise'	Hum.	1936–40
'Dehon'	Uni.	1936–40
'Delporte'	C.U.	1926–30
'Fontor'	Law	1948–52
'Jamiolle'	Law	1948–52
'Melonnier'	C.U.	1945–47
'Michel'	Uni.	1926–30
'Mignolet'	Law	1945–47
'Milnaert'	Hum.	1945–47
'Parmentier'	Law	1945–47
'Peletier'	C.U.	1945–47
'Peters'	Hum.	1948–52
'Praet'	C.U.	1948–52

'Ransquin'	C.U.	1945–47
'Schutter'	C.U.	1931–35
'Valence'	Law	1948–52
'Vastenakel'	C.U.	1948–52
'Verbrugge'	C.U.	1945–47
'Wilkin'	Hum.	1931–35

* The specific year of entry is not indicated in order to preserve the anonymity of the interviewees

Name	Degree	Year of Entry
Augustin	Law	1952
Depoorter	C.U.	1946
Domont	Hum.	1930
Lenain	C.U.	1947
Salmon	C.U.	1946
Vallaeys	C.U.	1948
Willaert	C.U.	1931

Key
C.U. : Colonial University graduate
Law : Holders of a law degree
Uni.: Other University graduates
Hum.: Holders of a humanities degree or of another degree not recognised to be equivalent to a University degree

Appendix 2: Questionnaire sent to former territorials in 1989

1. Would you consider the time you spent in the Congo as the best period in your life, or is it just one period amongst others?
2. What brought you to the Congo and why did you choose to join the Territoriale?
3. If you were to begin your life again, would you still go to the Congo? As a territorial? Why? (Please answer this question whether your answer is positive or negative).
4. At the time, did you encourage young men to go to the Congo? To join the Territoriale?
5. If the territorial job still existed today, would you recommend it to a young man?
6. What would you say are the good and the bad sides of the job?
7. Are you proud to have been a territorial?
8. Are there some aspects of the job that you would prefer to forget about or even not to have experienced?
9. Has your territorial experience been helpful in your life afterwards (for example to find a job)?
10. What image do you think the average Belgian has of the Territoriale? Is it positive or negative? Does he only know what this job consists of?
11. What do you think of recent TV programmes about the Congo?
12. Has your view on the territorial job changed over time (either whilst you were there or since your return)? If yes, what contributed to this change (reading, films, discussions, subsequent events …)?

13. Do you still talk about your territorial experience today? To whom?
14. Do you think that the expression 'To dominate and to serve' encapsulates the essence of colonialism?
15. If you do, is it particularly relevant for the territorials (rather than other people who also were in the Congo)?
16. Was the domination aspect of the territorial job less/more/as important than/as the service aspect? (When you answer this question – and indeed all the other questions of the questionnaire – can you please differentiate if necessary between what you thought then and what you think today?).
17. Through which means (violence, repression whether military, police-backed or legal, intimidation, persuasion …) was domination exercised? In which domains (all, some which can be specified …)?
18. Was domination a good thing? (Please indicate how your thinking has changed over the years if necessary).
19. Did some things shock you? (Please indicate how your thinking has changed over the years if necessary).
20. Taking the Second World War as a reference point, do you think you had less/more/as much power, authority and prestige than/as the territorial generation which came before (or after) you.
21. Do you think you knew the natives as well/less/more as/than the "elders" (or "youngsters")?
22. If you could be a territorial again at the period of your choice, what would the latter be (e.g. the 1930s, the years of the Second World War, the early 1950s, etc.)? Why?
23. What did the service aspect of the job consist of? How did it manifest itself?
24. Minister Wauters said the following on the 25th anniversary of the Colonial University: 'Those who graduate from our University know that what they are going to do is not a job, is better than a career, is indeed the fulfillment of a mission'. Do you agree with this statement? (Please indicate how your thinking has changed over the years if necessary).
25. If you agree, do you think the statement applied equally to all members of the territorial service, irrespective of training (whether they were Colonial University graduates or not)?
26. Do you think it also applied to other groups of Whites? If yes, which ones?

Appendices

27. Did you believe in the superiority of Western civilisation and do you believe in it today? If yes, in which domains would you say it manifested (and still manifests) itself?
28. If you were hoping to bring progress, did you think you were actually achieving results? In which areas? What do you think about it today?
29. If you have particularly enjoyed a task or a territory, can you explain why?
30. If, on the contrary, you have particularly disliked a task or a territory, can you explain why?
31. Do you think that territorials could be perceived as belonging to a single group in spite of the variety of their experiences (in territories which could differ greatly in character)? If yes, what links them?
32. Compared to other groups of Whites in the Congo (other administrative services, settlers, missionaries …), were there practices or ideas which were peculiar to the Territoriale?
33. Would it be possible to speak of a 'professional mindset' ('*déformation professionelle*') characteristic of the Territoriale? What would it consist in?

BIBLIOGRAPHY

Académie Royale des Sciences d'Outre-Mer (ed.). 1988. *Recueil d'études "Le centenaire de l'Etat Indépendant du Congo"*, Brussels: Académie Royale des Sciences d'Outre-Mer/Koninklijke Academie voor Overzeese Wetenschappen.

——— 1992. *Recueil d'études "Congo 1955–1960" Verzameling studies*, Brussels: Académie Royale des Sciences d'Outre-Mer/Koninklijke Academie voor Overzeese Wetenschappen.

Actes de la recherche en sciences sociales. 1986. 'L'illusion biographique' 62/63, pp. 3–134.

Agar, Michael H. 1980. *The Professional Stranger. An Informal Introduction to Ethnography.* Orlando: Academic Press.

Albertini, Rudolf von (with Albert Wirz). 1982. *European Colonial Rule, 1880–1940. The Impact of the West on India, Southeast Asia, and Africa* (transl. by John G. Williamson). Westport, Connecticut: Greenwood Press.

Alexandre, Pierre. 1971. 'De l'ignorance de l'Afrique et de son bon usage: note autobiocritique', *Cahiers d'Etudes Africaines* 43, pp. 448–54.

Amselle, Jean-Loup and Elikia M'Bokolo (eds). 1985. *Au coeur de l'ethnie. Ethnies, tribalisme et état en Afrique.* Paris: Editions La Découverte.

Annales. Economies, Sociétés, Civilisations. 1980. 'Archives orales: une autre histoire?', pp. 124–99.

Anstey, Roger. 1970. 'Belgian rule in the Congo and the aspirations of the "évolué" class', in L.H. Gann and P. Duignan (eds), *Colonialism in Africa, 1870–1960, Vol.2, The History and Politics of Colonialism, 1914–1960*, London: Cambridge University Press, pp. 194–225.

Ardener, Edwin. 1975. 'The "Problem" Revisited', in Shirley Ardener (ed.), *Perceiving Women*, London: Dent, pp. 19–27.

Arendt, Hannah. 1964. *Eichmann in Jerusalem: A Report on the Banality of Evil.* New York: Viking Press.

Asad, Talal (ed.). 1973. *Anthropology and the Colonial Encounter*. London: Ithaca.
Augustin, Paul. n.d. [circa 1985]. Mwalimu: Noirs et blancs, racontés à travers les souvenirs d'un administrateur au Congo, ms, 295 pp.
Bahloul, Joëlle. 1996. *The Architecture of Memory. A Jewish–Muslim Household in Colonial Algeria 1937-1962*. Cambridge: Cambridge University Press.
Balandier, Georges. 1951. 'La situation Coloniale: Approche Théorique', *Cahiers Internationaux de Sociologie* 11, pp. 44–79.
Barton, D., D. Bloome, D. Sheridan and B. Street. 1993. *Ordinary People Writing: The Lancaster and Sussex Writing Research Project*. Lancaster: Language in Social Life Occasional Paper 51.
Bayart, Jean-François. 1989. *L'Etat en Afrique: La Politique du Ventre*. Paris: Fayard.
Beidelman, T.O. 1982. *Colonial Evangelism: A Socio-Historical Study of an East African Mission at the Grassroots*. Bloomington: Indiana University Press.
Berman, Bruce. 1990. *Control and Crisis in Colonial Kenya. The Dialectic of Domination*. London: James Currey.
Berman, B. and J. M. Lonsdale. 1992. *Unhappy Valley. Conflict in Kenya and Africa*. London: James Currey.
Bertaux, Daniel. 1980. 'L'approche biographique: sa validité méthodologique, ses potentialités', *Cahiers Internationaux de Sociologie* LXIX, pp. 198–225.
——— 1981. 'From the Life-History Approach to the Transformation of Sociological Practice', in Daniel Bertaux (ed.) *Biography and Society. The Life History Approach in the Social Sciences*, Beverly Hills: Sage, pp. 29–46.
Beyens, Alain. 1992. 'L'histoire du statut des villes', in *Recueil d'études "Congo 1955-1960" Verzameling studies*, Brussels: Académie Royale des Sciences d'Outre-Mer/Koninklijke Academie voor Overzeese Wetenschappen, pp. 15–70.
Bhabha, Homi K. 1984. 'Of Mimicry and Man: The Ambivalence of Colonial Discourse', *October* 28, pp. 125–53.
——— 1986a. 'The Other Question: Difference, Discrimination and the Discourse of Colonialism', in Francis Barker, Peter Hulme, Margaret Iversen and Diana Loxley (eds), *Literature, Politics and Theory*, London: Methuen, pp. 148–72.
——— 1986b. 'Foreword', in Franz Fanon *Black Skin, White Masks*, London: Pluto, pp. vii–xxvi.
Bontinck, F.F. 1969. 'Les deux Bula Matari', *Etudes Congolaises* 13 (3), pp. 83–97.
Borofsky, Robert. 1987. *Making History. Pukapukan and Anthropological Constructions of Knowledge*. Cambridge: Cambridge University Press.
Bourdieu, Pierre. 1981. 'Décrire et prescrire', *Actes de la Recherche en Sciences Sociales* 38, pp. 69–74.
Bourgeois, R. 1987. *Témoignages. Fonctionnaire territorial (1931–1961)* T.1 – Vol.1 and 2. Tervuren: Musée Royal de L'Afrique Centrale.

Braeckman, Colette *et al.* 1990. *La colonisation, l'indépendance, le régime Mobutu et demain?* Bruxelles: CRISP.
Brausch, Georges. 1957. 'Le paternalisme: une doctrine belge de politique indigène (1908–1933)', *Revue de l'Institut de Sociologie* 2, pp. 191–217.
———— 1961. *Belgian Administration in the Congo.* London: Oxford University Press.
Brownfoot, Janice. 1984. 'Memsahibs in Colonial Malaya: A Study of European Wives in a British Colony and Protectorate, 1900–1940', in Hilary Callan and Shirley Ardener (eds), *The Incorporated Wife*, London: Croom Helm, pp. 186–210.
Browning, Christopher. 1992. *Ordinary Men. Reserve Police Battalion 101 and the Final Solution in Poland.* New York: Harper Collins.
Bruckner, Pascal. 1987. *The Tears of the White Man. Compassion as Contempt* (transl. from the French by William R. Beer). New York: The Free Press.
Buell, Raymond Leslie. 1928. *The Native Problem in Africa.* New York: Macmillan Company.
Bulletin des Tribunaux de Police Congolais. 1953, p.1.
Bustin, Edouard. 1971. 'Congo-Kinshasa. Guide bibliographique. Vol. I and II', *Les Cahiers du CEDAF* (3/4), 60 and 72 pp.
Byrnes, Giselle M. 1994. '"The Imperfect Authority of the Eye": Shortland's Southern Journey and the Calligraphy of Colonisation', *History and Anthropology* 8 (1–4), pp. 207–35.
Cahiers Internationaux de Sociologie LXIX. 1980. 'Numéro spécial: Histoires de vie et vie sociale', pp. 197–368.
Cahiers Marxistes. Août-septembre 1990. 'L'Afrique noire asphyxiée'.
Callaway, Helen. 1987. *Gender, Culture and Empire. European Women in Colonial Nigeria.* Houndsmills, Hampshire: Macmillan Press.
Caplan, Pat. 1997. *African Voices, African Lives. Personal Narratives from a Swahili Village.* London: Routledge.
C.E.C. asbl. n.d. *Zaïre 1885–1985. Cent Ans de Regards Belges.* Bruxelles: Coopération par l'Education et la Culture.
Ceyssens, Ryk. 1975. 'Mutumbula, mythe de l'opprimé', *Cultures et développement* VII (3–4), pp. 483–550.
Chanock, Martin. 1985. *Law, Custom and Social Order. The Colonial Experience in Malawi and Zambia.* Cambridge: Cambridge University Press.
Chaudhuri, Nupur and Margaret Strobel (eds). 1992. *Western Women and Imperialism: Complicity and Resistance.* Bloomington: Indiana University Press.
Chrétien, Jean-Pierre and Gérard Prunier (eds). 1989. *Les ethnies ont une histoire.* Paris: Karthala.
Clauzel, J. 1989. *Administrateur de la France d'Outre-Mer.* Paris: J. Lafitte et A. Barthélemy.
Clifford, James. 1988. *The Predicament of Culture. Twentieth-Century Ethnography, Literature and Art.* Cambridge, Massachussets: Harvard University Press.

Cochrane, Glynn. 1971. 'The Case for Fieldwork by Officials', *Man* 6 (2), pp. 279–84.
Cohen, Anthony P. 1992. 'Self-conscious Anthropology', in Judith Okely and Helen Callaway (eds), *Anthropology and Autobiography*, London: Routledge, pp. 221–41.
Cohen, William B. 1971. *Rulers of Empire: The French Colonial Service in Africa*. Stanford: Hoover Institution Press.
——— 1973. *Empereurs sans sceptre. Histoire des administrateurs de la France d'Outre-mer et de l'école coloniale* (transl. of the English by Louis de Lesseps and Camille Garnier). Paris: Berger-Levrault.
Cohn, Bernard. 1996. *Colonialism and Its Forms of Knowledge: The British in India*. Princeton: Princeton University Press.
Comaroff, Jane and John Comaroff. 1991. *Of Revelation and Revolution: Christianity, Colonialism, and Consciousness in South Africa*. Vol. 1. Chicago: The University of Chicago Press.
Connerton, Paul. 1989. *How Societies Remember*. Cambridge: Cambridge University Press.
Cooper, Frederick. 1996. *Decolonization and African Society. The Labor Question in French and British Africa*. Cambridge: Cambridge University Press.
Cooper, Frederick and Ann L. Stoler (eds). 1989. 'Special Issue: Tensions of Empire', *American Anthropologist* 16 (4).
Copans, Jean. 1974. *Critiques et politiques de l'anthropologie*. Paris: Maspero.
Cornélus, Henri. 1954. *Kufa*. Brussels: La Renaissance du Livre.
Cornevin, Robert. 1966. *Histoire du Congo Léopoldville-Kinshassa. Des origines préhistoriques à la République Démocratique du Congo*. Paris: Berger-Levrault.
——— 1972. *Le Zaïre (ex-Congo-Kinshasa)*. Paris: Presses Universitaires de France.
——— 1989. *Histoire du Zaïre. Des origines à nos jours*. Brussels: Hayez.
Cornil, P. 1953. 'Réflexions sur la Justice Pénale au Congo Belge', in *Journal des Tribunaux d'Outre-Mer* 33, pp. 33–9.
Crapanzano, Vincent. 1985. *Waiting: The Whites of South Africa*. New York: Vintage.
Crick, Malcolm. 1982. 'Anthropological Field Research, Meaning Creation and Knowledge Construction', in David Parkin (ed.), *Semantic Anthropology*, London: Academic Press, pp. 15–37.
Darbon, Dominique. 1990a. 'L'Etat prédateur', *Politique Africaine* 39, pp. 37–45.
D.D. [Dominique Darbon]. 1990b. Compte-rendu de 'Administrateur de la France d'Outre-Mer' de J. Clauzel. *Politique Africaine* 40, pp. 148–49.
Davis, John. 1992. 'Tense in Ethnography. Some Practical Considerations', in Judith Okely and Helen Callaway (eds), *Anthropology and Autobiography*, London: Routledge, pp. 205–20.
Davis, Kit. 1991. Words and Verbs: Magic, Realism and Ethnographic Writing. Paper presented at the Departmental Seminar of the Institute of Social Anthropology, Oxford, 18 January 1991.

Daye, Pierre. 1928. *Blancs*. Paris: Les éditions de France.
De Boeck, Filip. 1998. 'Beyond the Grave: History, Memory and Death in Postcolonial Congo/Zaïre', in Richard Werbner (ed.), *Memory and the Postcolony: African Anthropology and the Critique of Power*, London: Zed Books, pp. 21-57.
Dekoster, Louis. 1959. 'La fin de la Territoriale?', *Belgique d'Outremer* 14 (288), pp. 160–61.
De Lannoy, Didier, Mabiala Seda Diangwala et Bongeli Yeikelo Ya Ato (eds). 1986. 'Tango Ya Ba Noko. "Le temps des oncles". Recueil de témoignages zaïrois', *Les Cahiers du CEDAF* 5–6.
Dellicour, M.F. n.d. [1956]. *Les propos d'un colonial belge. Etudes et Portraits.* Brussels: Weissenbruch.
Dembour, Marie-Bénédicte. 1991a. 'La peine durant la colonisation belge', in Recueils de la Société Jean Bodin pour l'histoire comparative des institutions, *La Peine/Punishment* LVIII, Brussels: De Boeck-Wesmael, pp. 67–95.
——— 1991b. Vues actuelles d'anciens territoriaux sur leurs fonctions passées au Congo, ms.
——— 1992a. 'La physionomie du service territorial du Congo belge et du Ruanda-Urundi dans les années 1950 à travers quelques chiffres', in *Recueil d'études "Congo 1955–1960" Verzameling studies*, Brussels: Académie Royale des Sciences d'Outre-Mer/Koninklijke Academie voor Overzeese Wetenschappen, pp. 165–204.
——— 1992b. 'La chicote comme symbole du colonialisme belge?', *Canadian Journal of African Studies/Revue Canadienne des Etudes Africaines* 26 (2), pp. 205–25.
——— 1996. From Female Circumcision to Genital Mutilation Back to Circumcision: The French Lesson, ms.
Denzin, Norman K. 1989. *Interpretive Biography*. Newbury Park: Sage.
Depoorter, Roger. 1983. *Elle est loin l'étoile … Petite chronique congolaise*. Anvers: Roger Depoorter.
de Saint Moulin, Léo. 1988. 'Histoire de l'organisation administrative du Zaïre', *Zaïre-Afrique* 224, pp. 5–31.
de Valkeneer-Briard, S. 1950. *Au bout du sentier. Nouvelles Congolaises*. Charleroi: Heraly.
de Villers, Gauthier (avec la collaboration de Jean-Claude Willame). 1990. 'Belgique-Zaïre: Le grand affrontement', *Les Cahiers du CEDAF* (1–2).
de Villers, Gauthier. 1992. 'Zaïre, Années 1990. Vol. 2. Zaïre 1990–1991: Faits et dits de la société d'après le regard de la presse', *Les Cahiers du CEDAF* (1–2).
Dirks, Nicholas B. 1992. 'From Little King to Landlord: Colonial Discourse and Colonial Rule', in Nicholas Dirks (ed.) *Colonialism and Culture*, Ann Arbor: University of Michigan Press, pp. 175–208.
Djait, Hichem. 1989. *La grande discorde; religion et politique dans l'islam des origines*. Paris: Gallimard.

Domont, J.-M. 1988. 'Un territorial au pays des sectes politico-religieuses du Bas-Congo pendant les années 1939–1945', *Mémoires de l'Académie Royale des Sciences d'Outre-Mer, Classe des Sciences morales et politiques, Nouvelle série in-8* 50 (3) Brussels: Académie Royale des Sciences d'Outre-Mer, 133 pp.

Dumont, Jean-Paul. 1978. *The Headman and I: Ambiguity and Ambivalence in the Fieldworking Experience*. Austin: University of Texas Press.

Dumont, Louis. 1979 [1966]. *Homo Hierarchicus. Le système des castes et ses implications*. Paris: Gallimard.

Dupont, Théo. 1981. *Souvenirs d'Afrique*. Brussels: Valan.

—— 1983. *Souvenirs d'Afrique. Suite des témoignages*. Brussels: Valan.

Ellen, R.P. 1984. *Ethnographic Research. A Guide to General Conduct*. ASA Research Methods in Social Anthropology. London: Academic Press.

Engels, Dagmar and Shula Marks. 1994. 'Introduction: Hegemony in a Colonial Context', in Dagmar Engels and Shula Marks (eds), *Contesting Colonial Hegemony: State and Society in Africa and India*, London: British Academic Press, pp. 1–15.

Engels, Dagmar and Shula Marks (eds). 1994. *Contesting Colonial Hegemony: State and Society in Africa and India*. London: British Academic Press.

Fabian, Johannes. 1983. *Time and the Other. How Anthropology Makes its Object*. New York: Columbia University Press.

—— 1986. *Language and Colonial Power: The Appropriation of Swahili in the Former Belgian Congo, 1880–1938*. Berkeley: University of California Press.

—— 1990a. *History from Below. The 'Vocabulary of Elisabethville' by André Yav: Text, Translations, and Interpretive Essay*. Amsterdam, Philadelphia: John Benjamins Publishing Company.

—— 1990b. *Power and Performance. Ethnographic Explorations through Proverbial Wisdom and Theatre in Shaba, Zaire*. Madison: University of Wisconsin Press.

—— 1990c. 'Presence and Representation: The Other in Anthropological Writing', *Critical Inquiry* 16, pp. 753–72.

—— 1991. 'Dilemmas of Critical Anthropology', in Lorraine Nencel and Peter Pels (eds), *Constructing Knowledge. Authority and Critique in Social Science*, London: Sage Publications, pp. 180-202.

—— 1996. *Remembering the Present: Painting and Popular History in Zaire*. Berkeley: University of California Press.

Ferrarotti, Franco. 1983. *Histoire et Histoires de vie. La méthode biographique dans les sciences sociales*. Paris: Librairie des méridiens.

Fields, Karen. 1985. *Revival and Rebellion in Colonial Central Africa*. Princeton: Princeton University Press.

—— 1989. 'What one cannot remember mistakenly', *Oral History Journal* 17, pp. 44-53.

Filloux, Jean-Claude. 1952. *La mémoire*. Paris: Presses Universitaires de France. 'Que sais-je?'.

Fondation Royale des Amis de l'Institut Universitaire des Territoires d'Outre-Mer. 1987. *Middleheim. Mémorial de l'Institut Universitaire des Territoires d'Outre-Mer. Gedenkboek van het Universitair Instituut van de Overzeese Gebieden.* Belgique: Rossel.

Foucault, Michel. 1976. *Histoire de la sexualité. Vol.1. La volonté de savoir.* Gallimard.

Gann, L.H. and Peter Duignan. 1979. *The Rulers of Belgian Africa. 1884–1914.* Princeton: Princeton University Press.

Gardinier, David E. 1982. 'Decolonization in French, Belgian and Portuguese Africa: A Bibliographical Essay', in P. Gifford and Wm Roger Louis (eds), *The Transfer of Power in Africa 1940–1960*, pp. 515–66.

Gartrell, Beverley. 1984. 'Colonial Wives: Villains or Victims?', in Hilary Callan and Shirley Ardener (eds), *The Incorporated Wife*, London: Croom Helm, pp. 165–85.

Gevaerts, Franz. 1953. *Vade Mecum à l'usage des Fonctionnaires et Agents territoriaux du Congo belge.* s.l.

Ghiglione, Rodolphe and Benjamin Matalon. 1978. *Les enquêtes sociologiques. Théories et pratique.* Paris: Armand Colin.

Ghislain, Jean. 1992. 'Souvenirs de la Territoriale au Burundi. "Le brouillard sur la Kibira"', *Enquêtes et documents d'Afrique centrale* 11, 122 pp.

Gilsenan, Michael. 1986. 'Domination as social practice. "Patrimonialism" in North Lebanon: Arbitrary Power, Desecration, and the Aesthetics of Violence', *Critique of Anthropology* VI (1), pp. 17–37.

Gondola, Ch. Didier. 1997. 'Jeux d'argent, jeux de villains: Rien ne va plus au Zaïre', *Politique Africaine* 65, pp. 96–111.

Gould, David J. 1980. *Bureaucratic Corruption and Underdevelopment in the Third World. The Case of Zaire.* New York: Pergamon Press.

Gran, Guy (ed.). 1979. *Zaire: The Political Economy of Underdevelopment.* New York: Praeger.

Gravois, Martha and Martin W. Andresen. 1988. 'The Senior Officer Oral History Program: There's More to It Than "Have Tape Recorder, Will Travel"', *International Journal of Oral History* 9, pp. 227–33.

Grévisse, Fernand. 1949. 'La grande pitié des juridictions indigènes', *Mémoires de l'Institut Royal Colonial Belge, Cl. Sci. mor. polit., sér. in-8*, 19 (3), 128 pp.

—— 1984. 'La Territoriale en question', *Académie Royale des Sciences d'Outre-Mer, Bulletin des Séances* 30 (4), pp. 421–27.

Haarscher, Guy. 1998. 'Le temps du droit et l'expérience totalitaire', in François Host and Mark Van Hoecke (eds) *Temps et Droit. Le droit a-t-il pour vocation de durer?*, Brussels: Vruylant, pp. 159–69.

Hailey, W.M. 1938. *An African Survey: A Study of Problems Arising in Africa South of the Sahara.* Oxford: Oxford University Press.

Halbwachs, Maurice. 1925. *Les cadres sociaux de la mémoire.* Paris: Alcan.

Hansen, Karen Transberg. 1989. *Distant Companions. Servants and Employers in Zambia, 1900–1985.* Ithaca: Cornell University Press.

Harms, Roger. 1975. 'The End of Red Rubber: A Reassessment', *Journal of African History* XVI (1), pp. 73–88.

Hastrup, Kirsten. 1992. 'Writing Ethnography: State of the Art', in Judith Okely and Helen Callaway (eds) *Anthropology and Autobiography*, London: Routledge, pp. 116–33.

——— 1995. *A Passage to Anthropology: Between Experience and Theory.* London: Routledge.

——— 1996. 'Anthropological Theory as Practice', *Social Anthropology* 4 (1), pp. 75–81.

Hayes, Patricia. 1996. '"Cocky" Hahn and the "Black Venus": The Making of a Native Commissioner in South West Africa, 1915-46', *Gender and History* 8 (3), pp. 364–92.

Henige, David. 1982. *Oral Historiography.* Harlow, Essex: Longman.

Heussler, R. 1963. *Yesterday's Rulers. The Making of the British Colonial Service.* London: Oxford University Press.

——— 1983. *Completing a Stewardship: The Malayan Civil Service, 1942–57.* Westport: Greenwood.

——— 1987. *British Rule in Malaya: The Malayan Civil Service and Its Predecessors, 1867–1942.* Westport: Greenwood.

Higginson, John. 1988. 'Bringing the Workers Back in: Worker Protest and Popular Intervention in Katanga, 1931–1941', *Canadian Journal of African Studies/Revue Canadienne d'Etudes Africaines* XXII 2, pp. 199–223.

——— 1989. *A Working Class in the Making. Belgian Colonial Labor, Private Enterprise and the African Mineworker. 1907–1951.* Madison: University of Wisonsin Press.

Hoskyns, Catherine. 1965. *The Congo Since Independence. January 1960–December 1961.* London: Oxford University Press.

Hunt, Nancy Rose. 1988. '"Le bébé en brousse": European women, African birth spacing and colonial intervention in breast feeding in the Belgian Congo', *The International Journal of African Historical Studies* 21 (3), pp. 401–32.

——— 1990. 'Domesticity and Colonialism in Belgian Africa: Usumbura's Foyer Social, 1946–1969', *Signs* 15 (3), pp. 447–74.

——— 1991. 'Noise over Camouflaged Polygamy, Colonial Morality Taxation, and a Woman-Naming Crisis in Belgian Africa', *Journal of African History* 32 (3), pp. 471–94.

Hunt, Nancy Rose, Tessie R. Liu and Jean Quataert (eds). 1996. 'Special Issue: Gendered Colonialisms in African History', *Gender and History* 8 (3).

Hunter, Ian M. 1957 (2nd ed. 1964). *Memory: Facts and Fallacies.* Harmondsworth: Penguin Books.

Jackson, A. (ed.). 1987. *Anthropology at Home.* London: Tavistock.

Jacques, Gérard. 1995. *Lualaba, Histoires de l'Afrique Profonde.* Bruxelles: Racine.

Jacquet, Isabelle. 1987. 'Viens, je t'emmène de l'autre côté des nuages ... Aspects de la vie quotidienne au Zaïre', *Politique Africaine* 27, pp. 101–107.

Jenkins, Keith. 1997. *The Postmodern History Reader*. London: Routledge.
Jenkins, Richard P. 1979. 'Correspondence: The value of the evidence', *Man* 14, pp. 161–163.
Jewsiewicki, Bogumil. 1974. 'L'administration coloniale et la tradition. A propos de Giribuma, de R. Tonnoir', *Cultures et Développement* VI (3), pp. 589–604.
—––––– 1983. 'Modernisation ou destruction du village africain; l'économie politique de la "modernisation agricole" au Congo belge', *Les Cahiers du CEDAF* 5.
—––––– 1986. 'Collective Memory and its Images: Popular Urban Painting in Zaire – A Source of "Present Past"', *History and Anthropology* 2, pp. 389–96.
—––––– 1987. 'Vers une anthropo-sociologie historique des populations. Une proposition de macro-analyse des processus démographiques contemporains au Zaïre', *Cahiers d'Etudes Africaines* (105–106), pp. 107–21.
—––––– 1991. 'De la prestidigitation, de la démocratie et des morts "sans qualité particulière"', *Politique Africaine* 41, pp. 90–96.
—––––– 1993. *Naître et Mourir au Zaïre: Un demi-siècle d'histoire au quotidien*. Paris: Karthala.
Kanyinda, Lusanga. 1975. 'Le phénomène de la colonisation et l'émancipation des institutions socio-politiques traditionnelles au Zaïre', *Les Cahiers du CEDAF* 1.
Kapferer, Bruce. 1988. 'The Anthropologist as Hero: Three Exponents of Post-Modernist Anthropology', *Critique of Anthropology* 8 (2), pp. 77–104.
Keesing, Robert. 1989. 'Exotic Readings of Cultural Texts', *Current Anthropology* 30 (4), pp. 459–69.
Kennedy, Dane. 1987. *Islands of White: Settler Society and Culture in Kenya and Southern Rhodesia, 1890–1939*. Durham: Duke University Press.
Kestergat, Jean. 1985. *Quand le Zaïre s'appelait Congo*. Brussels: Paul Legrain.
Kirk-Greene, A.H.M. 1980. 'The Thin White Line: The Size of the British Colonial Service in Africa', *African Affairs* 79, pp. 25–44.
—––––– 1991. 'Forging a Relationship with the Colonial Administrative Service, 1921–1939', in Alison Smith and Mary Bull (eds), *Margery Perham and British Rule in Africa*, London: Frank Cass, pp. 62–82.
Klatch, Rebecca E. 1988. 'The Methodological Problems of Studying a Politically Resistant Community', in Robert G. Burgess (ed.), *Studies in Qualitative Methodology. Vol.1. Conducting Qualitative Research*, London: Jai Press, pp.73–88.
Kuklick, Henrika. 1979. *The Imperial Bureaucrat: The Colonial Administrative Service in the Gold Coast, 1920–1939*. Stanford: Hoover Institution Press.
Kuper, Adam. 1992. 'Post-modernism, Cambridge and the Great Kalahari Debate', *Social Anthropology* 1 (1A), pp. 57–72.
Lance, James. 1990. 'What the Stranger Brings: The Social Dynamics of Fieldwork', *History in Africa* 17, pp. 335–39.

Langness, L.L. 1965. *The Life History in Anthropological Science*. New York: Holt Rinehart and Winston.

Langness, L.L. and Geyla Frank. 1981. *Lives: An Anthropological Approach to Biography*. Novato: Chandler and Sharp.

Laude, Norbert. 1959. 'Le service territorial', *Belgique d'Outremer* 14 (297), p. 26.

Lemaire, Tom. 1991. 'Anthropological Doubt', in Lorraine Nencel and Peter Pels (eds), *Constructing Knowledge: Authority and Critique in Social Science*, London: Sage, pp. 22–39.

Lemarchand, René. 1964. *Political Awakening in the Belgian Congo*. Westport, Connecticut: Greenwood Press.

Lenain, M. 1989 (July). 'Lettre ouverte à Madame Colette Braeckman'. *Congorudi*, 8–9.

Lequin, Yves and Jean Métral. 1980. 'A la recherche d'une mémoire collective: Les métallurgistes retraités de Givors', *Annales. Economies Sociétés Civilisations* 35 (1), pp. 149–66.

Leroy, Pierre. 1963 to 1977. Débuts; Le temps d'Usumbura; Journal de la Province Orientale; Les Presses de la Buanderie. Mons: Les Presses de la Buanderie, photocopied.

Lewis, I.M. 1993. 'Misunderstanding the Somali Crisis', *Anthropology Today* 9 (4), pp. 1–3.

Lewis, Oscar. 1961. *The Children of Sanchez. Autobiography of a Mexican Family*. New York: Random House.

Livre Blanc. Apport scientifique de la Belgique au développement de l'Afrique centrale, T. I, II and III. 1962 and 1963. Brussels: Académie Royale des Sciences d'Outre-Mer.

Louis, Roger Wm and Jean Stengers. 1968. *E.D. Morel's History of the Congo Reform Movement*. Oxford: Clarendon Press.

Lovens, Maurice. 1974. 'La révolte de Masisi-Lubutu (Congo belge, janvier-mai 1944)', *Les Cahiers du CEDAF* 3/4.

——— 1975. 'L'effort militaire de guerre du Congo belge (1940–1944)', *Les Cahiers du CEDAF* 6.

Lowenthal, David. 1985. *The Past is a Foreign Country*. Cambridge: Cambridge University Press.

Lyons, Maryinez. 1992. *The Colonial Disease. A Social History of Sleeping Sickness in Northern Zaire, 1900–1940*. Cambridge: Cambridge University Press.

MacGaffey, Janet. 1988. 'Evading Male Control: Women in the Second Economy in Zaire', in Sharon B. Stichter and Jane L. Parpart (eds), *Patriarchy and Class. African Women in the Home and the Workforce*, Boulder: Westview Press, pp. 161-76.

——— 1991. *The Real Economy of Zaire. The Contribution of Smuggling and other Unofficial Activities to National Wealth*. London: James Currey.

MacGaffey, Wyatt. 1978. 'African History, Anthropology and the Rationality of the Natives', *History in Africa* 5, pp. 101–20.

——— 1982. 'The Policy of National Integration in Zaïre', *The Journal of Modern African Studies* 20 (1), pp. 87–105.
——— 1986. *Religion and Society in Central Africa: The BaKongo of Lower Zaire.* Chicago: University of Chicago Press.
——— 1992. 'Kimbanguism in the Independence Process', in *Recueil d'études "Congo 1955–1960" Verzameling studies,* Brussels: Académie Royale des Sciences d'Outre-Mer/Koninklijke Academie voor Overzeese Wetenschappen, pp. 329–42.
——— 1994. 'Dialogues of the Deaf: Europeans on the Atlantic Coast of Africa', in Stuart B. Schwartz (ed.), *Implicit Understandings: Observing, Reporting and Reflecting on the Encounters Between European and Other Peoples in the Early Modern Era,* Cambridge: Cambridge University Press, pp. 249–67.
Magotte, J. n.d. [1952]. *Les circonscriptions indigènes.* La Louvière: Imprimerie Louviéroise.
Malengreau, Guy. 1950. 'La politique coloniale de la Belgique', in Colston Research Society and the University of Bristol (ed.) *Principles and Methods of Colonial Administration,* London: Butterworths, pp. 35–52.
Markowitz, Marvin D. 1973. *Cross and Sword: The Political Role of the Christian Missions in the Belgian Congo, 1908–1960.* Stanford: Hoover Institution Press.
Mayer, Adrian C. 1989. 'Anthropological Memories', *Man* 24 (2), pp. 203–18.
McCabe, James. 1990. 'Address on "Nations and Nationalism"', *St John's College Notes,* ms, pp. 80–85.
McCullagh, C.B. 1997. *The Truth of History.* London: Routledge.
McLachlan, Hugh V. 1981. 'Is "power" an evaluative concept?', *British Journal of Sociology* 32 (3), pp. 392–410.
Merriam, Alan P. 1961. *Congo. Background of Conflict.* Evanston: Northern University Press.
Michiels, A. and N. Laude. n.d. [1938]. *Notre Colonie: Géographie et notice historique.* Brussels: Edition universelle.
Middleton, John (ed.). 1997. *Encyclopedia of Africa South of the Sahara.* Vol.1–4. New York: Simon and Schuster.
Moore, Sally Falk. 1986. *Social Facts and Fabrications. "Customary" Law on Kilimanjaro, 1885–1980.* Cambridge: Cambridge University Press.
Myerhoff, Barbara. 1982. 'Life History Among the Elderly: Performance, Visibility and Re-Membering', in Jay Ruby (ed.) *A Crack in the Mirror. Reflexive Perspectives in Anthropology,* Philadelphia: University of Pennsylvania Press, pp. 99–117.
Myerhoff, Barbara and Jay Ruby. 1982. 'Introduction', in Jay Ruby (ed.) *A Crack in the Mirror. Reflexive Perspectives in Anthropology,* Philadelphia: University of Pennsylvania Press, pp. 1–35.

Bibliography

Nader, Laura. 1974. 'Up the Anthropologist. Perspectives Gained from Studying Up', in D. Hymes (ed.), *Reinventing Anthropology*, New York: Vintage Books, pp. 284–311.
Nahoum-Grappe, Véronique. 1996. 'L'usage politique de la cruauté: L'épuration ethnique (ex-Yougoslavie, 1991–1995)', in Françoise Héritier (ed.), *De la Violence*, Paris: Opus, pp. 273–323.
Nencel, Lorraine and Peter Pels (eds). 1991. *Constructing Knowledge: Authority and Critique in Social Science*. London: Sage.
O'Brien, Rita Cruise. 1972. *White Society in Black Africa: The French in Senegal*. London: Faber and Faber.
Okely, Judith and Helen Callaway (eds). 1992. *Anthropology and Autobiography*. London: Routledge.
Parker, Melissa. 1995. 'Rethinking Female Circumcision', *Africa* 65 (4), pp. 506–23.
Passerini, Luisa. 1988. 'Oral History in Italy After the Second World War: From Populism to Subjectivity', *International Journal of Oral History* 9, pp. 114–24.
Pels, Peter and Oscar Salemink. 1994a. 'Introduction: Five theses on Ethnography as Colonial Practice', *History and Anthropology* 8, pp. 1–34.
―――― (eds) 1994b. 'Special Issue: Colonial Ethnographies', *History and Anthropology* 8 (1–4).
Perks, Robert and Alistair Thomson (eds). 1998. *The Oral History Reader*. London: Routledge.
Perrings, Charles. 1979. *Black Mineworkers in Central Africa. Industrial Strategies and the Evolution of an African Proletariat in the Copperbelt 1911–41*. London: Heinemann.
Personal Narratives Group. 1989. *Interpreting Women's Lives: Feminist Theory and Personal Narratives*. Bloomington: Indiana University Press.
Poirier, J., S. Clapier-Valladon and P. Raybaut. 1983. *Les récits de vie. Théorie et pratique*. Paris: Presses Universitaires de France.
Politique Africaine. 1991. 'Zaïre. Un pays à reconstruire' 41, 110 pp.
Powdermaker, H. 1966. *Stranger and Friend: The Way of an Anthropologist*. New York: W.W. Norton.
Pratt, Mary Louise. 1986. 'Fieldwork in Common Places', in James Clifford and George E. Marcus (eds), *Writing Culture: The Poetics and Politics of Ethnography*, Berkeley: University of California Press, pp. 27–50.
―――― 1992. *Imperial Eyes: Travel Writing and Transculturation*. London: Routledge.
Problèmes d'Afrique Centrale. 1951. 'Le "drame de la territoriale"' 4 (2), pp. 152–58.
Prochaska, David. 1990. *Making Algeria French: Colonialism in Bône, 1870–1920*. Cambridge: Cambridge University Press.
Quinet, Paul. 1955. 'Quelques considérations sur les problèmes du service territorial', *Problèmes d'Afrique centrale* 1, pp. 10–15.

Raymaekers, P. and H. Desroche. 1983. 'L'administration et le sacré', *Mémoires de l'Académie Royale des Sciences d'Outre-Mer, Classe des Sciences morales et politiques, Nouvelle série in-8*, 396 pp.

Réalités Africaines. 1957. 'Le Congo belge et le Ruanda-Urundi'. Casablanca: Editions Fontana.

Reed-Danahay, Deborah. 1996. *Education and Identity in Rural France: The Politics of Schooling.* Cambridge: Cambridge University Press.

Reyntjens, Filip. 1985. *Pouvoir et droit au Rwanda. Droit public et évolution politique, 1916–1973.* Tervuren: Musée Royal de l'Afrique Centrale.

Romains, Jules. 1972 [1928]. *Le dieu des corps.* Gallimard, collection Folio.

Rosaldo, Renato. 1989. *Culture as Truth. The Remaking of Social Analysis.* Boston: Beacon Press.

Rousso, Henry. 1991. *The Vichy Syndrome: History and Memory in France since 1945.* Cambridge: Harvard University Press.

Rousso, Henry and Eric Conan. 1994. *Vichy: Un passé qui ne passe pas.* Fayard.

Ryckmans, Geneviève (ed.). 1995. *André Ryckmans: Un territorial du Congo belge. Lettres et documents 1954–1960.* Paris: L'Harmattan.

Ryckmans, Pierre. 1948. *Dominer pour servir.* Brussels: L'édition universelle.

[Rubbens, Antoine]. 1945. *Dettes de Guerre.* Elisabethville: Editions de "L'essor du Congo".

Sacré, Marcel. 1989 (July). 'Carte blanche: Le Zaïre: dettes et créanciers'. *Congorudi*, 7–8.

Said, Edward W. 1978. *Orientalism.* London: Routledge and Kegan Paul.

Salmon, Jacques. 1953. 'Le droit matrimonial des Warega', *Bulletin des Juridictions indigènes et du Droit Coutumier Congolais* 21 (6), pp. 121–28 and 229–48.

Samarin, William J. 1989. *The Black Man's Burden: African Colonial Labor on the Congo and Ubangi Rivers, 1890–1900.* Boulder, Colorado: Westview Press.

Schaffer, Bernard. 1985. 'Policy-Makers Have Their Need Too: Itinerance and the Culture of Poverty', in Jeff Wood (ed.), *Labelling in Development Policy,* London: Sage, pp. 33–66.

Schatzberg, Michael G. 1988. *The Dialectics of Oppression in Zaire.* Bloomington: Indiana University Press.

Schieffelin, Edward L. and Robert Crittenden (eds). 1991. *Like People You See in a Dream. First Contact in Six Papuan Societies.* Stanford: Stanford University Press.

Scohy, André. 1952. *Etapes au soleil.* Brussels: Editions du chat qui pêche.

Sharwood-Smith, Joan. 1992. *Diary of a Colonial Wife.* Radcliffe Press.

Slade, Ruth. 1960. *The Belgian Congo.* London: Oxford University Press.

—— 1962. *King Leopold's Congo.* London: Oxford University Press.

Smith, Robert Eugène. 1976. 'L'administration coloniale et les villageois. Les Yansi du nord de Bulungu, 1920–1940 (Zaïre)', *Les Cahiers du CEDAF* 1.

Spencer, Jonathan. 1989. 'Anthropology as a Kind of Writing', *Man* 24 (1), pp. 145–64.

Stengers, Jean. 1963. *Belgique et Congo: L'élaboration de la Charte coloniale.* Brussels: La renaissance du livre.
―――― 1982. 'Precipitous decolonization: the case of the Belgian Congo', in P. Gifford and W.R. Louis (eds) *The Transfer of Power in Africa, 1940–1960*, New Haven: Yale University Press, pp. 305–35.
―――― 1989. *Congo. Mythes et réalités. 100 ans d'histoire.* Paris, Louvain-la-Neuve: Duculot.
Stoler, Ann Laura. 1989a. 'Rethinking Colonial Categories: European Communities and the Boundaries of Rule', *Comparative Studies in Society and History* 31 (1), pp. 134–61.
―――― 1989b. 'Making Empire Respectable: The Politics of Race and Sexual Morality in 20th Century Colonial Cultures', *American Ethnologist* 16 (4), pp. 634–59.
Strathern, Marilyn. 1987. 'The Limits of Auto-Anthropology', in Anthony Jackson (ed.), *Anthropology at Home*, London: Tavistock, pp. 16–37.
Strobel, Margaret. 1991. *European Women and the Second British Empire.* Bloomington: Indiana University Press.
Szombati-Fabian, Ilona and Johannes Fabian. 1976. 'Art, History, and Society: Popular Painting in Zaïre', *Studies in the Anthropology of Visual Communication* 3, pp. 1–21.
Tancré-Van Leeuw, C. 1992. 'Les territoriaux et la décolonisation', in *Recueil d'études "Congo 1955–1960" Verzameling studies*, Brussels: Académie Royale des Sciences d'Outre-Mer/Koninklijke Academie voor Overzeese Wetenschappen, pp. 401–12.
Tedlock, Dennis. 1983. *The Spoken Word and the Work of Interpretation.* Philadelphia: University of Pennsylvania Press.
―――― 1987. 'Questions concerning Dialogical Anthropology', *Journal of Anthropological Research* 43 (4), pp. 325–37.
Terrain. 1997. 'Miroirs du colonialisme' 28.
Thomas, Nicholas (ed.). 1992. 'Special Issue: Colonialism and Culture', *History and Anthropology* 5.
―――― 1994. *Colonialism's Culture: Anthropology, Travel and Government.* Oxford: Polity Press.
Thompson, E.P. 1975. *Whigs and Hunters: The Origin of the Black Act.* London: Allen Lane.
Thompson, Paul. 1988 [1975]. *The Voice of the Past: Oral History.* Oxford: Oxford University Press.
Thomson, Alistair. 1990. 'The Anzac Legend: Exploring National Myth and Memory in Australia', in Raphael Samuel and Paul Thompson (eds) *The Myths We Live By*, London: Routldege, pp. 73–82.
Tinel, Marcel. 1956. *Elianga. Roman de la forêt iturienne.* Brussels: La renaissance du livre.
Tonkin, Elizabeth. 1982. 'The Boundaries of History in Oral Performance', *History in Africa* 9, pp. 273–84.

―――― 1990. 'History and the Myth of Realism', in Raphael Samuel and Paul Thompson (eds), *The Myths We Live By*, London: Routldege, pp. 25–35.

―――― 1992. *Narrating our Pasts. The Social Construction of Oral History.* Cambridge: Cambridge University Press.

Tonnoir, R. 1970. *Giribuma. Contribution à l'histoire et à la petite histoire du Congo équatorial.* Tervuren: Musée Royal de l'Afrique Centrale.

Turnbull, Colin. 1984. *The Forest People.* London: Paladin.

Tyler, Stephen. 1987. 'On "Writing-Up/Off" as "Speaking-for"', *Journal of Anthropological Research* 43 (4), p. 338–42.

Union des femmes du Congo belge et du Ruanda-Urundi (L'). 1956. *La femme au Congo. Conseils aux partantes.* Brussels: L. Cuypers.

Vanderlinden, Jacques. 1962. 'Vers la rédaction des droits coutumiers congolais', in John Gilissen (ed.) *La rédaction des coutumes dans le passé et le présent.* Brussels: Institut de Sociologie.

―――― 1985. *La crise congolaise.* Bruxelles: Editions Complexe.

―――― 1988. 'Le gouverneur et les militaires', *Mémoires de l'Académie Royale des Sciences d'Outre-Mer, Classe des Sciences morales et politiques, Nouvelle série in-8* 49 (3), 99 pp.

―――― 1994. *Pierre Ryckmans 1891–1959: Coloniser dans l'honneur.* Bruxelles: De Boeck-Wesmael.

―――― 1996. 'Le biographe entre le vice et la vertu. A propos de Pierre Ryckmans', *Bulletin des Séances* 42 (3), pp. 371–91.

Vanderstraeten, L.F. 1992. 'La Force Publique et le maintien de la "Pax belgica" 1944–Janvier 1955', in *Recueil d'études "Congo 1955–1960" Verzameling studies*, Brussels: Académie Royale des Sciences d'Outre-Mer/Koninklijke Academie voor Overzeese Wetenschappen, pp. 495–524.

Vangroenweghe, Daniel. 1986. *Du sang sur les lianes. Léopold II et son Congo* (transl. from the Dutch). Brussels: Didier Hatier.

Van Leeuw, Claire. 1981. L'administration territoriale au Congo belge et au Ruanda-Urundi. Fondements institutionnels et expérience vécue. 1912–1960. Mémoire présenté en vue de l'obtention du grade de Licencié en Philosophie et Lettres (Histoire), Université Catholique de Louvain.

―――― (ed.). 1987. 'Femmes coloniales au Congo belge. Essais et documents', *Enquêtes et documents d'histoire africaine*, 7.

Van Maanen, John. 1988. *Tales of the Field. On Writing Ethnography.* Chicago: University of Chicago Press.

Vansina, Jan. 1972. 'Les Kuba et l'administration territoriale de 1919 à 1960', *Cultures et développement. Revue internationale des sciences du développement* IV (2), pp. 275–325.

Vaughan, Megan. 1991. *Curing Their Ills: Colonial Power and African Illness.* Stanford: Stanford University Press.

Vellut, Jean-Luc. 1980. 'Les Belges au Congo (1885–1960)', in Albert d'Haenens (ed.) *La Belgique. Sociétés et Cultures depuis 150 ans. 1830–1980.* Brussels: Ministère des Affaires étrangères, pp. 260–65.

——— 1981. 'Les bassins miniers de l'ancien Congo Belge. Essai d'histoire économique et sociale (1900–1960), *Les Cahiers du CEDAF* 7.

——— 1982. 'Matériaux pour une image du Blanc dans la société coloniale du Congo Belge', in Jean Pirotte (ed.) *Stéréotypes nationaux et préjugés raciaux aux XIXe et XXe siècles. Sources et méthodes pour une approche historique*, Leuven: Editions Nauwelaerts, pp. 91–116.

——— 1983. 'Le Katanga industriel en 1944: Malaises et anxiétés dans la société coloniale', in *Le Congo durant la Seconde Guerre Mondiale: Recueil d'Etudes. Bijdragen over Belgisch-Congo Tijdens de Tweede Wereldoorlog*, Brussels: Académie Royale des Sciences d'Outre-Mer, pp. 495–523.

——— 1987. 'Résistances et espaces de liberté dans l'histoire coloniale du Zaïre: avant la marche à l'Indépendance (1876–1945)', in Catherine Coquery-Vidrovitch, Alain Forest and Herbert Weiss (eds), *Rébellions, Révolution au Zaïre. 1963–1965*. T.1, Paris: L'Harmattan, pp. 24–73.

————- 1991. 'La communauté portugaise du Congo belge', in J. Evaraert and E. Stols (eds), *Flandre et Portugal: Au confluent de deux cultures*, Antwerp: Fonds Mercator, pp. 341–45.

Verdeaux, François. 1987 'Au coeur de l'ethnie: Anthropo ma non topo', *Politique Africaine* 26, pp. 115–21.

Verdier, Raymond. 1985. 'De l'ignorance à la méconnaissance des traditions juridiques africaines', *La connaissance du droit en Afrique*, Brussels: Académie Royale des Sciences d'Outre-Mer, pp. 295–298.

Verhaegen, Benoît. 1983. 'La guerre vécue au centre extra-coutumier de Stanleyville', in *Le Congo durant la Seconde Guerre Mondiale: Recueil d'Etudes. Bijdragen over Belgisch-Congo Tijdens de Tweede Wereldoorlog*, Brussels: Académie Royale des Sciences d'Outre-Mer, pp. 439-93.

——— 1995. 'Commentaires sur la biographie de Pierre Ryckmans (1891–1959) par Jacques Vanderlinden', *Bulletin des Séances* 41 (2), pp. 173–81.

Waldren, Jacqueline. 1996. *Insiders and Outsiders. Paradise and Reality in Mallorca*. Oxford: Berghahn.

Watson, Lawrence C. and Maria-Barbara Watson-Franke. 1985. *Interpreting Life Histories: An Anthropological Inquiry*. New Brunswick, NJ: Rutgers University Press.

Weiss, Herbert F. 1967. *Political Protest in the Congo. The Parti Solidaire Africain During the Independence Struggle*. New Haven: Princeton University Press.

White, Luise. 1997 [1993]. 'Cars Out of Place: Vampires, Technology, and Labor in East and Central Africa', in Frederick Cooper and Ann Laura Stoler (eds), *Tensions of Empire: Colonial Cultures in a Bourgeois World*, Berkeley: University of California Press, pp. 436–60.

Willaert, Maurice. 1990. *Servir au Congo. Carnets d'un territorial 1931-1961*. Brussels: Didier Hatier.

Willame, Jean-Claude. 1987. 'Chronique d'une opposition politique: l'UDPS (1978-1987)', *Les Cahiers du CEDAF* (7–8).

——— 1988. 'Eléments pour une lecture du contentieux belgo-zaïrois', *Les Cahiers du CEDAF* (6).
——— 1991. 'Zaïre, Années 90. Vol. 1. De la démocratie "octroyée" à la démocratie enrayée (24 avril 1990 – 22 septembre 1991)', *Les Cahiers du CEDAF* (5–6).
——— 1992. *L'automne d'un despotisme. Pouvoir, argent et obéissance dans le Zaïre des années quatre-vingt*. Paris: Karthala.
Young, Crawford. 1965. *Politics in the Congo. Decolonization and Independence*. Princeton: Princeton University Press.
——— 1994. *The African Colonial State in Comparative Perspective*. New Haven: Yale University Press.
Young, Crawford and Thomas Turner. 1985. *The Rise and Decline of the Zairian State*. Madison: University of Wisconsin Press.
Young, Robert. 1990. *White Mythologies: Writing History and the West*. London: Routledge.

INDEX

'Adam' 79, 81–82, 92–92, 94, 95, 121
Alexandre 165
Allport 114
'Amory' 153–54, 167
Andresen 131
anonymity xii, 100–105, 129, 130
anthropology 194, 196–202, 205–207; and arrogance 190–91, 201–202, 206; dialogical 8–11, 96; and distance 198–201; and immersion 172; and knowledge 10, 45, 197, 202, 203, 206; reflexive 7–8, 14, 16; and understanding 196–202, 206–207
anti-colonial prejudices: by author 7, 45-50, 125–29, 140, 170–72, 179–86, 190, 202, 206; of average Belgian 69–72; former colonials' response to 74–77, 81–82, 92; in media and academia 70–77, 80–81, 95, 106, *see also* colonialist label; illegalities
Arendt 63, 170
army recruitment 23-24, 83, 97
Augustin 14, 56–57, 81, 102, 104, 159, 168

Bahloul 16
Balandier 76, 176
Bartlett 117–18
Beidelman 178, 192

Belgian colonialism: British view on 12, 16, 53, 85, 98; comparison with Nazi Germany 60–64, 84; and model colony 182, 184; ordinary character of 170–73, 188, 190, 196, 202; and paternalism 48, 76, 115, 142, 146, 151, 168, 205, *see also* colonialism; territorial service; prestige; colour bar; occupation; memories of Belgian Congo; debt
Belgian Congo, *see* Belgian colonialism; memories of Belgian Congo; territorial service
belgicains 69–70, 79
belgo-zairian dispute 76–77
Berman 167
Bertaux 54, 79
'Bertrand' 50, 81, 83, 116, 121, 125, 134, 136–37, 143, 146–47, 149, 152, 167
Bhabha 15, 167
Birindwa 193
Bontinck 155
Bourdieu 168
Braeckman 14, 75–76, 77, 97, 104
Brausch 132, 182-183
British view on Congo, *see* Belgian Colonialism
Browning 63
Bruckner 47, 203

231

Index

Bucher 131
Buell 43
Bula Matari 155–56
bush 79, 90, 112, 127, 143, 149–53

Caplan 16, 131
Chanock 28, 143
Chaudhuri 43
chicote, *see* whip
chiefs, local 23, 26, 43, 55, 143
Chilver 16
Clauzel 174, 184
Clifford 166
Cochrane 165
Cohen 9, 14
Cohn 132
'Colman' 80–81
colonial discourse studies 11, 15
Colonial University 20, 42, 108, 150–51, 167
colonialism 202–205; as action 186–90; term 2-3, 14, 76, *see also* Belgian colonialism; anti-colonial prejudices; domination; colonial discourse studies
colonialist label 2, 71, 81–82, 124, 204, *see also* anti-colonial prejudices
colour-bar 27, 38–39, 76, 126–29, 136–37, *see also* segregation; racism
Conan 123
Congo Free State, *see* Leopold II
Connerton 16
Cooper 15, 167
Cornélus 97, 161, 163, 164
Cornil 48-49
corporal punishment 76, *see also* whip
council of chiefdom 22–24, 156
Crick 172
cruelty 56
custom: and chiefs 23; and détribalisés 23, 40, 166; evolution of 145; knowledge by territorials of 31, 73, 135, 165; and native courts 26, 28

Darbon 173–74, 184–86
'Dauw' 138, 166
'd'Ave et d'Ove' 80, 84, 103, 160–61, 164, 185
Davis 13, 130

de Bellefroid 184
debt, colonial 74, 76–77
'de Glaise' 42, 51–52, 54, 56, 60, 61, 64, 65, 66–67, 84–85, 131, 191, 207
'Dehon' 87–88, 91–92, 93, 95, 98, 102, 109, 111, 112, 117, 125–26, 141, 153, 161–62, 189
Dekoster 42
Dellicour 160, 168
'Delporte' 110–11, 131
Dembour 42, 43, 64, 67, 97, 102, 130, 180, 208
Depoorter 141–42
Desroche 168
de Valkeneer-Briard 165
dialogical anthropology, *see* anthropology
dilemmas, moral and epistemological 53–54, 61–65, 92–93, 189, 194, 199, *see also* knowledge; legitimisation
Dirks 15
distance, *see* immersion; prestige
Djait 178–79
domination 4, 24, 68, 112, 133, 138–39, 147–48, 154, 167, 176, 178, 181, 185–86, 187, 192, 195, 200, *see also* force; legitimisation; colonialism
Domont 157–58, 159
Duignan 18, 21, 44
Dumont, J.-P. 53
Dumont, L. 62
'Duruisseau' 80, 106

Engels 43, 67
epistemology, *see* anthropology; dilemmas
épopée, *see* memories of Belgian Congo
évolués 40, 149-150, 163, 167

Fabian 8, 15, 97, 103, 142, 14, 198, 200, 203, 204–205, 206, 207
Ferrarrotti 81
Fields 43, 121–22
Filloux 113, 118–19, 120, 122
flogging, *see* whip
'Fontor' 110, 143–44, 192
force 35–36
Fritz 131

Gann 18, 21, 44

Index

Garfinkel 98
Gavaerts, *see* Vade Mecum
Ghiglione 66, 108
Gilsenan 50, 62, 79
Gould 14, 193
Gravois 131
Grévisse 72–74, 121
guilt 103, 147–48, 189, 193, 202, 203–204, 206

Haarscher 14
Hailey 16
Halbwachs 6
Hansen 44
Harms 42
Hastrup 10–11, 13, 14, 15, 194, 196–98, 201, 202, 203, 207
Hayes 67, 207
Henige 132
Heussler 15
Higginson 40, 43
history 63, 82, 92, 96, *see also* objectivity
Hochschild 16
Hunt 44, 166, 192
Hunter 113–16, 120, 131

illegalities 55, 58, 61, 83, 84, 88, 100–103, 179, *see also* rule of law; anticolonial prejudices; territorial service
immersion 134–37, 142, 171–76
independence 1–2, 13, 21, 46, 71, 108, 115, 134
interviewees: as eager participants 78–81; as historical witnesses 82–85
interviewer: misunderstandings by 124–29, 171; tactics by 50–54; respect for interviewees 51, 62, 191, 199–200; and young female student image 50–51, 52, 59, 79, 95, 128, 195, *see also* dilemmas
interviewing process: agenda covered 105, 109–12, *see also* anonymity; tape recording
itinerance, *see* touring

'Jamiolle' 78, 102–103, 110–11
Jenkins 130
Jewsiewicki 44, 97, 165, 166, 167, 192

judicial system 24–29, 48, 143

Kabila 14, 74, 77, 192
Keesing 191
Kennedy 15, 96, 158, 168, 192
Kestergat 42, 43, 98, 165, 166
Kimbanguism 168
Kirk-Greene 168
Kitawala 57
knowledge: as judgment 189; and elusive facts 63, *see also* anthropology; dilemmas; objectivity
Klatch 200
Kluver 114
Kuklick 15
Kuper 9

Lance 204
leave 21, 30, 38, 43, 71
legitimation as object of study 53, 61–64, 165, 189, 200
Lenain 75–76, 104
Leopold II 12, 16, 17–18, 42, 46, 98, 110, 171, 205
Leopoldville 1, 156
Lequin 79, 131, 191
Lévi-Strauss 123, 181
Lonsdale 167
Lovens 126, 165
Lubumbashi 97, 154
Lyons 192

McCabe 148
MacGaffey 15, 41, 43, 166, 168
McLachlan 62
Masisi-Lubutu revolt 126
Matadi 154, 156
Markowitz 40, 44, 98, 154, 167
Marks 43, 67
Matalon 66, 108
Mayer 130
media, *see* anti-colonial prejudices
memories of Belgian Congo: by author 45–49; as beautiful period in life 2, 69, 106; conflicting 3–4, 72–74, 133; as épopée 81–82, 92, 94–95, 96; as oeuvre 78, 81; as oppression 61, 72–73; as process 5–6; and risk of

233

Index

anachronism 49, 94, 124, 126, 180–81; by territorials 2, 124, *see also* memory; Belgian colonialism; anti-colonial prejudices; nostalgia; pride; guilt
memory 5–7, 8, 112–24, 131–32; and chronology 115, 131; collective 4, 6, 45, 49; as distortion 5, 63, 114, 118, 120–21, 124; and eidetic imaging 114; and forgetting 115–16, 123; and identity 123–24; and the present 5–6, 113–20, 124, 129; as rendering the past 86–92, 120–22, *see also* memories of Belgian Congo
'Melonnier' 125, 132
ménagère 108, 111, 139–42, 165
Métral 79, 131, 191
'Michel' 92, 94, 106–107, 131
'Mignolet' 116, 121
military intervention 139, 155, 167
'Milnaert' 9-10, 42, 43, 50 54–56, 57–58, 60–61, 62, 64, 65, 83, 83-84, 85, 86, 89–92, 93, 94–95, 96, 97–98, 103–104, 107–108, 111, 116, 117, 118–19, 128–29, 131, 132, 133, 134, 138–39, 140, 141, 157, 163, 166, 168, 169–93, 196, 202
missionaries 38, 40, 89, 90, 147, 167, 176, 178, 204
Mobutu 13, 14, 74, 97, 184, 192–93
Morel 17
M'Peti 184
Myerhoff 14, 97

Nahoum-Grappe 56, 64
native circumscriptions 23, 27, 135
native tribunals, *see* judicial system
Nazi Germany, *see* Belgian colonialism, *see also* occupation
nostalgia 2, 110, 143, 146–48, 184

objectivity 79, 82, 86, 95
occupation 60, 138–39

Parker 208
'Parmentier' 62, 93–94, 104, 108, 117, 127–28, 140, 196
Passerini 131

paternalism, *see* Belgian colonialism
'Peletier' 60, 94, 144–46, 149–50, 152, 155–56, 161, 166, 167, 168, 196–97, 201, 202–202, 206
Pels 115, 165, 200
Perks 15
Perrings 40, 43, 154
'Peters' 42, 58–60, 62, 83, 85, 95, 131, 136, 142
planton 41, 142, 166
police-state 125–26
polygamy 145–46, 147, 178
Poirier 79, 131
postmodernism 11
Powdermaker 172
power 61–62, 181, *see also* domination
Pratt 192
prejudices, *see* anti-colonial prejudices; dilemmas
prestige 23, 80, 136, 153–65, 168, 177–78, 186
pride 37, 183, 185
'Praet' 102, 105–106, 131

Quarantelli 131
Quinet 167

racism 11, 48–49, 76, 136–37, 142, 176, *see also* colour-bar
'Ransquin' 140, 150–51, 185
Raymaekers 168
red rubber atrocities 12, 17–18, 42, *see also* Leopold II
Reed-Danahay 132
reflexivity, *see* anthropology
relève 21, 73, 130, 138, 164
'Robert' 109
Romains 7–8
Rosaldo 143, 147–48, 167
Ruanda-Urundi 42
Rubbens 97, 132
Ruby 14
rule of law 57, 60
Ryckmans, A. 98, 165
Ryckmans, P. 35–36, 84, 177, 185, 191, 193, 205, 207

Sacré 77

Index

sadism 56-57, 60
Salemink 15, 165
Salmon 145
Samarin 97, 128, 191
Second World War 1, 5, 6, 21, 37, 42, 57, 121, 123, 130, 139, 153, 158, 186; as turning point 32–33, 38, 135, 140, 164
segregation 38–39, 89–91, 126, 163–64, 168, *see also* colour-bar; immersion; racism
Stanley 155
Stanleyville 121, 144
Stengers 14, 42, 182
Stoler 15, 40, 140, 204
Strathern 197–98, 199, 203, 207
Strobel 43
Szombati-Fabian 103

Tancré-Van Leeuw 3, 31, 120, 134–35, 175, *see also* Van Leeuw
tape-recording 81, 107–108, 131
Tedlock 9–10
territorial service 1, 17–44, 176–177; and risk of abuse 35, 56-57; and action through small projects of development 183, 185; African absence within 38–39; control within 33–35, 57, 171; creation of 17–18; denigrated achievements of 72, 183; functions attributed to 22–30; generational differences within 135–36, 138, 149, 160, 163–64, 168; judicial control over 27–28, 35, 56, 101; negative image about 70–71; numbers within 21; and paperwork 33, 135, 152; ranks within 18–20; rigid description by author of 176–77; transfers within 30–31; and women 37–38, 41, 43, *see also* Bula Matari; Colonial University; leave; relève; touring; immersion; army recruitment; illegalities; Belgian colonialism; memories of Belgian Congo
Thomas 15, 66
Thompson, E.P. 58
Thompson, P. 108, 131, 132
Thomson 15, 132

Tinel 159
Tonkin 79, 97, 117, 123, 167
Tonnoir 165
touring 3, 28, 31–34, 127, 134, 135, 152
Tshibumba 73, 182
Tshisekedi 184, 193
Turnbull 98, 132
Turner 3–4, 14, 73, 156
Tyler 9–10

understanding in anthropology, *see* anthropology

Vade Mecum 22-24, 28, 29, 31, 33–34
Vallaeys 115
Vanderlinden 14, 43, 47–48, 52, 75, 165, 166, 191, 193
Vanderstraeten 155
'Van Gansbeke' 138
Vangroenweghe 42
Van Leeuw 39, 42, 52, 66, 102, 153, 167, *see also* Tancré-Van Leeuw
Van Maanen 199-200
Vansina 40, 43, 44, 97, 142
'Vastenakel' 86–87, 89, 91–92, 134, 149, 166, 168
Vaughan 192
Vellut 40, 66, 75, 98, 158, 165, 166, 182, 191–192
'Verbrugge' 100–101
Verdier 73
Verhaegen 75, 76–77, 121, 166, 191, 193
violence 56–60

Wajda 60
war effort 139
whip 59–60, 63–64, 66, 73, 83, 84, 88, 100, 101–103, 108, 155, 160–62, 164
Wigny 42
'Wilkin' 100
Willaert 139
women, *see* territorial service

Young 3–4, 14, 21, 27, 38, 40, 72–73, 156, 167, 191

www.ingramcontent.com/pod-product-compliance
Lightning Source LLC
Chambersburg PA
CBHW052019070526
44584CB00016B/1812